T0408007

JOURNEYS OF BLACK WOMEN IN ACADEME

DIVERSITY IN HIGHER EDUCATION

Series editor: Henry T. Frierson

Volume 1: *Mentoring and Diversity in Higher Education* – Edited by H. T. Frierson

Volume 2: *Examining Protégé-Mentor Experiences* – Edited by H. T. Frierson

Volume 3: *Latinos in Higher Education* – Edited by David J. León

Volume 4: *Beyond Small Numbers: Voices of African American PhD Chemists* – Edited by Willie Pearson Jr.

Volume 5: *Lessons in Leadership: Executive Leadership Programs for Advancing Diversity in Higher Education* – Edited by David J. Leon

Volume 6: *Black American Males in Higher Education: Diminishing Proportions* – Edited by H. T. Frierson, Willie Pearson, Jr., and James H. Wyche

Volume 7: *Black American Males in Higher Education: Research, Programs and Academe* – Edited by H. T. Frierson, James H. Wyche, and Willie Pearson Jr.

Volume 8: *Support Systems and Services for Diverse Populations: Considering the Intersection of Race, Gender, and the Needs of Black Female Undergraduates* – Edited by Crystal Renée Chambers

Volume 9: *Women of Color in Higher Education: Turbulent Past, Promising Future* – Edited by Gaetane Jean-Marie and Brenda Lloyd-Jones

Volume 10: *Women of Color in Higher Education: Changing Directions and New Perspectives* – Edited by Gaetane Jean-Marie and Brenda Lloyd-Jones

Volume 11: *Beyond Stock Stories and Folktales: African Americans' Paths to Stem Fields* – Edited by Henry T. Frierson and William F. Tate

Volume 12: *Black Female Undergraduates on Campus: Successes and Challenges* – Edited by Crystal Renée Chambers and Rhonda Vonshay Sharpe

Volume 13: *Latino College Presidents: In Their Own Words* – Edited by Rubén O. Martinez and David J. León

Volume 14: *Seeding Success in Indigenous Australian Higher Education* – Edited by Rhonda G. Craven and Janet Mooney

Volume 15: *Maori and Pasifika Higher Education Horizons* – Edited by Fiona Cram, Hazel Phillips, Pale Sauni, and Clark Tuagalu

Volume 16: *Black Males and Intercollegiate Athletics: An Exploration of Problems and Solutions* – Edited by Robert A. Bennett III, Samuel R. Hodge, David L. Graham, and James L. Moore III

Volume 17: *Infusing Undergraduate Research Into Historically Black Colleges and Universities Curricula* – Edited by Jeton McClinton, Mark A. Melton, Caesar R. Jackson, and Kimarie Engerman

Volume 18: *The Coercive Community College: Bullying and Its Costly Impact on the Mission to Serve Underrepresented Populations* – Edited by Leah P. Hollis

Volume 19: *The Crisis of Race in Higher Education: A Day of Discovery and Dialogue* – Edited by William F. Tate IV, Nancy Staudt, and Ashley Macrander

Volume 20: *Campus Diversity Triumphs: Valleys of Hope* – Edited by Sherwood Thompson

Volume 21: *Underserved Populations at Historically Black Colleges and Universities: The Pathway to Diversity, Equity, and Inclusion* – Edited by Cheron H. Davis, Adriel A. Hilton, and Donavan L. Outten

Volume 22: *Broadening Participation in STEM: Effective Education Methods, Practices, and Programs for Women and Minorities* – Edited by Zakiya Wilson-Kennedy, Goldie S. Byrd, Eugene Kennedy, and Henry T. Frierson

Volume 23: *Diversity and Triumphs of Navigating the Terrain of Academe: International Perspectives* – edited by Raphael Heaggans and Henry T. Frierson

Volume 24: *The Beauty and the Burden of Being a Black Professor* – Edited by Cheron H. Davis, Adriel Hilton, Ricardo Hamrick, and F. Erik Brooks

Volume 25: *Young, Gifted and Missing: The Underrepresentation of African American Males in Science, Technology, Engineering and Mathematics Disciplines* – Edited by Anthony G. Robins, Locksley Knibbs, Ted N. Ingram, Michael N. Weaver Jr., and Adriel Hilton

DIVERSITY IN HIGHER EDUCATION VOLUME 26

JOURNEYS OF BLACK WOMEN IN ACADEME: SHARED LESSONS, EXPERIENCES, AND INSIGHTS

EDITED BY

BRENDA L. WALKER
University of South Florida, USA

United Kingdom – North America – Japan
India – Malaysia – China

Emerald Publishing Limited
Emerald Publishing, Floor 5, Northspring, 21-23 Wellington Street, Leeds LS1 4DL

First edition 2024

British Library Cataloguing in Publication Data
A catalogue record for this book is available from the British Library

ISBN: 978-1-83549-269-7 (Print)
ISBN: 978-1-83549-268-0 (Online)
ISBN: 978-1-83549-270-3 (Epub)

ISSN: 1479-3644 (Series)

Printed and bound by CPI Group (UK) Ltd, Croydon, CR0 4YY

To our mothers, grandmothers, and other ancestors whose educational backgrounds belied their wisdom and who truly inspired this book.

To our communities who invested in and supported us throughout our academic journeys.

To our mentors who graciously met us where we were and generously poured into us.

To the doctoral scholars and early- and mid-career faculty and administrators who sounded the call and trusted us enough to seek and hold dear our advisement and counsel.

To my dear colleagues and chapter contributors who without hesitation responded to the call despite having to deal with disquieting and unsettled memories.

To our children, grandchildren, and future generations whom we hope will be ultimately impacted by our work.

CONTENTS

ABOUT THE EDITOR

Dr Brenda L. Walker is a Professor at the University of South Florida and an Attorney. Her research focuses on improving outcomes among African American learners in urban and low-income schools and communities. She addresses faculty shortages, school suspension, special education overrepresentation, and school-to-prison pipeline phenomena. Dr Walker has written numerous journal articles, book chapters, and a children's book, *One Love*. She also coauthored a textbook on positive classroom management and has secured external grants to recruit and retain traditionally underrepresented scholars. Dr Walker mentors doctoral students and junior and mid-level faculty nationally on successful doctoral program completion and tenure and promotion attainment, respectively.

ABOUT THE CONTRIBUTORS

Gwendolyn Cartledge is a Professor Emerita at the Ohio State University (OSU), College of Education and Human Ecology. She began teaching in general and special education but taught most extensively in higher education. Her professional research and writings have centered on the social and reading skills of children with and without disabilities, particularly those from culturally and linguistically diverse backgrounds. She documents over 100 publications, including 5 books: *Teaching Social Skills to Children, Cultural Diversity and Social Skill Instruction, Teaching Urban Learners, Diverse Learners with Exceptionalities,* and *There's More to the Story: Using Literature to Teach Diversity and Social-Emotional Skills in the Elementary Classroom*. Among her various awards, Gwendolyn Cartledge is recognized for Distinguished Teaching (2003, OSU), Educator of Year (2006, Ohio Council of Exceptional Children), Distinguished Alumni (2010, University of Pittsburgh), and Women in Behavior Analysis Hall of Fame (2022, WIBA). She received her undergraduate and master's degrees from the University of Pittsburgh and her doctorate in education from the Ohio State University.

Cathy D. Kea, Professor Emerita at North Carolina Agricultural & Technical State University, is distinguished for her research in special education, particularly in developing culturally responsive teachers and supporting educators of color. With over 30 scholarly publications to her name, Dr Kea's expertise is widely recognized. She is a consistent beneficiary of federal education grants and has earned prestigious accolades, including the Felix S. Barker Special Education Leadership Award in 2021 and the Leadership to the Special Education Field Award from the University of Kansas in 2019. Her academic credentials include a BA from North Carolina Central University, an MS with a focus on learning and behavioral disorders from the University of Wisconsin-LaCrosse, and a PhD in Special Education and Administration from the University of Kansas. Furthering her specialization, she completed a postdoctoral fellowship in multicultural special education at the University of Virginia-Charlottesville.

Patricia J. Larke is a retired Professor Emerita from the Department of Teaching, Learning and Culture (TLAC), Texas A&M University, College Station, TX. She retired from the Department of Teaching, Learning as Culture after 34 years in 2017. She has been a scholar in the field of multicultural education for over 35 years. She was the first African American female who received the rank of Full Professor beginning at the rank of Lecturer. She has over 125 publications including journal articles, book chapters/monographs, and three coedited books.

Her latest coedited book is entitled, *Cultivating Achievement, Respect and Empowerment (CARE) for PreK-12 African American Girls: Implications for Access, Equity and Achievement*. She currently resides in Beech Island, SC, with her husband, Rev Dr Alvin Larke, Jr, retired Professor Emeritus, Texas A&M University.

Lillian B. Poats, EdD, is a Professor in the Department of Educational Administration and Foundations at Texas Southern University. She previously served as an Acting Provost and the Senior Vice President for Academic Affairs, the Dean of the College of Education, and the Associate Dean of the Graduate School. Dr Poats earned a bachelor's degree in Secondary Education from Purdue University, a master's degree in counseling, and a doctorate in Higher Education Administration from Texas Southern University. She has numerous professional publications which focus on academic success and diversity in education. They include: "The Predictable Relationship between Demographic Factors and Persistence of First-Year Students at a Historically Black College & University;" "The Predictability of Success for Minority Students Entering an Educator Preparation Program;" "Cultural and Ethnic Diversity in Texas Schools: Implications for Leadership Effectiveness;" and "A View from the Top: An Academic Affairs Take on the Scholarship of Integration."

Veronica G. Thomas, PhD, is a Professor in the Department of Human Development and Psychoeducational Studies at Howard University. She is also the Evaluation and Continuous Improvement (ECI) Director of Georgetown-Howard Universities Center for Clinical Translational Sciences (GHUCCTS). Dr Thomas has received the American Evaluation Association's Multiethnic Issues in Evaluation TIG Scholarly Leader Award for scholarship that has contributed to social justice–oriented, equity-focused, and culturally responsive literature. She has authored or coauthored numerous peer-reviewed publications, and her recent textbook, *Evaluation in Today's World: Respecting Diversity, Improving Quality, and Promoting Usability,* coauthored with Patricia B. Campbell, received a Most Promising New Textbook Award from the Textbook & Academic Authors Association.

Gwendolyn C. Webb currently holds a joint appointment as an Associate Professor in *Educational Administration and Human Resource Development* and *Teaching, Learning and Culture* at Texas A&M University (TAMU). She is the Associate Director of the Educational Leadership Research Center at TAMU. Her work explores (a) culturally responsive leadership, pedagogy, and teacher development, (b) equity audits, (c) the disproportionate representation of African American learners in Special Education, (d) culturally responsive family and community engagement, and (f) the exploration of academic achievement, and sociopolitical and emotional contexts among African American girls. Her current research focuses on examining the perceptions of young African girls who demonstrate "Talking With Attitude," as they are overrepresented in discipline and suspension data. She champions a strength/integrity model to share their voice, while affirming their cultural identity and promise. She is currently a Co-PI of a collaborative Teacher Performance Quality grant with Prairie View A&M University. Project Leading Equity Across Diverse Environments with Revolutionary Synergy (LEADERS) prepares principals to better serve high needs and Title I campuses in PreK-12 schools in the State of Texas.

Clara Y. Young is a strategic transformational leader who has served as a Department Chairperson, an Associate Vice President, and a President of organizations. She is skilled in strategic planning, implementing strategies to realize the vision and scholarly writing. She has progressed through the ranks in academia up to Interim Assistant Vice President. Dr Young implemented strategic initiatives to assist students in their progression in higher education as a Doctoral Student, Professor, Department Chairperson, and AVP. She led the Tenure and Promotion process at Tennessee State University and addressed progress and issues related to academic programs. She also led "New Faculty Orientation" and implemented the "New Faculty Institute." Dr Young's academic career has included being an advocate for students in which she has mentored students through the academic process by instructing how to ask questions, take exams, write papers, and communicate with professors.

PREFACE

INTRODUCTION

At first blush, this book, *Journeys of Black Women in Academe: Shared lessons, Experiences, and Insights*, appears to focus solely on our academic journeys in higher education institutions. But it is much more than that. Unlike airport security demanding that you either quickly consume or toss out certain items before boarding flights, we could not and would not jettison our family backgrounds and lived cultural experiences. Each chapter author had her own private reckoning with how her career in the academy was impacted by family, community, and cultural backdrops. The following chapters, both joyful and painful to write at times, meld the academy with the communities in which we grew up. When you've been in a field over three decades, it is natural to retrospectively examine your career. You begin to ask yourself questions such as: Have I made the impact that I wanted? What were my points of pride? What regrets, if any, do I have? What facilitated my success? By the same token, what prohibited my success? What would I do differently next time?

As I reflected on my own journey, replete with successes and challenges, I believe that it has covered multiple terrains. My conversations with Black women in the academy in the field of education have led to similar conclusions. Throughout our careers, we have traversed across varied terrains, pathways, and routes as we navigated the academy and its formal and informal reward systems. This book emerged from smooth and rough spaces and all those in between – intersections, crossroads, railroad tracks, and roundabouts.

I enjoy going to professional conferences. They provide great academic getaways to disseminate my work, stay abreast of what's going on in the field of education, and engage in professional development via plenary sessions, roundtables and panel discussions, and speaker series. As exciting and enlightening as those activities are, what I look most forward to is gathering informally with my academic "sisters," with whom I feel connected by culture and circumstances in the academy. We make time, cramming our social time into an already overprogrammed schedule. At these gatherings, we talk about our families, current events, and, of course, what is going on at our respective institutions. At times, we are conscious of lowering our voices as our excitement rises – other times, not so much. Regardless of our individual backgrounds, the conversation is often peppered with what we refer to as old folks' sayings that we heard frequently as children. They are those sayings that we heard from our mothers, grandmothers, and other elders and are passed down from generation to generation. While we used to call them old folks' sayings, we have come to realize that we say them now quite often. According to that line of logic, we have become old folks.

> Before you talk about others, sweep around your own front door.
>
> If you tell one lie, you gotta tell two.
>
> She didn't stay in school as long as John stayed in the army. (*She didn't stay in school* can be replaced with any occurrence that happened or didn't happen in a short period of time).
>
> The pot can't call the kettle black.
>
> What's done in the dark will come to light.
>
> I'll be there tomorrow, if the good Lord's willing and the creek don't rise.

These are some of the most common sayings. I'm sure every culture has its own ancestral sayings. As you read this book, I hope that you will reflect on your ancestral sayings and how they have or have not impacted you as a scholar preparing for, or in a professorial or administrative role in the academy. This book also comes from a place of realizing that most of us have either retired or will be sunsetting our careers in the academy in the not-too-distant future. As I stand on the sunsetting phase of my career, and take a rearview mirror approach, I'm reminded of those sayings even more. What is most striking is the realization that having earned a doctorate in education and a jurist doctorate, it was the ancestral sayings and lessons that facilitated the lessons and insights that I gleaned. In light of those foundational experiences, I believe that I was able to navigate the academy somewhat better. Moreover, that is what helped me reconcile many of my higher education experiences and dissonance.

When I was in fourth grade, my classmate "Carlton" threatened to beat me up when school got out every single day. I started watching the clock and getting anxious after lunch. I dreaded 3:00 p.m. rolling around. The dismissal bell. I'd grab my books and run as if there was no tomorrow – with "Carlton" on my heels. Each day, "Carlton" seemed to be getting closer and closer before I reached my front door. This went on for about two weeks. I reluctantly told my mother that as much as I loved school, I didn't want to go because of "Carlton." After I shared how I was fast becoming a track star, she asked me if I really wanted to stop him. I said that I wanted nothing more than for him to leave me alone.

She told me to go and find a big stick the next morning and on the way to school, to discretely put it behind a tree. When the 3:00 dismissal bell rings, she said to just run to the tree, duck behind it, grab the stick, and come out swinging. She forewarned me to make sure that I made it to the tree.

Sure enough, the next morning I found a nice-sized stick and put it behind a tree that I pass every day on the way home. Every time "Carlton" passed me at school, he said, "Imma beat you up after school." I had even more anxiety after lunch that day. At 3:00 p.m. sharp, the bell rang, and I sprang into action. I quickly grabbed the books perched on my desk for easy access and takeoff. And I ran and ran. I looked back and he was right behind me. *If I could just make it to the tree.*

I made it and ducked behind the tree. I came out swinging that big stick wildly and blindly (I think I even had my eyes closed). The next thing I knew, "Carlton" took off running in the opposite direction. In the academy, I thought of that incident often. Even though I don't think I hit or even made the slightest contact with "Carlton" while I was swinging the stick, it sent him a strong message that even though he was much bigger than me, I stopped running and stood up for myself. I'm sure my mother pondered whether she should go to the school and report it or teach me how to handle my business. To this day when faced with a challenge, I tell myself that everything will be all right if I just make it to the tree. Of course, I wouldn't advocate that big stick approach to addressing school bullies now, but that was a much different day and time.

There are so many other rich experiences that the contributing authors and I recount throughout this book. Those experiences, lessons, and insights shed light on our successes and challenges encountered along our academic journeys. Four of the contributing authors are retired professors, and four of us have not retired (three professors and an Associate Professor). The eight authors jointly amassed over 250 years in academe, with an average tenure of 30 years.

This book was also written and emerged during a time when many universities were undergoing legislative bans on diversity, equity, and inclusion that were disrupting and displacing initiatives, offices, and personnel (see https://www.npr.org/2024/03/04/1235725631/university-florida-cuts-dei-office and https://www.texastribune.org/2023/12/28/texas-new-laws-dei-ban-colleges-universities/). DEI positions often are assumed by persons of color who stand to be most impacted by the shuttering of those offices and initiatives. Teacher preparation programs are also impacted regarding promotion and teacher guidelines and sanctions for violations of the legislative bills. Perhaps this book can be instructive regarding the continued need for initiatives and services that take advantage of the exceptions that are identified in the legislative bills. Tenure and promotion strategies are addressed in each of the eight chapters.

Mentorship of Black women in the academy is more crucial now than ever before. Each of the eight authors discussed mentorship and what we deemed effective mentorship model components. Mentorship models must avoid a deficit-driven approach where the protégé is the one perceived on the receiving end of mentorship. Instead, developing a reciprocal mentorship-protégé model can be more beneficial. Several of us debunk the myth that only race-similar mentors are the best for Black women. While same-race mentors are sorely needed, we in no way downplay their importance and effectiveness. Some authors have experienced effective mentoring from men, including those who are racially dissimilar. In fact, my mentors in higher education have been men – both Black men and white men. They had the most profound impact on my growth and development in my Master's and doctoral programs and the early-, mid-, and senior-level faculty phases of my career. That said, this book is also intended to be instructive to non-Black faculty and administrators regarding the strategies that go beyond eliminating invisibility and microaggression phenomena to affirming the uniqueness of Black women using strength-based approaches.

To orient you on how this book came together, I sent letters out to Black women who have been in higher education for over two decades and who, despite challenges, have successful academic careers, however they defined "successful careers." I aimed to gauge their interest in crafting chapters that would be instructive for graduate students and early- and mid-career faculty and administrators in higher education. I also asked them to reflect on their ancestral or old folks' sayings that resonated with them throughout their careers.

It was amazing that among the eight of us who answered the call, four spent most of their careers in Predominately White Institutions (PWIs). Three spent most of their careers in Historically Black Colleges and Universities (HBCUs), and the last one had experiences in both institution types, with her last one in a HBCU.

Interestingly, I asked the authors one question to which they were to interpret and respond in their own way: The guiding question was: As you reflect on your career, what advice/lessons learned do you most want to impart to early- and mid-career faculty and administrators? The intent is to pass the baton to faculty, researchers, and administrators of color, especially African American or Black women.

Journeys of Black Women in Academe: Shared Lessons, Experiences, and Insights is where our academic wisdom squares up with our ancestral wisdom. We share and pass along this combined and culturally relevant wisdom to scholars and professionals in academia. The chapters are ordered in an alternating fashion by institution type – An author from a PWI is followed by an author from a HBCU.

Each chapter was individually crafted without conversations or communication with the other authors. In fact, the contributing authors did not know which authors were involved in this project until all chapters were completed and submitted for peer review. Notably, the overwhelming majority of the contributors provided glimpses into their family backgrounds and childhood lessons. Most of the authors were from working-class backgrounds, and one was from a poor or low-income background. There were similarities and some differences in the themes among the authors at PWIs and our counterparts at HBCUs. Racism among white colleagues was discussed more than gender among faculty at PWIs, and gender-related phenomena were more prominent among some authors at HBCUs. At least three of the authors discussed the phenomena of resistance they experienced from some Black colleagues. Self-esteem and ethnic identity were themes that emerged across five contributors, while six authors discussed family and community supports. Each author addressed the importance of mentorship in its various forms and provided clear strategies for successfully navigating tenure and promotion.

Other themes included the need for identifying passion and purpose and the role that spirituality and religion played in their careers in the academy. In conclusion, this book is not the culminating event of our work and journeys. It represents a beginning where we unabashedly honor our rich ancestral wisdom legacy and share experiences among ourselves and in mixed company. One of the authors quoted Shirley Chisolm, who said,

> I want history to remember me… not as the first black woman to have made a bid for the presidency of the United States, but as a black woman who lived in the 20th century and who dared to be herself. (n.d.)

As the Editor of this book, I am honored to present our well-traveled sojourns where we simply exhaled and dared to be ourselves.

ACKNOWLEDGMENTS

This book would still be a figment of my imagination and an object of my heart's desire if it were not for Dr Henry Frierson, my long-time mentor, colleague, and friend. I could always count on him, as the Diversity Series Editor, to give honest feedback, encouragement, and well-balanced critiques. Dr Frierson is one of the most astute, generous, and talented scholars and former university administrators that I know. I am so grateful that throughout my career, he has always been there fulfilling a host of roles. Despite his busy schedule and being in such high demand, Dr Frierson is never too busy to listen to my ideas, no matter how far-fetched, and share his expertise, advice, and words of wisdom. I am so appreciative of Dr Frierson who, because of his impact, makes me want to be a better scholar and humanitarian.

I am forever indebted to my awe-inspiring chapter contributors and sister-colleagues representing Predominately White Institutions (PWIs) and Historically Black Colleges and Universities (HBCUs). You texturized my vision and breathed life into this book. I sincerely do not have the lexicon to adequately express my gratitude for the way you responded to the increased calls urgently sounded by Black women in higher education institutions around the country. I marvel how you each continue to be that woman, postretirement for some.

Mentorship is at the core of this book. I constantly reflect on the culturally responsive and effective mentoring that I received in my graduate schooling. I am grateful for Dr Paul Zionts, who provided guidance as my Master's advisor at Central Michigan University and the Late Dr Richard Simpson, my co-major doctoral program professor at the University of Kansas. They were prime examples that effective mentoring transcends race and gender differences. I am also eternally grateful to the other men who mentored me throughout my career in the academy. In addition to Dr Henry Frierson, I will always appreciate Dr James L. Paul, Dr John L. Johnson, Dr Tennyson Wright, Dr Bernard Oliver, and Dr Ronald Rochon.

I also thank my colleagues across race and gender lines with whom I work. It has been refreshing and affirming to begin discussing some phenomena unique to Black women in the academy. I am encouraged that this book can be a vehicle for more open and honest dialogues. I thank you now and in advance.

I have been blessed to have had proud, hardworking, and spiritually uplifting women in my life. Every day, I'm thankful for the ancestral sayings and influence of my mother, the late Ms Louise Nutt, my grandmother, the late Ms Emma Lawrence, and my aunties, Ms Mildred Brent, the late Ms Gayle Ford, Ms Betty Dancer-Turner, Ms Velorice Collins, and my cousin, Ms Janet Hill.

Without Emerald Publishing Company, this book truly would not be possible. I am immensely thankful for their editing and publication teams including Kirsty Woods, Joshi Monica Jerome, Lydia Cutmore, Sangeetha Rajan, Lauren Kammerdiener, Varsha Velmurugan, and Denise Woolery. They made the technical aspects as painless as possible and graciously worked with us despite the time difference. I will forever be grateful for their diligence and commitment to a high-quality product.

Last, but certainly not least, I appreciate and am grateful for my family and friends who gave me sacred time and space to engage in my three R process – Reflecting, Reminiscing, and Reconciling. My husband, Andre M. Walker, has been a staunch supporter throughout this process and stood in the gap of life's daily demands so I could maximize my reflecting and writing times. Carolyn Barton, my sister-in-love, DeAndre and Cindy Walker, my son and daughter-in-love, and my two beautiful grandchildren never cease to encourage and inspire me and my work. Thank you to my dear cousins who also make me want to be a better version of myself, especially Valerie Miller in Flint, MI, the Honorable Michael Wagner in Detroit, MI, and Father Maurice Nutt in New Orleans, LA. I would be quite remiss if I did not thank Dr Samuel L. Wright, Sr, my dear friend and unofficial accountability partner who checked on my progress daily. His handprint is all over every one of my initiatives and projects. This book is no different. Much respect to All!

"FORE DAY IN THE MORNIN" AND BLACK WOMEN IN ACADEME: EMBRACING OPPORTUNITIES AND CONFRONTING MICROAGGRESSIONS

Brenda L. Walker

University of South Florida, USA

ABSTRACT

This author reflects on her academic career spanning three decades as a Black woman in higher education. Ironically, the elders' sayings she heard and detested as a child resonated throughout her career. While in eighth grade, her grandmother admonished her for being deceptive and trying "to pull one over" on her and said that this author would need "to get up 'fore day in the mornin'" to accomplish that feat. "Fore day in the mornin" must have been the time before her grandmother was fully alert, astute, and had the most clarity. For Black women to succeed in the academy, we must remain alert and recognize when faculty, administrators, and students attempt to pull one over with microaggressions and other forms of resistance. Microaggressions and resistance were perpetrated across race and gender lines, and occasionally by those who look like her. Having been reared in urban and low-income communities, the author acknowledged the investments she received throughout her schooling and career from both members of the academy and from Black communities. Consequently, her mission to improve outcomes in schools and communities, much like those in which she grew up, has not changed in 33 years. Understanding race and culture in self-definition and identity are discussed, followed by embracing opportunities and return on investments. There are increased calls for reciprocal and culturally responsive mentor–protégé relationships and successful strategies for tenure and promotion. The author

Journeys of Black Women in Academe
Diversity in Higher Education, Volume 26, 1–26

Published under exclusive licence by Emerald Publishing Limited
ISSN: 1479-3644/doi:10.1108/S1479-364420240000026001

makes meaning of both successful and challenging critical incidents in the academy.

Keywords: Black women faculty; microaggressions; academia; intersectionality; mentor and protégé relationships; Black women administrators; tenure and promotion

In junior high school, my friend "Simone" invited me to her birthday party. It was to be held on the upcoming Sunday. I wanted to attend, but there was one problem. It was on a Sunday. I went to church with my grandmother on Sundays – literally all day on Sundays. We went to Sunday School in the morning and stayed for the regular church service from late morning until the afternoon. We went home for some downtime and dinner and returned for the evening church service at 5:00 p.m. I reluctantly asked my grandmother if I could miss the evening service to attend "Simone's" birthday party. After some hesitation, she finally agreed. I was ecstatic! That Sunday, I excitedly walked around to "Simone's" house and discovered that she was not having a birthday party. Not only was she not having a birthday party, but her birthday was six months away. Since my grandmother was at church, we invited several friends over to my grandmother's house. We were having such a good time in the basement; we were laughing, talking, playing music on the record player, and dancing. What I did not know was that my grandmother suspected something was awry and returned home early. She was furious! I can still hear her saying, "You gotta get up 'fore day in the morning' to pull one over on me." Growing up, I heard that "'fore day in the mornin'" saying and cringed more times than I can count.

Ironically, as much as I didn't like to hear it as a child, "fore day in the mornin" resonated with me as I took a rearview look at my career in the academy and crafted this chapter. It became an automatic mantra whenever I suspected someone was trying to pull one over on me or be deceitful to achieve their goal. Even though I was unknowingly misled initially by my eighth-grade friend "Simone," I allowed the deception to play out by inviting friends over while my grandmother was at church. Similarly, in higher education, whether the deception is intentional or not is immaterial, especially when it is knowingly played out or committed. To this day, I have no idea what time "fore day in the mornin" is. I imagine it is not only relatively early, but more importantly, it must be before the time when you are most alert, have all your wits about you, and have the most clarity. Perhaps it is before you can readily discern when something is awry, not right, off-kilter, or the butter in the milk not clean. Maybe it is analogous to the advice that Thelonius Sphere Monk, the legendary jazz musician, gave to other musicians. He said that, "There are no wrong notes, only notes in wrong places" (https://www.bookey.app/quote-author/thelonious-monk).

Throughout my career in the academy, it was paramount that I remained alert and recognized and confronted micro- and macroaggressions and other forms of resistance while finding and amplifying my voice. I needed to provide advocacy and agency not just for myself but also for other Black women and men in higher education. To successfully navigate as a Black woman in the professoriate, I had to deliberately lean in to define my own "fore day in the mornin" and learn to read all the notes, including those in between and in the wrong places.

This chapter continues the recent national dialog on unsilencing Black women in higher education so that our voices are heard and we are more visible, respected, and affirmed. This author discusses the need for self-definition and identification incorporating race and culture. Culturally responsive opportunities are then shared to return investments in both academic and African American communities. Further, microaggressions and other forms of resistance are addressed that uniquely impede Black women's success in the academy. The author extolls the power of reciprocal mentor–protégé relationships and concludes with strategies that facilitate Black women in the academy attaining tenure and promotion.

UNDERSTANDING RACE AND CULTURE IN SELF-DEFINITION AND IDENTITY

My serene pastel pink suit and matching pumps were oddly deceptive. I glanced in the hotel room's full-length mirror and was even more convinced. My calm-looking outer appearance belied and was no match for the mounting anxiety and nervousness swirling inside me. It was March 1991, and I was interviewing for my very first Assistant Professor position at a university in the southeast. I was a doctoral candidate at the University of Kansas where I had conducted my dissertation research and was writing my results and discussion or chapters four and five of my dissertation. I flew in the day before the interview and was pleasantly surprised when I received my itinerary. It was the best!

The night before the interview, a Black woman faculty member hosted about six or seven other Black women who held various faculty roles at the university across several Colleges. It was an informal, kick-your-shoes-off meet and greet in her home. We watched the original movie, *The Color Purple*, sipped wine, and talked and talked. It was as if I knew them already. While I had interviewed at a few other universities, no other university provided a safe space for me to be with women who looked like me. No other university provided a no-judgment, no-apology-needed comfort zone where I could ask my uber-important interview questions. This hostess did. She created space so I could safely ask where to go to get my hair done and whether there were engaging African Methodist Episcopal Churches in the area. As an outsider moving there from the Midwest, I wanted a heads up on the city's Black communities, in which I planned to immerse myself. It was important that I develop trusting, reciprocal relationships to authentically gain entrée to those communities.

As delightful as the eve of the interview was, it added to my anxiety that next morning. I was pressured more than usual to do well. I really desired a tenure-earning position at that university. After spending the evening with my new academic sisters, I realized even more the critical roles that race, gender, and culture play in my professional and personal worlds. Making time and space for my multiple intersectionalities of race, gender, and my cultural being did not go unnoticed. My mind was made up. This was going to be the one – the perfect university for me.

When I received the call a week or so later from the Department Chairperson offering me the position, I knew that I would happily launch my career in the academy there. Knowing that the state had a hiring freeze at that time was even more confirming. The Department Chair made a case to hire me despite the freeze solely based on my credentials, qualifications, and what I would bring to the department. That did it! I was convinced that I would not have been happy at any other university. And to be perfectly honest, I was happy...until I wasn't. And I felt supported...until I didn't.

I deliberately started this chapter with a snippet of my university interview process. It may have been almost 33 years ago, but it remains symbolic and representative of who I am today. First and foremost, a pink pastel suit was not on the typical interview suit color palette at the time. Interview suits were more likely to be darker and more basic in color (i.e., navy, gray, black, etc.). In the interview, I intentionally disclosed both my culturally responsive research focus and my individual uniqueness in a true *caveat emptor* or buyer beware manner. Pairing a white starched button-down blouse with a cotton-candy pink suit symbolized my flair for the nontraditional, which is tempered by my need for some tradition at times. My individuality and uniqueness remain important to me and show up in my styles of dress, hair, office décor, and other aspects of my professional and personal realms.

I made a point to let everyone know that my research, teaching, and service have not occurred by happenstance. Emerging from my humble beginnings, my work would continue to be intentional. I am a proud product and beneficiary of urban and low-income schools and communities. That's what I know and am most passionate about. I would not want anyone to think that I duped them while interviewing. It would be egregious to say one thing in the interview and practice another. So, I explicitly shared how I am committed to improving outcomes for all children and youth but am primarily focused on improving outcomes for Black children and youth living in poverty.

I am proud of that commitment and dedication and how it continues to ground and center my academic journey 33 years later. The year 1991 was such a conflicting year because we were forced as a nation to have conversations about police brutality against Black men and sexual harassment accusations leveled against a Black man by a Black woman. Several Los Angeles Police Officers were videotaped brutally beating Mr Rodney King on March 3, 1991 (https://www.history.com/this-day-in-history/police-brutality-caught-on-video).

In that same year and only 2 months after I assumed my Assistant Professorship, Anita Hill testified in the Supreme Court confirmation hearing that Clarence Thomas sexually harassed her while she was his adviser at the Equal Employment Opportunity Commission. Despite her graphic testimonial details, Mr Thomas was confirmed with a vote of 52–48.

I was keenly aware of police brutality targeting Black males and sexual harassment to which Black women have been subjected in this country. However, I was less familiar with how Black women are targeted and dealt with in the academy. I came to the University with a social justice and equity penchant stemming from inequities I witnessed not just in K-12 classrooms but in every segment of society – law enforcement and criminal justice, housing, banking, medical, etc. What I was ill-prepared for, however, were the inequities perpetuated in higher education. Given my 33-year academic career, one overarching question guides this chapter: *As a Black woman in higher education, what are the most impactful lessons and insights that should be shared with Black women who are doctoral students or early- or mid-career faculty and administrators?* I also aimed to share lessons and insights that would be instructive for full Professors and administrators across race and gender. As a Black woman, of course, I intend for this chapter to be beneficial to Black women and other women of color, but the audience is not just Black women or women of color. I believe that White doctoral students, faculty, and administrators can benefit by viewing faculty and administrator experiences through the lens of a Black woman who has had bittersweet experiences throughout her career. Like many of my sister colleagues, I have enjoyed and achieved success but have also experienced gendered and racialized trauma and stress.

Sankofa is a West African term that means that we must return to or "fetch" our past to move forward. Sankofa is so fitting for this chapter to discuss and make sense of critical incidents that occurred throughout my academic career. As I go back and fetch my past in the academy, I must first go back and fetch my past growing up in low-income communities and being heavily influenced by my mother, grandmother, aunts, and cousins. I draw on my rich experiences in poor neighborhoods and communities, including the Norman Street Housing Projects under the Saginaw Housing Authority. When I think about it, that is where I learned to value individual uniqueness and appreciate collaborative problem-solving.

Some of my friends and colleagues appear perplexed when I tell them that I am proud to have grown up in urban and low-income communities. First and foremost, my mother was a single parent who raised five children in a firm but loving way. Contrary to popular opinion about low-income families, our home was filled with reading materials, including magazines, poetry books, and the *World Book and the Encyclopedia Britannica*. It was a running joke that despite having limited income, my mother faithfully paid every month so that we could have several encyclopedias or passports to the world at our fingertips. I am so grateful for the way she shored up my self-esteem long before I started kindergarten. She taught me to be proud of who I am, my racial background, and my dark brown skin tone.

When I was in kindergarten, my White teacher passed out drawing paper and told us to draw our best picture so she could hang it in the classroom. She was preparing our room for school administrators to visit the next day. I went to work on my best picture. I drew a picture of myself in the image my mother taught me and proudly reinforced it at home. After drawing the picture complete with correctly placed face, limbs, and clothing, I took out the special dark brown crayon my mother had bought me for occasions such as that. I shaded in my face, arms, and legs with that beautiful dark brown crayon. When I finished, I admired my drawing and beamed broadly. Suddenly, I felt someone looking over my shoulder and spun around. It was my teacher. I waited for her to tell me that I did a good job. And I waited and waited. Judging by the scowl on her face, she was not about to affirm me.

Instead, she reminded me that we had important guests coming to visit and that she had intended to hang the pictures up for them to see. She walked away without ever collecting my dark brown girl "masterpiece." The teacher proceeded to hang everyone's picture up except mine. Kindergarten then was half-day, so I didn't have long to wait until time to run home and tell my mother what had transpired. That gave my mother the perfect opportunity to reiterate what she always told me. I have everything to be proud of – who I am, the African kings and queens from whom I originated, and the many contributions of the likes of Paul Laurence Dunbar, Marian Anderson, and Langston Hughes. My mother marched me back to the school and sat me in the hallway while she went into the classroom to meet with the teacher. Despite my trying, I could only overhear bits and pieces of the conversation. I found out later that in her soft-spoken manner, my mother very calmly explained to the teacher how she took great pains to ensure that I started school with a positive self-esteem and identity. She was adamant about not wanting the teacher to destroy my self-esteem. In hindsight, that teacher's action or inaction was serendipitous. It made me even more conscious at a young age to be proud of who I am. At the university, it has translated to my self-affirmation and affirmations of my village or support group. I do not depend on others' acceptance or value of me and what I bring to the table. Most importantly, I learned to never allow anyone to define who I am, what I stand for, or my worth.

Collaborative problem-solving was another principle I learned in my childhood that was instrumental throughout my university career. One of my earliest and fondest recollections of collaborative problem-solving happened when our apartment was next door to another single-parent family with the same number of children. Our families were quite close as our mothers fiercely looked out for each other. In one of our apartments, the electricity was cut off for nonpayment. To this day, I cannot tell you which one was temporarily without electricity. What does stick out in my mind is that until one apartment's electricity was legitimately restored, both of our families had enough electricity to meet our basic needs. Do not try this at home, but at that time, we ran extension cords from one apartment to the other. In effect, both families cooked using hot plates for cooking and for boiling water for baths.

As a child, I had no understanding or appreciation for the danger of running those extension cords from one apartment to the next. However, I did appreciate the way we all worked together for a common goal with no judgments made. Moreover, we imagined that we were having a fun and light-hearted camping experience. While sharing electricity was illegal and unsafe, the value of collaborative problem-solving and shared community was ignited and stoked for me, especially how it could be used to mitigate some effects of poverty.

EMBRACING OPPORTUNITIES AND RETURNING INVESTMENTS IN THE ACADEMY AND BLACK COMMUNITIES

Without having the lexicon for it as a child, I also learned the importance of return on investment in its many forms. Growing up in urban and low-income communities, my return on investment has long been important to me. I returned to my hometown in Saginaw, Michigan, for my much anticipated 52nd-year high school class reunion. It was a reunion for the class of 1971 Black graduates from any of the Saginaw area high schools. As I imagined, reconnecting with my friends with whom I went to junior high and/or high school was so wonderful. From my peers, I heard the same resounding comments over and over. They consistently told me that they always knew that I would go far and that I would make a difference for others. Their sincere comments caused me to reflect on the many ways they held me in high esteem and invested in my future career and me. Remarkably, most were from low-income families quite like my own. Ironically, I managed to navigate elementary, junior high and high school without being involved in one fight and with minimal peer pressure to break academic or societal rules and norms. With the exception of "Simone," I believe that my classmates invested in me by applying little to no pressure to engage in behaviors that ran counter to being academically productive. My peers encouraged and celebrated my academic and social milestones.

I attended Central Michigan University for my undergraduate education. It was about an hour away from Saginaw. When I went home some weekends and summer, older adults and family members expressed how proud they were that I was in college. They would give me tightly folded-up fives, tens, or twenties for "spending money." Community service takes on new meaning when the community has invested in you, and you are compelled to return far more than what was invested.

When I assumed my Assistant Professor position, I asked what the criteria for tenure and promotion were. In the Fall of my sixth year, I was expected to meet the University's criteria for teaching, research, and service to be promoted and tenured. My return on investment had to yield benefits to Black communities. That was non-negotiable for me. Early in my career, the challenge was determining how to meet the University's tenure and promotion parameters while impacting and benefitting Black communities *and* my profession. That was no easy feat considering the low weight that service carries when tenure and promotion decisions are made.

To be clear, teaching effectiveness and cogent and impactful research records sway tenure and promotion decisions far more than service. To accomplish my professional and personal goals, I needed to infuse service throughout my service agenda and the two most important tenure and promotion expectations – teaching and research. Stated simply, I was able to maximize my return on investment to my profession and Black communities locally, regionally, nationally and internationally. For example, I intentionally incorporated culturally responsive and respectful pedagogy that focused on more equitable academic and social skill instruction for pre-and in-service teachers. My solution-based research consistently examined phenomena that affect Black learners far more disproportionately than other races and ethnicities.

We are expected to publish or disseminate our work in well-regarded academic journals for tenure and promotion. As important as they are in the Academy, our academic journals are less accessible to those most subjected to the phenomena I investigated. Parents, community agents, and some K-12 school personnel entrusted with Black children and youth are less likely to read published work in journals unfamiliar to laypersons. Thus, I also relied on popular press venues, including my guest speaking and interviewing in mainstream and Black newspapers, television, and urban and Black radio shows. Those platforms allowed me to translate published research and scholarship for laypersons. In addition to getting audience feedback, I ensured they always had access to and information about my research findings and initiatives to improve outcomes for our most disenfranchised learners.

My sustained community service has socially validated my teaching and research and led to a genuine reciprocal and tri-directional relationship. Not only has the community been a viable part of my teaching and research, but I am very much immersed in the community. To be successfully tenured and promoted *and* to return investments to your community, you must build and stoke symbiotic relationships among all three tenure and promotion dimensions of teaching, research, and service.

Most of my investors were Black women when I was growing up. In contrast, my mentors who invested in me in higher education were men – White men and Black men. In my second year as an Assistant Professor, I decided that I wanted to compete for a federal grant to partner with the local school district to develop a Drop-Out Prevention Center. I served on committees with the local school district and knew that the drop-out phenomenon was one of the most critical issues they needed to address. Consistent with the literature, fewer than half of the Black males who enrolled in the ninth grade persisted to 12th grade and graduated as seniors 3 years later (Bridgeland et al., 2006).

Though I had worked on sections of grants while in my doctoral program, I had never written an entire grant by myself. It was a daunting task, but I was up for it. I told my department chairperson, a White male, that I wanted to pursue a federal grant opportunity and partner with the school district to develop the Drop Out Prevention Center. I proceeded to explain and show him data on why such a center was needed for urban and low-income Black learners. I was prepared to rattle off more reasons why I would be remiss if I did not craft a competitive proposal. He had one question: What supports did I need to prepare a highly competitive grant application? I must admit his question caught me off-guard. I remember while in my doctoral program at the University of Kansas, I had worked with two known grant writers who were typically successful in securing external funding.

Adding to my surprise, he told me to call them to see if they would be interested and available to work with me for a week. He said he would find the money to pay for their accommodations if they came. They did, and we had a grant writing boot camp of sorts. I submitted the federal proposal, and a couple of months later, I was on my way to our department faculty meeting. Out of habit, I stopped by the mail room on my way to the conference room. A letter from the Department of Education awaited. I opened it in the conference room right before the meeting started. Big mistake! I was visibly upset and deeply disappointed. I was informed that my proposed Drop-Out Prevention center was *not* selected for funding in that competition.

As disappointing as that was, the following paragraph was even more unsettling. It stated the total number of applicants, the competitive nature of the grant, the number of funded projects, and the rank-ordering of my proposal. I couldn't hold back the tears when I read that mine was right below the cut-off line and would have been the next one funded if there were more money. Much later, my colleagues teased me for some time about opening that letter at the start of the department meeting. Despite the tears and the non-funding, that remains one of my fondest memories as an Assistant Professor. It spoke volumes of the extent to which my chairperson supported my fierce commitment and desire to invest in low-income communities, much like those I grew up and knew so well.

In essence, I was struck by the cyclical nature of investments. My Department Chairman invested in me so that I could return it both professionally and personally. I often reflect on my chairperson's actions. When I let him know that I wanted to write a grant, he immediately determined that he would make it happen, as opposed to telling me why it would not work or why he couldn't offer any support. I was thrilled that he did not approve verbally and sit back and do nothing, secretly hoping that I would flounder or, better yet, give up. I'm very proud to say that while I didn't get that project funded, I went after a second federal project.

We desperately needed to increase the presence of Black men who were teaching children with special needs. As a new teacher educator in a metropolitan city, I was pretty surprised to walk into my university classrooms filled with aspiring teachers and have such a limited presence of Black women and a literal absence of Black men. That was particularly disturbing for me each semester. Special education classrooms then and now were disproportionately composed of black children and youth (Blanchett, 2006; Harry & Anderson, 1994; Starling, 2012). It seemed quite logical to seek funding to recruit and prepare black male teachers who would be effectively prepared not to maintain the status quo but to assist in determining more accurately who belongs in special education classes and who doesn't.

I learned from our crafting of the unsuccessful federal dropout prevention grant proposal. I wrote the next proposal totally independent and poured into the grant proposal what I learned from the unfunded Drop-Out Prevention Center. I received funding for a special education male teacher project entitled "Project PILOT" (Preparing Innovative Men of Tomorrow) (Townsend & Harris, 2002). Since the first cohort of Project PILOT was funded in 1994, three cohorts of African American men have enrolled and graduated with special education degrees and special education teaching certifications in K-12 classrooms. In that project alone, over 40 African American male teachers were produced. Most assumed teaching positions in Florida and school districts within the university's catchment areas. Some still teach in K-12 or have become administrators in community colleges. I was so pleased that my university president and provost at the time provided funding for two additional years after the federal grant funds ended.

Those Black male scholars changed the complexion of our College of Education classes. I anticipated their voice and presence would disrupt some colleagues' traditional teacher education practices. I had no idea how much those Project PILOT young men were responsible for growth in my own teaching and learning interactions with my students. I heard accounts of the discussions in some of my colleagues' classes. Discussions and lectures on literacy and reading instruction were peppered with interjections and questions from the men of Project PILOT. For example, if the professor was facilitating a hearty discussion and demonstration of strategies for the teaching of reading or math, it was not uncommon for a Project PILOT man to say, "Excuse me, but what strategies do you have for children who come home from school to no electricity? Or children who have been up half the night because of something traumatic happening to a family member? What about children forced to take on adultlike caregiver roles in their families?"

Some faculty members embraced their questions and were delighted that the men of Project PILOT expanded my colleagues' teaching and ability to take on multiple perspectives, even when they had never been subjected to that experience or circumstance. I had some engaging conversations with several colleagues. On the other hand, some faculty resented the Project PILOT men for their voices of agency and advocacy for urban and low-income K-12 students and their families. They avoided conversations with me and, at times, even avoided eye contact. The Pilot men recounted how faculty began to ignore their raised hands and used other tactics to cut them off or silence them. As part of the Project, I arranged monthly mandatory seminars facilitated by Black male professors and administrators in universities around the country.

The seminars addressed topics not typically taught in teacher education programs. Namely, seminar topics included defining themselves and maintaining their identity while adhering to university course and field experience requirements and understanding and affirming Black students' hidden gifts and talents. Other seminars focused on helping Black men get in touch with their feelings and memories about their relationships with their own fathers to be better positioned to teach Black males with conflicted feelings about their fathers. That said, those seminars were instrumental in the Project PILOT men processing and reconciling their experiences in our university classes and field experiences in K-12 schools. Given their recounted experiences in the courses where their contributions were ignored or minimalized, I arranged for the seminar facilitators to address those issues and demonstrate strategies likely to yield productive responses and interactions in those classes.

While I saw myself as a cultural broker or mediator (Gay, 2002) for the Black men in my project, I was ill-prepared for their disruption of my own pedagogy and teacher education practices. I took great pride in being culturally and individually responsive and affirming. Approximately three weeks into the semester, I was teaching a behavior management class to 30 undergraduates preparing to become teachers. The Black men of Project PILOT composed one-half of the class. I distinctly remember that Fall day when the PILOT scholars lingered after class and asked if they could talk to me. It was clear that they had selected a spokesperson for the PILOT cohort. I told them that I was happy to meet with them. When everyone else left, the spokesperson revealed that they wanted to talk to me because I treated them differently than I did the White females in the class.

At first, I was quite defensive. I assured them that I in no way treated them differently. I believed in affirming all my students and meeting their needs. In fact, I believe in meeting them where they are. When I finished my litany of defense mechanisms, I listened as they went on and on about how their White female colleagues had sidebar conversations when we were discussing concepts, and I didn't miss a beat. They told me in no uncertain terms that when they had sidebars and were very much on task and discussing the topic at hand, I stopped talking midsentence and rolled my eyes. That was tough to hear, so I did what any self-righteous Assistant Professor would do: I denied, denied, and denied.

Late that night, I reflected on the Project PILOT men's conversation and replayed many class discussions in my mind. I had to confront and reckon with my own teaching and feminization in my university classroom. Simply put, I forced myself to see their experiences in my course through their lenses instead of my own. They were right, and I had to deal with it. I surmised that what caused me to react differently were the men's voice levels and amplification. They were louder and deeper than women's whispers. Thus, those men's sidebar conversations sounded more like dull roars. I vowed to be more conscious of my reaction to their sidebar conversations that were very much on the topic. I incorporated more time for students to process and discuss concepts in smaller dyads, triads, and groups. We would then have designated times when everyone focused on the speaker. Immediately following the speaker was time for individual and group reaction and processing. I also did a much better job articulating to the young men how loud sidebar conversations can detract from all our teaching and learning interactions. More importantly, I engaged the PILOT men in problem-solving and asked them to assist in generating viable solutions. They really liked the idea of incorporating time for sidebar conversations more frequently throughout class discussions.

CONFRONTING MICROAGGRESSIONS, ANONYMITY, RESISTANCE, AND OTHER FORMS OF CANCEL CULTURE

As stated earlier, when I look back over my childhood, I fondly reflect on the sayings of my grandmother and other elders in my community. Commonly referred to as "old folks" sayings, I heard them so much that I would roll my eyes and mouth the words when I thought no one was looking. Another one that agitated me was the admonishment that you should never ever "throw rocks and hide your hands." My grandmother was more likely to overlook your transgression or rock-throwing if you owned up to it. In her mind, far worse than the transgression was denying it and refusing to take ownership or accountability for your behaviors and actions.

As I reflect on my career in higher education, I am struck by how many times I uttered those exact words and lamented how some administrators, faculty, and students do precisely that – throw rocks and hide their hands. While some of my lessons and insights emanate from painful experiences, some critical incidents brought much happiness and were part and parcel of my academic journey, experiences, and lessons. What follows is a discussion of the anonymity, secrecy, and resistance I have experienced in the academy.

One of my most painful memories occurred relatively early in my career. I was an enthusiastic Assistant Professor teaching undergraduate students, many of whom I recruited for our program. I worked hard to foster positive relationships with my students, or so I thought. I remembered what a guest scholar said in a talk at my university. She said you need a critical mass of traditionally underrepresented students in your classes to have an authentic conversation about diversity. For once, I had a critical mass of African American students in my courses. I was delighted.

One of my students could not continue in our program for a reason that had absolutely nothing to do with me. However, when he told his peers why he was no longer in classes with them, he chose to lie and blame me for his circumstances. As you might imagine, the students believed his one-sided narrative. His hiding his hands put me in a compromised position. Professionally and legally, I could not, nor would I divulge that information as he had student rights to confidentiality and privacy. Unfortunately, I had no such protections and could not refute his untruthful accusations. Subsequently, I had to deal with newly fractured relationships with several of my students.

Apparently, two Black students lodged a complaint against me with the Department Chair following that student's misrepresentations. One evening, I used the copy machine and found a document that was inadvertently left on the machine. It was the summarized results where one of my colleagues interviewed several students in my class. Interestingly, neither the Chair at that time nor the faculty member, whom I considered a friend, informed me of the students' complaints or the process used to "investigate" the students' accusations. I remember thinking that the university is the last place one would expect so much to be done under the cloak of secrecy and the mask of anonymity. Little did I know that was a harbinger of things to come. Ironically, higher education is premised on open ideas and the search for truth, yet many of its procedures and practices are cloaked, masked in anonymity and secrecy, and steeped in outdated tradition.

I noticed when I assumed the role of Assistant Professor that only male faculty taught in our doctoral program. It was unsettling that tenure-earning and tenured women faculty in the Department were relegated to teaching undergraduate and master's students only, not doctoral students. Yet men who were adjuncts or nonpermanent faculty, along with tenured and tenure-earning men, taught doctoral students. That was confusing and caused me some dissonance. I knew that to be successful at tenure and promotion, faculty needed to have experience teaching, mentoring doctoral students, and serving on their committees. At a faculty meeting, I politely made that observation and asked what I needed to do to teach doctoral students. I earned a doctorate from the well-regarded University of Kansas, so I didn't think it would be problematic.

Like many others, my department verbally espoused the philosophy that no person "owned" the courses they taught. Yet I was told that if I wanted to teach doctoral students, I would need to develop a course of my own. Given that we had no courses in our program on urban education, I began developing a doctoral course in urban special education that evening. I learned that you must determine the best means for your self-advocacy and agency. It may be using your own voice or communicating your concerns to a trusted mentor willing to advocate for you when power dynamics are at play, and you are most vulnerable.

There is a growing body of literature on microaggressions (Louis et al., 2016) and the invisibility of Black women in the academy (i.e., Showunmi, 2023; Smith, 2015). The invisibility phenomenon refers to the ways that other faculty and administrators ignore, silence, or minimize Black women's voices and contributions. I had an interesting experience during my short tenure as an Associate Dean. The University consolidated three campuses – the main one with two regional campuses. Consequently, at the time, the Interim Dean, a White woman, met regularly with her leadership team consisting of three Associate Deans and a Director. There were two White Associate Deans on the main campus and we, two African American women, were college-wide leaders on the regional campuses. I was the Associate Dean on a regional campus, and my colleague was the Director of Education on the other regional campus.

In total, there were two White women and two Black women on the Interim Dean's leadership team. I noticed that in her leadership meetings, she would consistently refer to the two White Associate Deans by name and laud them with compliments. When she referred to my sister colleague and me, who provided leadership on the regional campuses, she referred to us by our titles. She totally ignored our campus contributions and our voices in the meeting, but referred to our White colleagues as Dr Jane Doe and Dr Jenna Smith (pseudonyms used). For example, she referred to me by my title as the Interim Associate Dean on the regional campus.

I found it interesting that she not only minimized our contributions but also rarely said our names. It was bothersome the first time it happened, but I gave her the benefit of the doubt. I then noticed that it happened again. I tried humor but to no avail. I said, "Like the singing group, 'Destiny's Child', Say my name, say my name, say my name." She laughed awkwardly, but it did not work. She avoided addressing us more personally and continued to minimize our contributions and accomplishments.

To be clear, I was not looking to the Interim Dean or anyone else at the University for affirmation or validation of my self-worth. Just like I enjoyed the support of my own village–family, friends, and community, I continued to have a convoy of support among family, friends, mentors, and community who provided social validation and encouragement. That is the support system that kept me uplifted and affirmed. I have never relied on a Predominantly White Institution (PWI) for that level of affirmation or culturally responsive support. Unfortunately, even though I was not dependent on the University for affirmation, as a Black woman, my being placed in administrative positions or taking advantage of the university reward structures are inextricably connected to other's perceptions of my value. When those in power hold diminished perceptions of your accomplishments, credentials, and value to the organization, they can more readily pass you over for leadership appointments and other coveted opportunities such as prestigious awards, representation, and seats at decision-making tables.

As my supervisor, the Interim Dean was in a position of power and control. Initially, I needed to bring it to her attention in case her actions were at a dysconscious level of racism (King, 1991).

> Dysconscious racism is a form of racism that tacitly accepts dominant White norms and privileges. It is not the absence of consciousness (that is, not unconsciousness) but an impaired consciousness or distorted way of thinking about race as compared to, for example, critical consciousness. (King, 1991, p. 135)

She would sometimes invite the two White Associate Deans to meetings with the provost, while my African American colleague and I received no such invitation. Despite my letting her know my disappointment in her failure to invite us, she continued to treat us dismissively and as an afterthought. Her actions were anything but dysconsious (King, 1991) or tacit slights. They were deliberate and intentional. It was her intention to erase, reduce, and literally keep us in our "places." After that, my motivation shifted from schooling her on phenomena uniquely experienced by Black women to letting her know that her increasingly blatant actions were duly observed and noted. My only comfort was knowing that because she didn't get up "fore day in the mornin," she certainly did not pull one over on me. I had even more clarity about my contributions, voice, and her futile attempts to minimize both.

While I have enjoyed the support and affirmation of most Black administrators, faculty, and staff at the university, I recall an occasion when a Black administrator also downplayed my accomplishments and voice. Accolades were readily given when White faculty earned awards or received grant funding. At times, I did not have the same congratulatory response when I received awards or grant funding. I had developed a substantial internal and external funded grant portfolio, that benefitted our university immensely. It was a tough lesson for me that "getting up fore day in the mornin" is not just applicable to my White faculty colleagues and administrators but at times was also relevant to some who looked like me.

It took me quite a while to reconcile the irony of Black women or men clipping the wings of other Black women in academia. It reminds me of a scene in the movie, "The Color Purple." There is a glaring and poignant scene in the first movie in 1985 and the second movie being screened in 2023, 38 years later. In that sobering scene, Harpo asks Celie for advice on how he can make his wife, Sophia, more submissive and less domineering like her. Celie, who was severely mistreated, told Harpo that he should beat Sophia. When Sophia got wind of Celie's advice, she marched over to Celie and confronted her.

Hurt and looking for an explanation for Celie's surprising directive, Sophia roared, "You told Harpo to beat me!" Celie sheepishly admitted that she told him that because she was jealous of Sophia. Based on stories from some Black women at PWIs and HBCUs, I thought that minimizing contributions of someone of similar race and gender spoke even more broadly and profoundly of self-hatred and discontent with their own situation. The hard lesson was not taking it personally or as an indictment of other Black women in general. The overwhelming majority of Black women with whom I have worked as colleagues, faculty, staff, and students have been most uplifting and affirming. It is essential to understand their perspectives and motivations and identify their motivation and needs. The ultimate in self-growth and actualization occurred when I began to look beyond what I perceived as their acts or transgressions against me to actually lift them up and celebrate them and their accomplishments.

I had another federal grant-funded project that allowed the recruitment and retention of doctoral scholars of color for university faculty positions to focus their research on children and families in urban and low-income schools and communities. We had productive teaching and learning interactions and course discussions and presented nationally at conferences. The project went well until I admonished some for failing to fulfill the grant requirement that they spend several hours in an urban school relative to their research needs. That field experience aimed to increase their familiarity with urban schools and gain entrée to schools long before they needed access to conduct their dissertation research.

I called a meeting to justify why they needed to fulfill that requirement as written in the grant proposal. To explain the difference between funding with minimal expectations and funding to complete the requirements promised in the proposal, I said that having field experiences in an urban school was a condition for receiving the monthly stipend and other perks provided by the grant. I then shared an analogy that was not received well at all. Some chose to complain to my colleagues or asked them to be their major professors, with no direct conversations with me.

Again, I had to move beyond my own hurt and avoid taking it personally. I continued to celebrate and cheer them on as they navigated their programs of study, but more from the sidelines since I was not a member of their committees. By my admission, I am a work in progress on self-growth and development. Still, I realized that my primary purpose in securing external funding was to increase the presence of faculty of color to conduct lines of inquiry to address academic and social issues in urban and high-poverty children and families. Given that my teaching, research, and service agendas focus on urban schools and communities, I would have loved to serve as their major professor, guiding them through their coursework and dissertations. However, it was more important that they successfully attain their PhDs and assume their rightful positions in higher education, even if it meant that I was not serving as their major professor.

According to Allen (2001), cancel culture is not unique to celebrities and popular culture. Cancel culture is typically reserved for celebrities who engage in offensive or inappropriate language and/or behaviors. Reported as a way for their victims to be empowered, supporters abandon or boycott the perpetrators and their music, products, movies, etc. Romano (2019) defined popular culture's notion of cancel culture as:

> A celebrity or other public figure does or says something offensive. A public backlash, often fueled by politically progressive social media, ensues. Then come the calls to cancel the person – that is, to effectively end their career or revoke their cultural cachet, whether through boycotts of their work or disciplinary action from an employer. (pp. 1–2)

Allen (2001) suggested that Black women professors at PWI law schools are in White spaces and subject to being canceled or silenced based on their multiple intersectionalities of gender and race. In my experiences and observations, Black women professors and administrators at PWIs are similarly canceled and silenced in the Academy for their advocacy and agency for social justice and equity, among other reasons. I have observed Black women and men administrators who were canceled simply because their appointed time, not their contracted time, was up.

At some PWIs, there may be only one or two who are higher-level administrators. That position, with the appearance of power and prestige, comes at a cost. It may mean the Black higher-level administrator holds that position until he or she falls out of favor with the powers that be. I have seen more times than I care to admit that the highest-ranking Black woman or man is put in that tenuous position until he or she says or does something that runs counter to the political or administrative winds in those White spaces. In a more sophisticated attempt to throw rocks and hide their hands, University powers that be may enlist other Black women or men to lead the cancel culture charge for no reason other than the person in that high-ranking position has fallen out of favor. That is the epitome of socially unjust and inequitable actions.

Interestingly, Moore (2008) suggested that Black women in Historically Black Colleges and Universities (HBCU) law schools face similar acts of racism and sexism. Noting that HBCU law schools were premised on White norms, she reported that Black women were silenced if it was perceived that they violated those norms. Consistent with Moore's research, I concur that Black faculty and administrators in higher education must maintain a sense of the sociopolitical climate. When injustices are committed against Black women, senior faculty and administrators must be more willing to take a stand and speak out when Black women are silenced or canceled for no justifiable reason. The limited representation of Black administrators, or tokenism, makes it difficult for Black women to speak out, as they may sense a need to reassure the leadership that they will comply with White norms (Moore, 2008).

Coded language and behaviors pose another form of secret, cloaked, and hidden agendas. When I developed the urban education course, I discussed it with the teaching faculty. There was one affiliated faculty member teaching in our program in particular who spent an inordinate amount of time wanting to talk about the definition of urban education. After this occurred across several faculty meetings, it became clear that his mission was to keep the conversation sidetracked on definitions to avoid more substantive discussions on how we could better meet the needs of urban and low-income schools and communities.

There were times when I observed faculty members throwing rocks and hiding behind coded language while serving on search committees. For example, I served on a search committee in another department in my college. When we discussed our top candidates based on their academic records and the preferred qualifications we previously identified, a candidate of color was unanimously considered our top candidate. We conducted phone interviews with our top candidates. That same applicant remained our #1 ranked candidate and we were excited to bring her on campus for a more in-depth interview. The candidate showed up in the most colorful and beautiful floor-length ethnic-inspired attire. It was stunning and affirming of the candidate's racial and ethnic group membership. I found the search committee's discussion following the candidate's visit most interesting and unsettling.

Based on my colleagues' summation of the candidate, I wondered if we attended the same interviews and job talk she so eloquently delivered. Some of my colleagues said she was dismissive when a faculty member asked a question. There was also some speculation that she might not be a good fit. When I pressed my colleagues for more specific commentary, they continued to be vague and subjective. I was quite bothered by that critical incident for several reasons. First, she was our top candidate based on her academic dossier, replete with research and publications in reputable journals in her field, her earned doctorate from our aspirational institution, and her on-point responses during the telephone interview.

I attended her interview with the search committee and with the faculty and found her to be thorough in her responses, gracious, indulging, and anything but dismissive. I believe she was too ethnic and self-assured for some search committee members. Of course, when the search committee narrative was crafted on her, it was expressly stated that she would not be a good fit and would not be a welcome member of that department. In effect, despite being asked by the Dean not to rank the applicants, they went out of the way to rule out that ethnic-inspired, confident, and accomplished candidate, despite my objections. I concluded that a strategy that made it convenient to ignore and give no weight to my objections was to ensure that Black women remain in the numerical minority when committees are formed.

While some colleagues noted my dissenting comments, since I was the only Black woman on the committee, I was outnumbered and outvoted in a democratic process. Having such a limited presence on search committees and other decision-making bodies in higher education serves no one well. In addition, my colleagues need more opportunities to value within-group diversity and observe and understand multiple perspectives.

I remained disturbed and surprised about that critical incident because those most opposed to hiring that candidate were not ultra-conservative. Before that, I considered them liberal and more receptive to issues of social justice and equity.

Those coded and misleading practices remain embedded in higher education structures that allow faculty and administrators to hide behind anonymity, invisibility, and secrecy. There also seems to be a visibility–invisibility spectrum that our colleagues situate themselves along relative to their openness or lack thereof about their roles in making adverse decisions impacting African American women in hiring decisions, tenure and promotion, and other university reward systems (i.e., sabbaticals, teaching and research awards, fellowships, etc.).

A struggle for me these past three decades has been to find ways to have open and honest conversations with my colleagues about issues of social justice and equity and how faculty and administrators will be the first to put language in our mission and value statements about honoring diversity in all forms. Yet, we continue to engage in actions that run counter to those statements. Sometimes, the conversations have been on an individual basis, and others have occurred in small groups. Years ago, I vividly remember a department faculty meeting where a colleague made some derogatory comments about a low-income community in Ohio based on an event that had recently happened in the news. I followed with a comment to get him to understand the stereotypical nature of his remarks. It didn't take long to figure out that it would have gone far south if we continued the conversation in that group setting. I told the faculty member I would love to continue our conversation but did not want to derail the department agenda.

After the meeting, I followed him to his office with my calendar in hand to schedule our follow-up meeting. We met and had a heart-to-heart conversation. I started the conversation by sharing with him how I grew up in the same kind of community about which he made such disparaging remarks. Entering the conversation on that note disarmed him. He could better understand why I was even more offended by his comments. Sometimes on-the-spot decisions must be made. Some conversations are more effective when held in group formats, while others are more effective in one-to-one or small-group conversation formats.

Resistance to social justice and equity can be amorphous. It can take on varied shapes and forms with various disguises, with some not so sophisticated. Delay tactics are forms of resistance. I have experienced and observed administrators make promises to women of color that never materialize. Instead, they stall and delay and are not forthcoming. For example, we're often expected to remain in "interim" administrative positions far longer than our White colleagues. When asked about the interim status or promised positions, they hide their hands and blame others for their own unwillingness and delay.

I was promised an Associate Deanship of Social Justice and Equity. The Dean at the time announced it to the College Faculty before he took another Deanship elsewhere. Neither the position nor a contract ever came to fruition. I am always amazed when White administrators are appointed without undergoing an internal or external search. If Black women are not afforded similar opportunities, that level of disregard and disrespect is unconscionable and flies in the face of most universities' missions, value statements, and strategic plans related to equity and social justice.

DEVELOPING RECIPROCAL MENTOR–PROTÉGÉ RELATIONSHIPS

Many of my early opportunities in higher education emanated from the productive and positive relationships forged with my mentors in my master's and doctoral programs at Central Michigan University and the University of Kansas, respectively. To yield something positive from a divorce, I decided because I was no longer tied to my hometown, I would fulfill my dream of pursuing a terminal degree in special education, emotional impairment, or behavior disorders in particular. I was visiting with my Master's Advisor, with whom I enjoyed a great open and honest mentor–protégé relationship. I told him of my decision to pursue my doctorate. He picked up the phone and called one of his best friends and colleagues. Before I left his office, he made sure the door was open for me for an interview at the University of Kansas.

I went for the interview, and much to my pleasant surprise, my soon-to-be major professor shared with me that KU's College of Education was affiliated with Juniper Gardens' Children's Research Project. Juniper Gardens is a community-based research center that conducts and disseminates research to improve children's and families' outcomes. Not only did I interview with KU faculty members, but I also interviewed with the Directors of Juniper Gardens.

My major professor had the wherewithal to realize that as the only African American doctoral student in the special education program at KU at that time, I needed to be connected and affiliated with Juniper Gardens for several reasons. First, their research focused on urban schools and communities. Second, several Black women were either researchers or behavior observers who went into the schools to observe and collect data on teacher and student behavior systematically. As a White male, he knew that I needed those academic and cultural connections to thrive. That was a perfect connection since I had no family or friends in Kansas.

I viewed my master's and doctoral program as on-the-job training grounds. In each program, I developed my own strengths and need assessments based on my career objectives. They provided opportunities for me to learn new concepts and apply them as if I was already on the job or in the role for which I was desiring and anticipating. For example, while in my master's program, I wanted to gain more expertise working with children and youth with emotional impairments. My master's advisor had a wealth of knowledge and expertise in that area. Because I was teaching children with emotional impairment, my classroom was the most naturalistic place to try out and modify new learnings. I was delighted with the relationship my advisor and I forged and his influence on my coursework, program, and master's thesis. I researched whether the child's race influences teacher placements of children in special education classes. Mutual trust, respect, and regard are critical to reciprocal mentor–protégé relationships.

Similarly, my doctoral major professor and I developed a mutually regarded mentor–protégé relationship. As much as I gained from our work together, I never felt the sharing of expertise was one-sided. It was bidirectional. Much like the old car-renting company commercial, I believed that I needed to take the driver's seat in my program. While he and my committee members guided me, I needed to keep track of the experiences and learning that I wanted to gain while I was in my training. As an example, KU is known internationally for its record in securing large federally funded grants. I would have been remiss if I hadn't gained some grant-writing practice while in my program. I started by asking faculty writing grants if I could serve as their research assistant throughout their grant-writing processes.

Of course, that was pre-internet, so it meant going to the library and pulling, copying, and annotating journal articles that could be used to support their grant ideas. Considering my work with my major professor, I had the luxury of being funded on a federal grant as a full-time doctoral student research assistant. Subsequently, I had an office in the special education suite. As a doctoral student, maintaining a physical presence in the program or department is vital for embracing various opportunities for new experiences and gleaning information on conferences, internships, scholarships, and leadership roles that impact policies and practices. In essence, as a doctoral student who aspired to assume a tenure-earning higher education position in special education, it was important to be under the tutelage of a professor and committee members who were actively engaged in the roles I envisioned myself after completing my dissertation and graduation.

My socialization process as a future faculty member began in my doctoral program. Socialization is "the process by which students acquire the attitudes, beliefs, values, and skills needed to participate effectively in the organized activities of their profession" (Nettles & Millett, 2006, p. 89). While necessary for all doctoral students, socialization is especially critical for underrepresented group members because they are less integrated into the graduate community (Simpson, 2003). Students' academic success is affected by poor integration and lack of socialization. According to Gardner (2010), doctoral students face challenges during three phases of their doctoral preparation process. Developmentally, when students can resolve or navigate the challenges, growth occurs. However, students are more likely to exit their programs prematurely when presented with too many challenges or inadequate supports. Gardner suggests that the optimal condition for doctoral student growth and development occurs when a balance is struck between the challenges of the process and the supports provided.

That intentional socialization of doctoral students is well-supported in the literature. Researchers reported the need for doctoral programs to integrate their scholars' anticipated career expectations with their doctoral experiences and programs (i.e., Gardner & Doore, 2020). Multidimensional approaches are needed to meld coursework theory and research with applied experiences consistent with the increasingly rigorous university faculty expectations (e.g., scholarly writing for publication in high-impact journals, grantsmanship, designing and conducting impactful research, and sustaining community engagement consistent with universities' missions and values).

There is a chronic shortage of tenured Black women faculty in academe (National Center for Education Statistics, 2023). Those national data show that

Black women compose only 5% of assistant professors, 3% of associate professors, and a mere 2% of full professors. Racism, microaggressions, biases, and intersectionality have been attributed to the lack of tenured and promoted Black women professors (i.e., Rucks-Ahidiana, 2021). One strategy for increasing the presence and participation of Black women in the academy is for search committees to be vigilant about uncovering policies and practices that undermine and negate even the most well-intended efforts to be more inclusive and equitable.

As a case in point, reward structures are in place in some universities that incentivize universities to be more rigorous and selective in student admissions and faculty hires. Those policies and practices may restrict certain Black students and faculty access to admission, tenure, and promotions. If search committees, for example, are instructed to only seek faculty members from research-designated institutions, productive faculty from Historically Black Colleges and Universities (HBCUs) and other Minority-Serving Institutions (MSIs) may be overlooked. It will take faculty and administrators across races and ethnicities to be vigilant and challenge each other on the policies and practices that lead to further inequities.

Also, the leadership must take a stand regarding inclusiveness in every phase of faculty searches, from how the position is written and advertised to the final selection and hiring of new faculty. Similarly, when productive White faculty members get job offers to go elsewhere, I have witnessed university leadership extend counteroffers to entice those faculty to remain at their current universities. In contrast, when equally productive Black faculty have received offers to go elsewhere, they have at times literally been shown the door and received no counteroffers from the university.

Having mentors who are similar in race and gender is ideal when they have a presence in higher education. The reality, however, is that there is a dearth of Black faculty and administrators to fulfill those roles. Considering some of the concerns expressed in this chapter, we desperately need social justice, equity, and inclusion in the representation and decision-making processes in the academy. Like my master's and doctoral major professors, White faculty and administrators of other races are sorely needed also to develop reciprocal trusting and beneficial mentor–protégé relationships.

One of the Kwanzaa principles is Ujima, which means collective responsibility and that I got your back, you got my back. Over my career in higher education, I have seen White faculty members go from silently and privately observing inequities directed at Black women to speaking out about them using somewhat anonymous formats. That is progress. While I would love nothing more than for them to take up the mantle of advocacy and agency more directly, I recognize that some faculty are starved for leadership around those issues in the academy, especially when some issues have been politicized. Hopefully, more faculty across races will adopt the Kwanzaa principle of Kujichagulia.

ATTAINING TENURE AND PROMOTION WHILE MAINTAINING IDENTITY

Given the already dire shortage of Black women in the academy (Griffin, 2019), a superficial and short-term solution would be to merely recruit and prepare more Black women doctoral students for university faculty positions. However, the literature on doctoral student preparation could not be more explicit. In addition to diversifying faculty, doctoral students must be well prepared to integrate their anticipated faculty roles of teaching, research, and service or community engagement (i.e., Anderson & Anderson, 2012; O'Meara et al., 2013). They must also be better prepared to recognize and address inequities from racism, microaggressions, intersectionality, and resistance.

As a doctoral scholar or early-career faculty member, focusing primarily on assuming a tenure-earning faculty position in higher education is inadequate. The focus must also be on successfully attaining tenure and promotion. As I mentor doctoral scholars and early-career Black women and women of other racial groups preparing for tenure and promotion and review their curriculum vitae or dossiers, I often notice their engagement in excessive amounts of professional and community service. Given my commitment to investing my time and talents in my community, I wholeheartedly understand their desire to "give back" to their communities and the need to publish in journals that the persons that I most wanted to impact may never access. That was a dilemma that I had to face early on.

I was honored to be called on by African American communities in a metropolitan area, especially since I was an outsider who was not reared in the area or the state of Florida. The first action I took upon assuming my Assistant Professor position was to find out the expectations and timeline for attaining tenure and promotion. I then set up my files in accordance with those guidelines and began to collect data documenting my accomplishments and challenges in the areas of teaching, research, and service.

The university assigned me a mentor, but it wasn't someone with whom I readily connected. Much like in my doctoral program, I knew I had to self-assess, get behind the wheel, and steer my professional development and growth opportunities. I decided that rarely is there a faculty member who excels in all three Tenure and Promotion expectations of university teaching, research, and engaged community service. Therefore, I identified an effective teacher-educator about whom students ranted and raved. I observed her classes and asked her to observe my teaching and offer feedback. Upon arrival at the University, I was excited about teaching my first classes. I was super prepared and knew I was one of the most effective teacher educators ever. Much to my chagrin, my first university evaluations were horrible. Some students commented that I was unclear about expectations; I spent too much time talking about race, I gave too many assignments, and I was too rigid about due dates.

The literature abundantly documents that Black women professors frequently receive lower evaluations than their white colleagues (Aruguete et al., 2017). Those researchers found that when students rated professors based solely on a photograph of the professor and a description, Black and White students rated

Black professors lower than White professors. Based on clothing style, they reported that Black professors were rated higher when they were photographed wearing formal or more dressy clothing. Conversely, White professors were rated higher wearing casual or less formal clothing.

Despite the long-standing research on Black women being rated more harshly and less favorably than our White counterparts, I was shaken to my core when I reviewed my student ratings. Some of their comments came from left field, but I "owned" them. In addition to the syllabus, I knew I needed to find varied ways to communicate course expectations. I also needed to continue incorporating issues of race, class, and gender in ways that engaged the students more and connected them better to their teaching effectiveness. I took advantage of workshops and readings designed to increase my own teaching effectiveness of adult learners and documented those efforts.

Since that time, I have served on many annual review and tenure and promotion review and evaluation committees. The reality is that Black women professors will likely receive less than optimal student course evaluations that may not accurately reflect their teaching effectiveness and preparation. As a reflective faculty member, I encourage Black women and other women to be accountable for favorable and less favorable evaluations, even when you disagree with the latter. In addition, describe and show the extent to which you addressed student concerns and perceptions about your teaching. Have a colleague observe your teaching and send written feedback. Other strategies include attending university-wide workshops on varied aspects of teaching and learning (i.e., technology that increases student motivation and engagement, discussion techniques, student-centered learning, etc.).

In research, ensure you know the expectations relative to publishing, grant proposal writing, conference presentations, and research awards. Seek research mentorship(s) based on your self-assessment with the university's expectations. Look for opportunities to collaborate on publications while recognizing that the order of authorship is important for tenure and promotion, with first and second authorships being more valued and indicative of your contribution to that research endeavor. Early on, define and carve out a compelling research agenda upon which your research and scholarship will focus. Black women professors are asked to engage in many initiatives, with many being service-oriented. Be judicious about your research and scholarship time and focus. Service initiatives are more impactful and carry more weight when you develop them into manuscripts for publication in journals in your field and layperson venues. Some universities have raised their research profiles and have clear indicators or metrics of faculty research impact. University librarians are helpful resources to facilitate a better understanding of researchers' h-index (Hirsch, 2005), a calculation indicative of the publications and citation counts (Thuna & King, 2017). Those researchers noted that other sources of impact data include Web of Science, SCOPUS, and Google Scholar.

The best advice I was given as an Assistant Professor was to carve out my writing time and preserve it. I started using Wednesdays as an uninterrupted writing day and still preserve that day with minimal other commitments. Writing groups are ideal for bouncing ideas off each other and holding each other accountable. Writing groups are particularly useful when composed of colleagues with varied and complementary skill sets. My current writing group has colleagues who are deft with technology and productive software, effective editors, skilled organizers, and efficient time managers.

Develop a flow chart or cycle of intentional research productivity and schedule or timeline. My major professor emphasized a viable cycle to increase research productivity. It involved (1) developing an Institutional Review Board (IRB) application; (2) conducting a research study; (3) crafting a manuscript for publication; (4) presenting it at a conference and getting audience feedback; (5) revising and submitting the manuscript; (6) As soon as it is submitted to a high impact journal, the cycle starts over for the next research study.

Securing external funding is valued at many universities and provides a means to fund the initiatives about which you are most passionate. In addition to learning from grant-writing mentors, I served on federal grant review panels and was privy to panel members' perceptions of grant proposals. In so doing, I learned more about what reviewers look for in competitive grant proposals. Find out the varied external funding opportunities in your discipline. That is, seek out the Request for Proposals (RFPs) from federal, state, and regional grants and contracts. Additionally, you may consider corporate and foundation funding opportunities for your proposed initiatives.

In conclusion, Black women in the academy continue to be silenced, invisible, disrespected, and canceled. To counter these phenomena, we must define ourselves and maintain our values and cultural identity while ensuring we attain tenure and promotion. It is imperative to develop and draw on your support system that, more often, may be external to the university and not dependent on the university for affirmation and validation. Many of us are fiercely committed to serving not just the academic community, but our own urban and low-income communities. Recognizing and taking advantage of culturally responsive opportunities to return investments is most gratifying.

Moreover, microaggressions, anonymity, and other attempts to cancel Black women in the professoriate must be confronted. Forging reciprocal mentor–protégé relationships can eliminate barriers to Black women's academic success. The literature is replete with strategies for attaining tenure and promotion relative to the two most valued aspects of teaching and research. Many of us have supportive colleagues who are members of other racial groups, as well as those who minimize and mute our presence, voices, and contributions. However, to be maximally successful in the academy, Black women must intentionally square our academic knowledge and skills with our ancestral wisdom and wit. Like my grandmother, we must remain vigilant, define our own "fore day in the mornin," and recognize when folks think they're pulling one over on us.

REFERENCES

Allen, R. (2001). From academic freedom to cancel culture: Silencing Black women in the legal academy (June 1, 2020). 68 UCLA L. Rev. 364 (2021). *UCLA Law Review*, *68*, 2021. https://ssrn.com/abstract=3951935

Anderson, S., & Anderson, B. (2012). Preparation and socialization of the education professoriate: Narratives of doctoral student-instructors. *International Journal of Teaching and Learning in Higher Education*, *24*(2), 239–251.

Aruguete, M. S., Slater, J., & Mwaikinda, S. R. (2017). The effects of professors' race and clothing style on student evaluations. *The Journal of Negro Education*, *86*(4), 494–502. http://www.jstor.org/stable/10.7709/jnegroeducation.86.4.049

Blanchett, W. J. (2006). Disproportionate representation of African American students in special education: Acknowledging the role of white privilege and racism. *Educational Researcher*, *35*(6), 24–28.

Bridgeland, J. M., DiIulio, J. J., & Morison, K. B. (2006). *The silent epidemic: Perspectives of high school dropouts*. Civic Enterprises.

Gardner, S. K. (2010). Doctoral student development. In *On becoming a scholar: Socialization and development in doctoral education* (pp. 203–222). Routledge.

Gardner, S. K., & Doore, S. A. (2020). Doctoral student socialization and professional pathways. In *Socialization in higher education and the early career: Theory, research, and application* (pp. 113–127). Springer.

Gay, G. (2002). Preparing for culturally responsive teaching. *Journal of Teacher Education*, *53*(2), 106–116. https://doi.org/10.1177/0022487102053002003

Griffin, K. A. (2019). Institutional barriers, strategies, and benefits to increasing the representation of women and men of color in the professoriate: Looking beyond the pipeline. *Higher Education: Handbook of Theory and Research*, *35*, 1–73.

Harry, B., & Anderson, M. G. (1994). The disproportionate placement of African American males in special education programs: A critique of the process. *The Journal of Negro Education*, *63*, 602.

Hirsch, J. E. (2005). An index to quantify an individual's scientific research output. *Proceedings of the National Academy of Sciences*, *102*(46), 16569–16572.

King, J. E. (1991). Dyconscious racism: Ideology, identity, and the miseducation of teachers. *The Journal of Negro Education*, *60*(2), 133–146.

Louis, D. A., Rawls, G. J., Jackson-Smith, D., Chambers, G. A., Phillips, L. L., & Louis, S. L. (2016). Listening to our voices: Experiences of Black faculty at predominantly White research universities with microaggression. *Journal of Black Studies*, *47*(5), 454–474.

Moore, W. L. (2008). *Reproducing racism: White space, elite law schools, and racial inequality*. Rowman & Littlefield.

National Center for Education Statistics. (2023). *Characteristics of postsecondary faculty. Condition of education*. U.S. Department of Education, Institute of Education Sciences. https://nces.ed.gov/programs/coe/indicator/csc. Accessed on August 30, 2023.

Nettles, M. T., & Millett, C. M. (2006). *Three magic letters: Getting to Ph. D*. JHU Press.

O'Meara, K., Knudsen, K., & Jones, J. (2013). The role of emotional competencies in faculty-doctoral student relationships. *The Review of Higher Education*, *36*(3), 315–347.

Romano, A. (2019, December 30). Why we can't stop fighting about cancel culture: Is cancel culture a mob mentality or a long overdue way of speaking truth to power? *Zac Freeland Vox*, 1–12. https://courses.bowdoin.edu/sociology-1101-spring-2020/wp-content/uploads/sites/319/2020/05/What-is-cancel-culture_-Why-we-keep-fighting-about-canceling-people.-Vox.pdf

Rucks-Ahidiana, Z. (2021, July 16). The systemic scarcity of tenured Black women. *Inside Higher Ed*. https://www.insidehighered.com/advice/2021/07/16/black-women-face-many-obstacles-their-efforts-win-tenure-opinion

Showunmi, V. (2023). Visible, invisible: Black women in higher education. *Frontiers in Sociology*, *8*, 974617. https://doi.org/10.3389/fsoc.2023.974617

Simpson, M. T. (2003). *Exploring the academic and social transition experiences of ethnic minority graduate students*. Doctoral dissertation, Virginia Tech.

Smith, C. (2015). Reflection of a Black female scholar: I know what it feels like to be invisible. *The Conversation*. https://theconversation.com/reflections-of-a-black-female-scholar-i-know-what-it-feels-like-to-be-invisible-39748

Starling, C. E. (2012). *Testimonies of African American male high school dropouts*. Doctoral dissertation, Florida A & M University.

Thuna, M., & King, P. (2017). Research impact metrics: A faculty perspective. *Partnership: the Canadian Journal of Library and Information Practice and Research*, *12*(1).

Townsend, B. L., & Harris, K. (2002). Preparing African American male teachers for urban special education environments. In J. Paul, L. Lavely, & A. Cranston-Gingras (Eds.), *Professional issues in special education: Intellectual, ethical, and professional challenges to the profession*. Greenwood Publishing Group.

PERSEVERANCE IS IN OUR DNA

Cathy D. Kea

North Carolina Agricultural and Technical State University, USA

ABSTRACT

With the ongoing educational disparities and an increasingly diverse special education student population, the need for Black special education teacher faculty at Historically Black Colleges and Universities (HBCUs) has never been greater. The role of Black women in higher education is indispensable as a means of addressing the social injustices faced by students of color with disabilities, diverse communities, families, and historically underserved groups by training Black educators. In this chapter, the author introduces her authentic self and academic journey as foundational to the proposed ideas expressed. The roles of novice special education faculty are discussed, including the challenges these emerging professionals face in obtaining tenure, promotion, and grant procurement. This is followed by suggestions for how to respond to the microaggressions (e.g., classism and colorism) encountered by both Black and White peers. Based on that groundwork, a series of best practices are proposed for creating safe spaces, nurturing and mentoring our future special education teachers. The chapter ends with a reinforcing and supporting summary of lessons learned to promote persistence and retention among Black special education teacher education faculty.

Keywords: Black woman; family; Historically Black Colleges and Universities (HBCU); mentorship; perseverance; resilience; special education faculty; support

WHERE ARE THE BLACK WOMEN FACULTY IN HIGHER EDUCATION SPECIAL EDUCATION PROGRAMS?

The absence of Black special education faculty in higher education, specifically women, is striking. As of 2022, Black doctoral candidates in special education accounted for only 9% of the total (National Center for Education Statistics [NCES], 2023). In their survey of special education faculty members at doctoral

Journeys of Black Women in Academe
Diversity in Higher Education, Volume 26, 27–48

Published under exclusive licence by Emerald Publishing Limited
ISSN: 1479-3644/doi:10.1108/S1479-364420240000026002

degree-granting institutions, Maggin and colleagues (2021) found a general commitment by faculty and doctoral programs to increase diversity, yet comprehensive recruitment and retention plans or ways to infuse diversity and cultural relevancy throughout the programs (e.g., coursework, internships, research frameworks, and Whiteness ideology) were lacking.

The disproportionate representation of special education graduates of color, in turn, negatively impacts a range of related roles (e.g., educator preparation faculty, researchers, policy experts, and advocates) that contribute to diverse intellectual leadership, including continuously questioning the biases of the dominant cultural perspectives on special education. Further, negative experiences during doctoral programs and graduate studies are reported to squelch the desire for some students of color to continue in these programs (Carter, 2002; Drame et al., 2022; Maggin et al., 2021; Slay et al., 2019). Specifically, the following six deterrents were prominent: (a) overall unwelcoming program climate created by White faculty and peers (e.g., "I was invisible to them."); (b) only one or two faculty of color in the department; (c) beneficial experiences readily given to White peers over doctoral students of color (e.g., research opportunities, manuscript co-authorships, grant projects, and national conference presentations); (d) lack of mentors and role models; (e) faculty unfamiliar with cultural needs and culturally relevant resources to support scholars of color; and (f) insufficient financial and motivational support.

The latter two areas were found to have a particularly negative effect on scholars of color – often assigned advisors or mentors were missing in action physically and were ineffectual. They had limited exposure to and understanding of the lived experiences of doctoral students of color and were unaware of how to support them. Additionally, the disparity in monetary support (e.g., scholarships, paid internships, grant projects) benefited White peers. Financial support is critical for doctoral students of color, especially Blacks. Black borrowers carry the heaviest student debt burden, and debt can trigger mental health problems (Jackson & Mustaffa, 2022). Financial wealth impacts one's ability to enter, remain, or exit from educational programs. To illustrate, Drame et al. (2022) found that financial support was sometimes withdrawn after originally granted. "When I [Norman] first got to my doc program, I was told that there was funding or grants that could fund me the entire time for my doctoral program. Of course, that never came to fruition, so I had to kind of maneuver around to get additional funding with the help of the Black Graduate Student Association" (p. 31).

Experiences such as these may cause scholars of color to leave academia and choose professions that are more financially rewarding and less prone to marginalization (McCray, 2011). In sum, while recruitment of doctoral students of color in special education programs is important, so is retention of these scholars of color. If Black doctoral students are not being retained and are not adequately prepared in all aspects of higher education, we have failed them. And, ultimately, we have failed all students of color in the nation's schools.

Against, this background, this chapter opens with an overview of the current and historical reality of education of and by teachers of color. This includes the roles of novice special education faculty along with the challenges faced by these emerging professionals in obtaining tenure, promotion, and grant procurement. Ways to respond to microaggressions (e.g., classism and colorism) from Black and White peers are then proposed followed by a series of best practices for creating safe spaces, nurturing, and mentoring future special education teachers. The chapter concludes with a recap of lessons learned to promote persistence and retention among our Black special education teacher education faculty.

THE RIPPLE EFFECT

Approximately 80% of all K-12 public school teachers are non-Hispanic White (U.S. Department of Education [USDOE], 2022a), whereas children of color make up approximately 54% of public-school enrollment (USDOE, 2022b). Further, 50% of infants and toddlers with disabilities ages birth through two are children of color; 49% of preschool children with disabilities, ages three through 5 (not in kindergarten), are from racially and ethnically diverse backgrounds; and 54% of students with disabilities, ages 5 (in kindergarten) through 21, are from racially and ethnically diverse backgrounds (USDOE, 2022b). By comparison, in 2021, 79.8% of special education teachers identified as White followed by 9.36% Black and 5.22% two or more races (Data USA, 2022). The shortage of highly qualified special education teachers and the glaring ethnic and racial imbalance between students of color and special education teachers of color is of great concern (Billingsley & Bettini, 2019; Peyton et al., 2021).

The prevalence of educators with limited diversity and with narrow exposure to students from culturally and linguistically diverse backgrounds, compounded by a lack of preparedness and culturally responsive pedagogy, may partially explain the continuing achievement gap of diverse students in the nation's schools. These issues are particularly worrisome since research shows that having just one Black teacher in elementary school positively impacts the social and academic progress of all students, but especially students of color and students with disabilities (Farinde-Wu et al., 2020; Gershenson et al., 2021). Unfortunately, opportunities to have role models are limited since we have a scarcity of teachers of color across all educational levels – from K-12 to postsecondary institutions. This lack of role models may discourage individuals from pursuing teaching or remaining in the teaching workforce (El-Mekki, 2023). Indeed, in a recent study, Ravenell and Cole-Malott (2023) found that when asked about the pros and cons of becoming teachers, students of color and Indigenous students emphasized that they wanted to see someone who looks like them in the profession.

HOW WE GOT HERE

Between 1890 and 1940, Black educators in the South's segregated and inequitable education system were dedicated to empowering Black youth to transcend the limitations set before them (Fultz, 1995). Battling the intersectional challenges of class, race, and gender within the oppressive confines of the Jim Crow era, they provided education to their pupils in substandard conditions with remarkable success (McCluskey, 2017). By weaving the real-life experiences and immediate concerns of their students into the fabric of their teaching, these educators cultivated a spirit of resilience, endurance, and aspiration for societal equity in their students. Despite the significant disparity in educational facilities and materials compared to those available in White schools, these academically adept Black teachers championed the cause of equality and justice while also serving as daily sources of encouragement to both their students and the broader community, nurturing scholastic attainment (Long, 2020).

Despite the ostensibly fair-minded objectives of desegregation, the enactment of integration policies still operated under the presumption of White educational superiority. In the process, significant harm was inflicted on Black students, their families, and entire communities. Thus, the intended outcomes of the landmark *Brown v. Board of Education* decisions of 1954 and 1955, which sought to secure the economic advantages and educational provisions typically available to White children for Black children (Foster, 1997), remained largely unfulfilled. In addition, the widespread closure of segregated Black schools resulted in the demotion of Black school leaders and the dismissal of more than 31,000 Black teachers in the period from 1954 to 1966 (Bettini et al., 2021; Foster, 1997; Fultz, 2004; Thompson, 2020; Walker, 2009). In the words of historian Vanessa Siddle Walker, "In exchange for access to the resources White schools had, Black educators had to give up aspirations and advocacy" (Long, 2020, p. 1).

Despite intensified hiring initiatives to remedy this imbalance, the issue of racial diversity among educators in American schools remains critical post-*Brown v. Board of Education* (1954, 1955). For example, while the number of teachers of color hired from 1988 to 2018 grew, these new hires departed the profession at higher rates than their White colleagues, primarily because their working realities in both general and special education are markedly different from those of their White peers (Scott et al., 2021; Terada, 2021). Indeed, studies in general education reveal that Black teachers often prioritize the impact of racism and everyday microaggressions over other issues like salary, administrative support, or resource availability when deciding to leave teaching (Frank et al., 2021). Additionally, teachers of color in special education tend to exit the profession already during their initial probationary period, often due to issues related to diversity, equity, inclusion, and a sense of belonging (Scott, 2020; Scott et al., 2021).

Similarly, the traditional structure of higher education has not included Black faculty – whether men or women. As a result, the Black women who manage to enter these so-called ivory towers are often met with hostility, gendered racism, and less favorable tenure prospects, leading to feelings of exclusion that prompt self-examination (Ferguson et al., 2021). Even with degrees from top-tier, including Ivy League, doctoral programs, the intellectual capabilities and qualifications of these women are often unfairly scrutinized based on a pervasive assumption that they are inherently less scholarly, are unable to secure research funding, and are just generally less productive than their White peers (Drame et al., 2022; Shealey et al., 2014). Additionally, the damaging myth persists that the employment of Black faculty primarily serves as a superficial nod to diversity, further perpetuating racial and ethnic prejudices in the hiring process.

Black women scholars in higher education deal with pay inequity, gender discrimination, stereotyping, and systemic sexism (McCray, 2011; Shealey et al., 2014). They are burdened with a greater teaching and service load than White peers and are frequently relegated to non-tenure-track roles and labeled "professors of practice," which offer less job security and fewer opportunities for career advancement (Porcher & Austin, 2021). In the journey toward tenure and promotion, Black women faculty face additional obstacles rooted in covert racial and ethnic biases embedded within the system. Specifically, the academic culture often lacks adequate mentorships and tends to steer these faculty members toward research agendas that align with Eurocentric perspectives, thus undervaluing research focused on minority issues (Ferguson et al., 2021; McCray, 2011; Shealey et al., 2014).

With the ongoing educational disparities and an increasingly diverse special education student population, the need for Black special education teacher faculty at Historically Black Colleges and Universities (HBCUs) has never been greater. The role of black women faculty is indispensable in the field of special education as a means of addressing the social injustices faced by students of color with disabilities, diverse communities, families, and historically underserved groups by training Black educators.

WHO AM I?

Our past and our lived experiences are immutable, yet their profound influence on our future often goes unrecognized. The values and lessons instilled in me during my upbringing have shaped who I am and the decisions I make. As the second eldest of four children, I was raised in a tightly knit, two-parent household in a working-class area. Our parents placed a strong emphasis on education, with my father dedicating evenings to assisting us with our studies at the kitchen table. Since both our parents held three jobs to provide for our family, we frequently joined them in their additional part-time endeavors after school hours, which included cleaning offices and doing household and yard maintenance for a White family.

The White family members were highly educated. The wife was a university professor, the husband a medical doctor, and their adult children were lawyers. Each grading period throughout our schooling, the wife asked my siblings and me to show her our report cards and then gave us a monetary reward for good grades. Over the years, we additionally received clothes from this family to wear and/or share with those in our community.

Beyond the actual work involved, these experiences were lessons in themselves; we were encouraged by our parents to pay close attention, take in our surroundings, and reflect on what each experience taught us. During summers, we were sent to family in the country to assist with farm work, such as in tobacco fields or on blueberry farms – a practice my mother believed would fortify our character. My brothers worked in tobacco while I worked on the blueberry farm. As blueberry pickers, we were paid $0.50 per pail. At the end of the day, after completing household chores, our cousins, my siblings, and I would draw sticks to determine the bathing order. The person with the shortest stick bathed first, with the remaining order based on the length of your stick. Our rural relatives lived without indoor plumbing, so an evening bath required a multi-step process: pumping water from the well, heating it on the wood stove, and then pouring the hot water into a huge tin wash tub. The water was not changed between baths, so each night, there were bets on who would be the first or last to bathe. We slept three to a bed in one room, with all the girls in one bed and the boys in another.

In the close-knit community we called home, my father was known for giving haircuts on our back porch, while my mother had a reputation for her delicious cooking, often treating the neighborhood children to what became their most-loved meals. My siblings and I were given the responsibility of delivering meals from our kitchen or the produce from our garden to local residents who were ill or housebound. Our house also served as a hub for various activities, including cub scout gatherings and traditional street games like jacks, double dutch, and hopscotch. My parents were deeply engaged in the fabric of our church and in educational and community events. As property owners, they faced prejudice and bore witness to the systemic racism and gentrification that threatened to erode the cultural and historical fabric of Black neighborhoods. Black-owned urban community businesses, cultural communalism, the presence of educational activists and leaders, and wealth existed prior to gentrification. Gentrification destroyed bustling businesses, eliminated historic neighborhoods, and drove away most residents of color, thus creating systemic inequities for those remaining and newcomers.

From the childhood experiences detailed above, I learned that pursuing and attaining education is critical. I also realized that terms like "impoverished," "poverty," and "poor" are subjective. For instance, neither my cousins nor I had children's books at home, yet our environments were literacy-rich. Everyday items in our homes (such as canned or packaged food, church bulletins, grocery store flyers, and patterned quilts) and in our community (like fast-food restaurants, street signs, roadside vegetable stands, gardens, fishing, and hunting) offered countless opportunities to learn literacy, mathematical calculations, and critical thinking.

When I entered integrated school settings, it became clear to me that my family didn't possess the material wealth others did, and in our predominantly white schools, we were labeled "poor." However, I never saw us as poor. Everyone in my neighborhood had similar possessions; we were clothed, fed, and loved. More important, we were the products of segregated schools led by Black administrators and teachers who were deeply connected with the community. Some lived in our neighborhood, and all made home visits and connected classroom learning with our lived experiences. Described as "warm demanders" (Griffin & Tackie, 2017), these educators held high expectations for us and were committed to nurturing high-achieving scholars. From them, I learned not to judge someone by their material wealth, but by their intellectual depth – and to educate those who may lack it.

Other life lessons centered around community and family. The support of both is needed for both personal and professional growth, and if absent, it's essential to create them for yourself. For us, the White family, our rural kin, and the neighborhood community demonstrated collaboration and ways of working together toward positive outcomes.

The final major lesson learned involves giving. We learned to always reach back and give to others in real-time and to pay it forward because, for Black communities, none of us are free until all of us are free. This means that giving is a lifetime commitment to our people and our community.

These childhood experiences profoundly influence my life to this very day, including my academic path. Mother told us to never be ashamed of where we come from, to work hard and make a way where there seems to be none, to understand that all that glitters is not gold, and to remember that we will face tests throughout our lives, but that perseverance is part of your DNA.

My Academic Journey

I identify as a cisgender woman and the first in my family to graduate from college. As a culturally responsive educator and a practitioner-based researcher, I see myself as an advocate for Black education. My journey began in a segregated elementary school, after which I transitioned through integrated middle and high schools, continued at a Historically Black College and University (HBCU) for my undergraduate studies, and concluded at Predominantly White Institutions (PWIs) for my master's, doctoral, and postdoctoral work, thus being exposed to very diverse educational settings. With more than 40 years in the educational sector beyond my training, my roles have included serving as a special education resource teacher, a consultant for a State Department of Public Instruction, and most recently, a faculty member in higher education for 35 years. Here, I spent time at two small PWIs and one HBCU, dedicating 31 years to a major HBCU in the Southeast, focusing on curriculum and program development, training educators to be culturally responsive, and securing federal funding.

FOSTERING UNDERSTANDING OF THE UNKNOWN FOR NEW FACULTY OF COLOR

Out of a total of 107 HBCUs, 11 are classified as Research II (R2) – defined as institutions offering doctoral degrees and engaging in high research activity. Over the years, I have often been asked by my White peers why I chose to work at an HBCU, especially since I had been trained at the top doctoral institution for special education. My answer has always been rooted in an African proverb: "Giving leaves an imprint that endures forever." That is, my aim has been to impart the knowledge gained from my own academic experiences, foster a nurturing community akin to a family for students, inspire them to surpass their own expectations and commit to guiding them through their academic and personal endeavors. Above all, I have always wanted my students to understand that resilience and persistence are embedded in their heritage.

For new faculty, it's vital to be introspective and truly understand your passion and let it guide your choice of institution, whether small, mid-sized, or large, whether public or private, and whether focused on teaching or research. My experiences as a classroom teacher, and later observing and delivering professional development to special educators in my role with the State Department of Public Instruction, confirmed my calling to be a culturally responsive educator. I have aimed to prepare educators who could connect with students of all academic levels, recognize and celebrate each student's intrinsic value and potential, and nurture their sense of self-worth and excellence. Beyond academic skills, it was imperative for me to shape educators who would stand against social injustices and racism, advocating for those from historically marginalized communities in a society that too often overlooks them.

Know Your Worth

Before you accept a position, "know your worth." This means doing your homework! What do you bring to the table? Now is not the time to be shy about your assets. Present your expertise without hesitation. Be prepared to discuss your vision, goals, strategic implementation and evaluation plan, and salary expectations. What will it cost the institution to acquire and keep you? For example, after securing both personnel preparation and research grants, suitors began to woo me away from my university. I did not want to leave, so I brought this offer up to my dean, who subsequently went to the provost and asked that I be given market-value pay, making me the highest-paid faculty member outside of the administrators in my college. Be fierce and advocate for yourself. Remain marketable and set standards for other faculty to follow in your footsteps.

Tenure, Promotion, and Grant Writing

Novice faculty members must seek out a work environment that resonates with them and meticulously chart their career paths. Mastering the art of networking, honing collaborative abilities, and harnessing self-drive and tenacity are key to achieving successful tenure and promotion. The path is daunting, leading through the murky complexities of explicit and implicit academic norms that must be decoded. Faculty are expected to perform daily feats across teaching, research, and service, all while nurturing personal development and maintaining a balance between work and life, as illustrated in Fig. 1.

As part of this journey, it is important to cultivate relationships within your department, across the college, and beyond the university to foster your intellectual growth, gain diverse viewpoints, and explore varied opportunities that yield fresh experiences. As shown in Table 1, regular engagement with your academic peers for feedback, whether through check-ins or joint ventures like grant applications and publications, is crucial. Effective collaboration calls for a

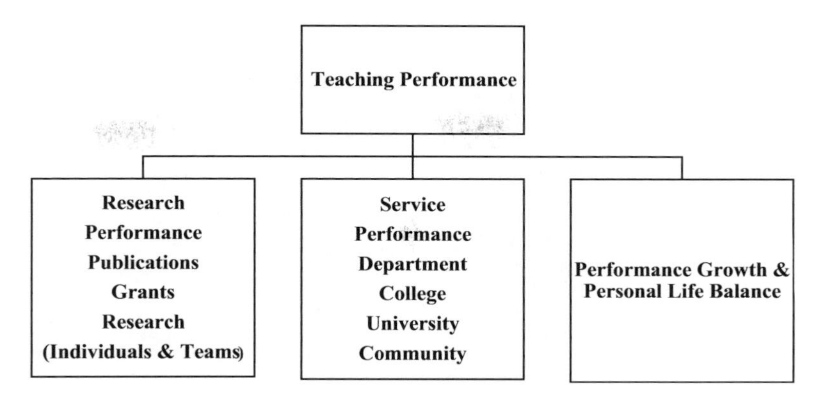

Fig. 1. Example of Tasks Performed by Higher Education Faculty.

Table 1. Networking and Collaboration Skills.

Networking Skills	*Formal Networking Skills* • Seek advice from a qualified professional • Seek information from a qualified professional • Seek a mentor • Collaborate	*Informal Networking Skills* • Seek information from peers • Initiate activities (e.g., grant writing research) • Maintain contact with others
Collaboration Skills	*Collaboration Skills* • Develop goals together • Plan goal implementation • Evaluate goal achievement	*Group Problem-Solving* • Be a team player • Do your share of the work • Choose your team players carefully

well-defined plan, clear objectives, and a commitment to a shared schedule. Choose your collaborative partners and team members judiciously to ensure open, honest, and trusting relationships.

Self-motivated faculty should also introspectively assess their interpersonal skills, self-evaluation capabilities, and resilience (see Table 2). Engaging in dialog with a mentorship circle that acts as a team of life coaches for both professional and socio-emotional guidance is an excellent initial step. Through discussions, goal setting, and planning with these mentors, you will be able to develop and execute an action plan that includes self-monitoring and evaluation.

As one of only two special education faculty members at my HBCU, I proactively formed a mentor circle that extended across my state and the country. My former undergraduate advisor, a Black female and professor of literacy at a Big Ten university in the Midwest, helped me to develop my research agenda and publication schedule, organizing monthly meetings to keep me on track. Another mentor, a Black male serving as Dean of Graduate Studies at a Southeastern HBCU, introduced me to professional networking and often included me in opportunities that arose. Additionally, a White male mentor from a

Table 2. Self-Determination and Persistence.

Self-Determination	*Social Skills* • Giving positive feedback • Giving negative feedback • Accepting negative feedback • Negotiating • Engaging in conversations • Solving problems	*Self-Evaluation Skills* • Self-evaluation of present skills • Self-evaluation of skills needed to achieve future goals
Self-Direction and Persistence	*Self-Direction Skills* • Action planning • Goal Setting • Goal planning • Self-monitoring • Self-evaluation	*Persistence Skills* • Persistence through problem-solving • Risk Taking Through Decision-Making • Dealing with stress – Recognizing and expressing feelings appropriately – Personal relaxation – Pursuit of happiness – Time management – Health-related behaviors – Spiritual behaviors

Carnegie-ranked Tier 1 university and Hispanic Serving Institution in the Southwest encouraged me to leverage my culturally responsive expertise, to publish, and to present nationally. Finally, another White male mentor embodying a warm and caring ethos taught me to command attention during conference presentations and to approach them with fearlessness. When meeting other Black novice special educators, I inquired about their mentorship experiences. A few had established a mentor circle like mine, but most had a single mentor. With my mentor circle's support, I was able to construct a research agenda, as depicted in Fig. 2, and adopt a guiding model that demanded continual problem-solving using the PEER approach.

A Shroud of Secrecy – Tenure and Promotion

I have always been a planner and detest being informed of things at the last minute. Therefore, it made sense to prepare myself for a successful tenure and promotion outcome. This involved reading the faculty handbook, consulting with recently tenured colleagues, and organizing my documentation files. Once, when I approached a seasoned colleague for her insights about the tenure and promotion process, she cautioned me, "Always approach tenure and promotion discussions with discretion and brevity." Puzzled by the veil of mystery that seemed to envelop the process, I questioned her further. She suggested we meet privately at her residence for a more open discussion. Despite feeling somewhat confused, I kept our appointment at her house and prepared myself to pay close attention to her words. She explained that there's a tendency in higher education for

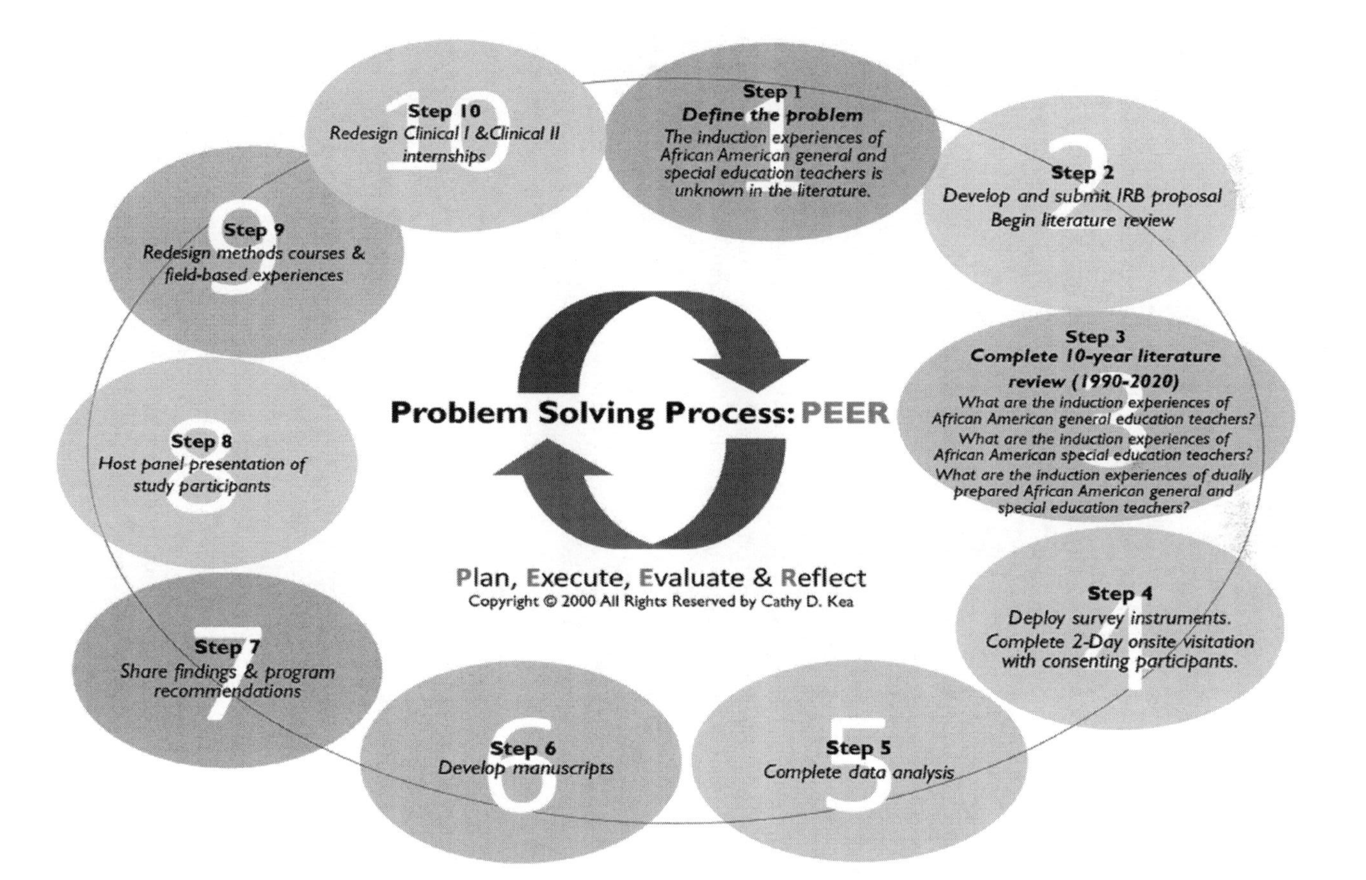

Fig. 2. Problem-Solving Process: PEER.

skepticism toward those, especially women and newcomers, who ask too many questions. She reassured me that my inquiries were reasonable and important, emphasizing that it's not just what you ask, but how you ask that matters. "Approach your senior colleagues as if you are seeking their sage advice, and always be polite and respectful," she advised, noting that this was part of socialization within the academic setting, where there's an expectation for younger faculty to show dependency. In closing, she complimented my boldness in asking questions, saying, "You have a spirit that reminds me of myself four decades ago. I'll guide you through this process, but let's keep our mentoring sessions off-campus. It's important to understand the nuances of the academic game to successfully navigate and excel in it!"

During my years at my HBCU, I witnessed colleagues secure tenure with fewer qualifications than others who were denied, despite having more substantial materials in their dossiers. This took me aback. If somebody followed the faculty handbook and possessed the required documents and letters of support, why were they denied tenure or promotion? Some were not promoted to full professor because they had not achieved national recognition, while others were promoted even though their dossiers paled in comparison to others. You quickly learn that "different people's differences are treated differently." How would I, as new faculty, and my dossier be viewed, I wondered. I began to keep more to myself, not being overzealous or walking the line, but rather holding the line, and I slowly came to understand why the "river of venom" ran so deep among the faculty and why cliques formed. Finding one or two colleagues to trust was not easy, but it eventually happened. I was tenured and promoted through the ranks to full professor, eventually garnering Professor Emerita status. It was not easy, but nothing worth having ever is. You must know the rules of the game to be in the game, to play the game, and, ultimately, to win the game!

Grant Writing

Securing grants can yield numerous advantages. It allows early-career faculty to bring their unique "vision" to life, fosters growth and innovation in educational programs, and facilitates the production of scholarly articles. Considerations for successful grant writing and implementation process include examining the institutional infrastructure, available clerical assistance, support from colleagues, and adequate release time, as depicted in Fig. 3.

Obtaining grants is key to forming important partnerships, for example, with colleagues and school districts, raising the institution's profile, and displaying the achievements of both the project and the director through conference presentations and publications. Yet, this kind of visibility can also lead to less favorable reactions among faculty. For instance, I once heard a colleague tell a new tenure-track faculty member that she had previously secured grants equal to those of the newcomer's first grant, only to acknowledge that the dean would soon be celebrating another faculty member's grant success. Such commendations are short-lived, especially when you are the latest addition to the faculty.

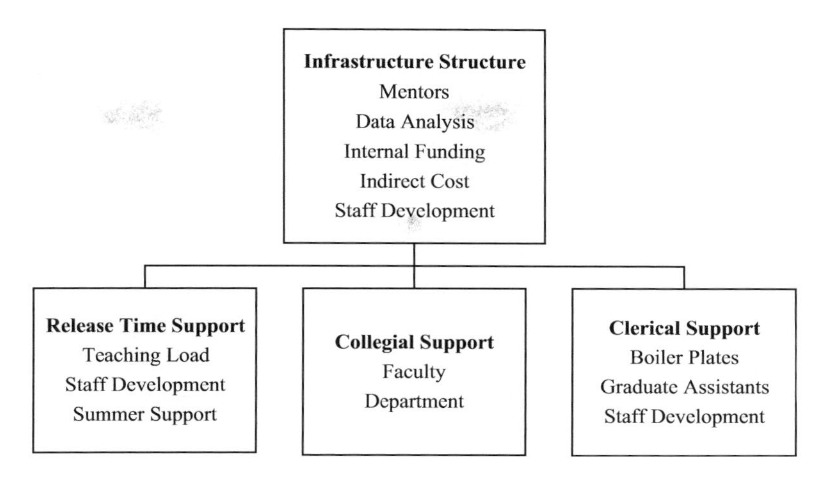

Fig. 3. Considerations for Successful Grant Writing.

If you secure external grants, I advise you to practice humility, offer to share resources when possible and suggest to your deans and chairs to refrain from using you as an example of grant procurement success as a way to prevent being isolated from colleagues and avoid professional jealousy. For example, the annual departmental travel budget for each faculty at my HBCU varied from $0 to $500, contingent upon the allocations of the state budget. Since my OSEP grants included travel funds for conferences, I chose not to utilize the departmental faculty funds. Instead, I nominated a junior faculty member to receive the departmental travel dollars that would have been allocated to me.

When you are one of only two or three special education faculty members at an institution, managing a grant can be daunting and overwhelming until you develop a system that works for you. I have been fortunate to have secured OSEP grant funds for 25 years. Even though it is akin to another full-time job, the effort is well worth it. The benefits and opportunities that you can provide for your scholars are your true reward.

Unwavering Resilience

During my time at an HBCU, I noticed that my counterparts at PWIs often treated me with less esteem. Unfortunately, this is not an unusual reaction, which seems to stem from a lack of understanding of HBCUs' importance, achievements, historical context, and current status. Black colleges and universities have a storied legacy that dates back to before the Civil War, particularly in educating Black teachers – one of the oldest vocations at these institutions. The enduring mission of the 107 HBCUs in the United States has been to educate Black Americans. Yet, colleagues at PWIs often doubt the quality of our students and the intellect of our faculty. Because they are not a part of the Higher Education Consortium for Special Education (HECSE), HBCUs remain largely enigmatic to many, often because they have not visited an HBCU campus or participated in joint projects. Faced with such negative perceptions, HBCU educators must consistently seize moments to educate their White colleagues and demonstrate resilience and adaptability, especially when engaging in dialogs about their institutions. Developing the strength to endure and adapt to such interactions, although tough, is an integral part of our role as advocates for the continued importance of these institutions.

Grace Under Fire

During your career, you are likely to encounter subtle but offensive comments or assumptions directed at underrepresented groups, known as microaggressions. The detrimental effects of such interactions are well documented, with research indicating they can adversely affect both one's physical and mental health, potentially leading to depression, stress, trauma, headaches, high blood pressure, and sleep disturbances (Washington, 2022). Over time, microaggressions can also contribute to burnout and decreased job satisfaction, which may, in turn, negatively affect staff turnover and retention rates.

For instance, at national or state conferences, attendees often express surprise when I discuss my latest research or suggest innovative and significant transformational strategies. The feedback I typically receive includes remarks like, "That was an insightful observation. Which university are you affiliated with? What kind of special education programs do you offer? Perhaps we could collaborate on a grant in the future."

I have spent more than three decades training preservice teachers to implement culturally relevant teaching methods in urban schools. My scholarly work and involvement are centered on the nexus of culturally relevant and sustainable teaching approaches in both general and special education. My research has explored how preservice teacher candidates incorporate cross-cultural experiences and culturally relevant tactics into their coursework, lesson planning, clinical experiences, and early career teaching. When I present my findings at national conferences, I receive praise for my systematic approach to data collection and the results yielded. A White director from the State Department of Public Instruction on the West Coast once commented, "Your data results are outstanding. Could you send me your presentation so I could share it with my team?" I responded that while I was eager to collaborate with her and her team, I was the person most qualified to present my research and, therefore, was not comfortable sharing it with another person. An incident like this reflects a form of intellectual undervaluation.

Similarly, early in my career, I encountered a telling incident with someone I had previously only conversed with via telephone. Upon our first face-to-face meeting, they expressed surprise at my articulate use of English, questioning, "You're Black! How do you speak so well? Who taught you?" My response was straightforward: "My eloquence comes from my parents, Catherine and Bill. Who taught you to speak?"

It's important to recognize that stereotypes, misconceptions, preconceived notions, and subtle forms of discrimination, including classism and colorism, are not exclusive to interactions with White colleagues or predominantly White institutions. They are also present in HBCUs, perpetuating legacies of enslavement.

Classism imposes varying degrees of worth based on an individual's economic standing, often leading to attitudes of superiority toward those at a lower economic tier or even contempt for individuals from the working class or poverty-stricken backgrounds who share one's racial identity. In the context of HBCUs, classism may manifest through probing inquiries known as the "5 Ws": (1) Who are your people (class and heritage)? (2) Where did you and your people attend college? (3) In what neighborhood do you currently reside? (4) What church do you attend? and (5) Why did you choose this HBCU for employment? Such questions, when posed during initial interactions with faculty, can lead to feelings of being diminished among individuals from more privileged classes, and induce shame regarding one's familial socioeconomic patterns, or result in a rejection of one's ancestry.

Colorism refers to the bias or discrimination that favors people with lighter skin tones within a racial or ethnic group – a phenomenon with deep roots stretching back to the era of slavery. Women of color, particularly in academic and community settings, have historically grappled with the emotional and psychological challenges that colorism presents as it affects job recruitment, promotions, and professional appointments. Phrases such as "she doesn't have the look" or would not be a "good fit" are often coded language referring to characteristics like skin shade, hair texture, body size, and family background.

The impact of colorism on self-esteem, interpersonal relationships within academia, and everyday experiences can be significant. Continually refining one's approach to handling microaggressions and challenging situations with dignity is crucial to prevent compromising one's self-respect and purpose. When responding to colorist remarks, evaluate your relationship with the person involved, find a respectful setting for discussion, and stay conscious of the historical context of microaggressions. Recognizing the distinction between someone's intent and the actual impact of their words is key here, as microaggressions are deeply embedded in our society. Hold your position firmly and demand respect. When developing your career, be sure to copyright all creative works and models, insist on equality in collaborative initiatives and grants, especially in academic fields where faculty of color are underrepresented.

Offering a Safe Space

The current landscape of education, marked by disparities and a special education student body that is increasingly diverse, along with a critical shortage of special education teachers of color (SETOC), has disproportionately negative consequences for students of color with disabilities, as manifest in elevated occurrences of disciplinary actions, increased instances of school dropout, assignment to segregated classroom settings, and a stark overrepresentation in special education programs, as reported by the Office of Special Education Programs (OSEP, 2022, 2023). Moreover, these students seldom encounter educators who reflect their racial and ethnic backgrounds (Gershenson et al., 2018, 2021).

The significant presence of Black students in special education, contrasted with the scarcity of Black Americans with degrees in this field, highlights the pressing need to attract, educate, and retain SETOC. To illustrate, in 2019, White students earned 80.6% (7,146) of all special education bachelor's degrees, compared to 8.7% (785) for Hispanic/Latino students and 3.6% (317) for Black/African American students (Cormier et al., 2021). Thus, it falls upon Black special education faculty to establish a nurturing environment for SETOC, aiming to diminish turnover and encourage longevity in our teacher training programs. For years at my HBCU, I served as the program coordinator for both our undergraduate and Master's of Art degrees in teaching special education programs.

It is our responsibility to ensure that our universities foster an inclusive atmosphere where every student feels their voice matters. Continuous self-education about the unique struggles and histories of our students is essential. Our curricula must represent a broad array of viewpoints, and we must openly tackle biases, equip our students with resources, and engage in dialog that supports a learning environment where students are acknowledged, heard, and understood. Above all, we must protect and preserve the integrity of our classrooms, even in the face of differing opinions from our students.

For example, during a discussion in my course on urban schools, a White preservice candidate expressed a strong attachment to the confederate flag, which led to her being vocally criticized by her Black peers. My students were puzzled when I intervened to safeguard her from further reproach. They had anticipated that I would align with their perspective. However, as time passed, these students, now educators themselves, have come to understand that my role at that moment was to protect all students, including her. It was my duty to ensure a safe learning environment for every individual in the classroom, regardless of my personal views on the expressed opinions. At the same time, it is important to utilize instances like this as "teachable moments," maintaining confidentiality regarding your students' errors by ensuring that the focus remains on the action or event that requires attention and improvement, not on the individual student. Such an approach teaches students that if they err, they can anticipate a serious private discussion with me, but their mistakes will not be exposed to public scrutiny.

It is essential for Black educators to adopt a "family approach," providing unwavering support to preservice candidates, regardless of their academic performance or socio-emotional challenges. The aim is to nurture them as one would one's own children, encouraging them to become the truest and best version of themselves. They are the torchbearers of our future, and our success in guiding them is imperative. Our Black youth rely on us as we advocate for fairness in the ongoing struggle for social justice.

BEST PRACTICES FOR SUCCESS

The mission of HBCUs has always been to cultivate an understanding in pre-service candidates about the significance of culture and its influence on educational planning, teaching, and classroom management, guided by the following three best practices: Personal Identity, Support Systems, and High Expectations.

Best Practice 1: Personal Identity

HBCUs actively incorporate elements of African American culture into their educational practices and curricula to foster student involvement rooted in cultural identity. They strive to help students cultivate a robust personal identity and harness their cultural heritage to enhance academic achievement. Through daily affirmations that celebrate their inherent beauty, intelligence, adequacy, and distinction, HBCUs affirm each student's value and honor their uniqueness.

Best Practice 2: Support Systems

HBCUs are known for fostering strong networks of support by facilitating frequent interactions between students and faculty, hiring faculty from a range of backgrounds, and adopting approaches such as intrusive advising (e.g., emails, phone calls, text messages, dorm and apartment visitation) to cultivate a sense of community and care among students. Such efforts also encourage students to engage deeply with their reading, develop their writing, think critically, and achieve proficiency in course material and academic standards.

Best Practice 3: High Expectations

Establishing high expectations reflects the commitment of HBCUs to provide impactful mentorship, foster aspirations for advanced studies, and encourage entrepreneurial ventures among their students. By addressing students as "Dr. (Last Name)" from the outset (e.g., undergraduates, masters, and doctoral levels), we send a powerful message of faith in our students' capabilities, often before the students themselves realize their own potential. This practice lays the groundwork for how students should perceive themselves and their peers, reinforcing a culture of mutual respect and intellectualism when they interact with one another. Calling students scholars and thinkers serves to spark an intellectual identity.

IT TAKES A VILLAGE

We typically associate the word "family" with blood-related individuals living together as a unit. However, families are people who care and provide support to students whether related by blood or not (Milner, 2020). I define family as those persons who respect you, care about your well-being, show up for you, are present for your joys and sorrows, and love you unconditionally in spite of your shortcomings. More important, they help you to grow and figure out who you really are.

Foster a sense of family among your preservice candidates, ensuring they feel a strong sense of support. Cultivate a vibrant learning community, but also equip students with the skills to forge networks beyond their immediate academic sphere. Remember, your students are a reflection of your legacy, and it is entirely appropriate to exhibit nurturing behavior; after all, you are shaping our future leaders. Afford them chances to stand out not only during their time at the HBCU but also as they begin their professional journeys and onwards – whether through guest lecturing, teaching, manuscript co-authorships, presenting at conferences, or forming business partnerships.

Also, make an effort to stay connected with your alumni. When you're visiting a city where they live, plan to get together. Keep updated on their activities and continue to support them. For instance, an alumnus once remarked to me, "You are the only professor who visited my classroom during your trip to Miami. You consistently share an abundance of resources to help us thrive and shine. Your commitment to nurturing your students extends far beyond the classroom walls. THANK YOU for all that you do for us."

SOWING SEEDS IN FERTILE MINDS: THE LASTING IMPACT OF MENTORSHIP

Deep-Rooted Mentorship

Up to this point, we have looked at the essential job functions and duties of a novice faculty member in higher education, explored challenges Black women may face when interacting with colleagues at both HBCUs and PWIs, and emphasized the necessity of offering support to students of color at whichever institution you choose. The significance of mentorship in this context cannot be overstated. The concept of mentorship is dual in nature. On one hand, it is imperative for you to have a circle of dependable and dedicated mentors who can offer you consistent guidance as you navigate through the various roles and situations you will face in higher education. On the other hand, it is crucial for you to act as a mentor to your preservice candidates – listening intently, giving exceptional feedback, and motivating them to achieve their highest potential. Your commitment must extend beyond mere career advice and suggestions of professional opportunities. It should encompass the imparting of life wisdom, providing emotional support, and fostering authentic relationships. Mentorship that is deeply ingrained is a lifelong commitment and is of immense value.

Anchoring Wisdom: Cultivating Brilliance at an HBCU

Reflecting on my 31-year tenure at my HBCU, it is clear to me that it was the students that kept me anchored. My aim was to cultivate their nascent qualities, foster their intellectual growth, and refine their talents to ensure they could thrive in a society that often fails to honor Black history and the contributions of Black people to this country. More important, I sought to equip aspiring special education teachers with the strength to remain steadfast in the face of challenges, to instruct them to be resilient, and to distinguish themselves in a field where they are a minority – whether through masterful communication, be it an academic paper, an impassioned lecture, or a simple email that reflects your acumen. The capacity to turn adversity into a teachable moment and to exhibit determination amidst daily obstacles should not only motivate students but also empower them to carve out their own space. This is the art of influence, skill, and gift that enriches every space you and your graduates will enter.

LESSONS LEARNED

As Black women in higher education, we encounter a range of complex issues, regardless of the institution we serve. Among these, working conditions often present significant obstacles, creating a stressful and exhausting environment that undermines our sense of control. We are frequently subject to role abuse, such as excessive teaching responsibilities, having to act as cultural mediators between students and faculty, and being expected to represent the Black community in general. Additionally, we may receive inadequate mentoring in critical areas such as scholarly writing, publishing, and grant procurement, compounded by insufficient access to resources, such as technology, travel funding, and graduate research assistants.

Moreover, racial battle fatigue is ever present, akin to an open wound that refuses to heal (Drame et al., 2022; McCray, 2011; Shealey et al., 2014). Our professional competence, credentials, qualifications, and leadership abilities are constantly under scrutiny and in doubt. The daily microaggressions we face from administrators, colleagues, and students, coupled with a lack of cultural sensitivity and respect for the diverse communities we serve, exacerbate the strain and frustration we experience in an already inequitable environment. The resulting feelings of isolation are intensified by lack of peer collaboration and with similar lived experiences. Our understanding and implementation of diversity, equity, inclusion, and belonging (DEIB) differs significantly. Rather than integrating DEIB thoroughly in an institution's structure, it is often addressed with a minimalist approach, failing to make meaningful change and, therefore, causing disdain.

Life in higher education is not for the faint-hearted. Your body armor must be reinforced with perseverance, resilience, and a robust support system to withstand the multitude of storms you will encounter. When the first devastating blows strike – whether that is not achieving tenure, being passed over for promotion, missing out on a new position, or facing scholarly mistreatment – you must find the strength to rise again, as you must each time you are knocked down. It will take your village to keep you grounded and steadfast.

Thriving in higher education necessitates a strategic approach, one that fosters intellectual vitality and the resilience required to realize your aspirations. As related earlier, I have drawn from my own cultural keystones – faith, family, and

Acknowledge barriers Create innovative solutions Hibernate, be humble & humane Identify goals & develop an action plan Enhance grant writing and research productivity Venture into new partnerships Exceed your expectations Reflect, relate, release

Fig. 4. A.C.H.I.E.V.E.R. *Source:* Copyright ©1998 All Rights Reserved by Cathy Kea.

heritage – which, along with the lessons imparted by the Black educators of my segregated elementary school, have been foundational to my journey. They taught me that what truly matters may often be found in the wisdom of restraint: "Silence is golden; listen and observe, for the truth will always be revealed." Besides, constant self-inquiry is vital: Know who you are, but also continually ask, "Who am I?" It is essential to assess, prioritize, and plan while setting healthy boundaries to ensure your aspirations are not sidelined. The three family snapshots featured at the beginning of this chapter reflect on power, privilege, and differences. They also highlight the significance of community, education, and family – pillars of strength in the Black community.

What gifts will you impart and what will your legacy be? Echoing Shirley Chisholm's words, "You don't make progress by standing on the sidelines, whimpering and complaining. You make progress by implementing ideas." So, pick up your pen and develop your blueprint for success because you can be the A.C.H.I.E.V.E.R., as depicted in Fig. 4. Regardless of where you work, acknowledge the barriers that exist; create innovative solutions to manage your multiple roles; hibernate, be humble, and humane while implementing civility; identify goals and develop an action plan yearly and engage in progress monitoring; enhance grant writing and research productivity; venture into new collaborative partnerships with caution; exceed your expectations; and last but not least, engage in self-care by reflecting, relating, and releasing your inner self.

As you tackle the responsibilities and daily challenges of your position, keep in mind Lena Horne's wise words: "It's not the load that breaks you down; it's the way you carry it."

REFERENCES

Bettini, E., Cormier, C. J., Ragunathan, M., & Stark, K. (2021). Navigating the double bind. A systematic literature review of the experiences of novice teachers of color in K-12 schools. *Review of Educational Research*, *92*(4), 495–542. https://doi.org/10.3102/00346543211060873

Billingsley, B., & Bettini, E. (2019). Special education teacher attrition and retention: A review of the literature. *Review of Educational Research*, *89*(5), 697–744. https://doi.org/10.3102/0034654319862495

Brown v. Board of Education of Topeka, 347 U.S. 483. (1954).

Brown v. Board of Education of Topeka, 349 U.S. 294. (1955).

Carter, J. A. (2002). A dialogue with divas: Issues affecting a scholarly agenda in special education, from Africana feminist perspectives. *The Journal of Negro Education*, *71*(4), 297–312. https://doi.org/10.2307/3211182

Cormier, C. J., Houston, D. A., & Scott, L. A. (2021). When salt ain't enough: A critical quantitative analysis of special education and education degree production. *Teachers College Record (1970)*, *123*(10), 3–30. https://doi.org/10.1177/01614681211059006

Data USA. (2022). *Special education teachers*. https://datausa.io/

Drame, E. R., Pierce, N. P., & Cairo, H. (2022). Black special education teacher educators' practice of resistance. *Teacher Education and Special Education*, *45*(1), 27–42. https://doi.org/10.1177/08884064211070570

El-Mekki, S. (2023). 4 ways to make your school better for black and brown teachers: Here's what teachers of color need from their principals. *EducationWeek*. https://www.edweek.org/leadership/opinion-4-ways-to-make-your-school-better-for-black-and-brown-teachers/2023/01

Farinde-Wu, A., Butler, B. R., & Handy, A. A. (2020). Conceptualizing a black female teacher pipeline: From recruitment to retention to retirement. *Theory into Practice*, *59*(4), 337–347. https://doi.org/10.1080/00405841.2020.1773160

Ferguson, T. L., Berry, R. R., & Collins, J. D. (2021). "Where is our space within this ivory tower?" The teaching experiences of Black women faculty in education programs. *Journal of Research on Leadership Education*, *16*(2), 140–157. https://doi.org/10.1177/19427751211002229

Foster, M. (1997). *Black teachers on teaching*. The New Press.

Frank, T. J., Powell, M. G., View, J. L., Lee, C., Bradley, J. A., & Williams, A. (2021). Exploring racialized factors to understand why Black mathematics teachers consider leaving the profession. *Educational Researcher*, *50*(6), 381–391. https://doi.org/10.3102/0013189X21994498

Fultz, M. (1995). Teacher training and African American education in the South, 1990–1940. *The Journal of Negro Education*, *64*(2), 196–210.

Fultz, M. (2004). The displacement of Black educators post-Brown: An overview and analysis. *History of Education Quarterly*, *44*(1), 11–45.

Gershenson, S., Hansen, M. J., & Lindsay, C. A. (2021). *Teacher diversity and student success: Why racial representation matters in the classroom*. Harvard Education Press.

Gershenson, S., Hart, C. M. D., Hyman, J., Lindsay, C., & Papageorge, N. W. (2018). *The long-run impacts of same-race teachers*. National Bureau of Economic Research. https://doi.org/10.3386/w25254

Griffin, A., & Tackie, H. (2017). Through our eyes: Perspectives from black teachers. *Phi Delta Kappan*, *98*(5), 36–40. https://doi.org/10.1177/0031721717690363

Jackson, V., & Mustaffa, J. B. (2022). Student debt is harming the mental health of Black borrowers. *The Education Trust*. https://edtrust.org/resource/how-student-debt-harms-black-borrowers-mental-health/

Long, C. (2020). A hidden history of integration and the shortage of teachers of color. *NEA Today*. https://www.nea.org/advocating-for-change/new-from-nea/hidden-history-integration-and-shortage-teachers-color

Maggin, D. M., Collins, T. A., Foster, J. A., Scott, M. N., Mossing, K. W., & Dorsey, C. M. (2021). Faculty perspectives on the recruitment, retention, and preparation of special education doctoral students of color. *Teacher Education and Special Education*, *45*(3), 227–245. https://doi.org/10.1177/08884064211046230

McCluskey, A. (2017). *A forgotten sisterhood: Pioneering Black women educators and activists in the Jim Crow South*. Rowman & Littlefield Publishers.

McCray, E. D. (2011). Woman(ist)s' work: The experiences of Black women scholars in education at predominantly White institutions. In *Women of color in higher education: Turbulent past, promising future* (Vol. 9, pp. 99–125). Emerald Publishing Limited. https://doi.org/10.1108/S1479-3644(2011)0000009010

Milner, H. R. (2020). *Start where you are, but don't stay there: Understanding diversity, opportunity gaps, and teaching in today's classrooms* (2nd ed.). Harvard Education Press.

National Center for Education Statistics [NCES]. (2023). *Racial/ethnic enrollment in public schools. Condition of education*. U.S. Department of Education, Institute of Education Sciences. https://nces.ed.gov/programs/coe/indicator.cge

Office of Special Education Programs (OSEP). (2022). *44th annual report to Congress on the implementation of the Individuals with Disabilities Education Act*. U.S. Department of Education. https://sites.ed.gov/idea/44th-annual-report-to-congress-on-idea

Office of Special Education Programs (OSEP). (2023). *OSEP fast facts. Individuals with Disabilities Education Act*. U.S. Department of Education. https://sites.ed.gov/idea/osep-fast-facts/

Peyton, D. J., Acosta, K., Harvey, A., Pua, D. J., Sindelar, P. T., Mason-Williams, L., Dewey, J., Fisher, T. L., & Crews, E. (2021). Special education teacher shortage: Differences between high and low shortage states. *Teacher Education and Special Education*, *44*(1), 5–23. https://doi.org/10.1177/0888406420906618

Porcher, K. M., & Austin, T. (2021). "Black women are the mules of the world": Black women professors of practice in teacher education programs. *Journal of African American Women and Girls in Education*, *1*(3), 109–129. https://doi.org/10.21423/jaawge-v1i3a54

Ravenell, A., & Cole-Malott, D.-M. (2023). The center for Black educator development. In S. Benromdhane, A. Kanarr, R. Townsend, & T. Taylor (Eds.), *Seeing myself: Student of color on the pros and cons of becoming teachers*. Teach Plus. https://teachplus.org/teachplus-cbed-seeingmyself/

Scott, L. A. (2020). Reasons early career Black special education teachers quit their positions. *American Journal of Educational Research and Reviews*, *5*(79), 1–17. https://doi.org/10.28933/ajerr2020-11-2305

Scott, L. A., Powell, C., Oyefuga, E., Padhye, I., & Cormier, C. J. (2021). Complementary review of the literature on attrition and retention patterns of special education teachers of color: What we know and how we move forward. *Multiple Voices for Ethnically Diverse Exceptional Learners*, *21*(1), 3–39. https://doi.org/10.56829/2158-396X-21.1.3

Shealey, M. W., Alvarez McHatton, P., McCray, E., & Thomas, U. (2014). "Sista doctas" taking a seat at the table: Advocacy and agency among women of color in teacher education. *Journal about Women in Higher Education*, *7*(1), 19–46. https://doi.org/10.1515/njawhe-2014-0003

Slay, K. E., Reyes, K. A., & Posselt, J. R. (2019). Bait and switch: Representation, climate, and tensions of diversity work in graduate education. *The Review of Higher Education*, *42*(5), 255–286. https://doi.org/10.1353/rhe.2019.0052

Terada, Y. (2021). *Why Black teachers walk away*. Edutopia. https://www.edutopia.org/article/why-black-teachers-walk-away

Thompson, O. (2020). School desegregation and Black teacher employment. *The Review of Economics and Statistics*, 1–45. https://doi.org/10.1162/rest_a_00984

U.S. Department of Education. (2022a). *Characteristics of 2020–21 public and private K-12 school teachers in the United States: Results from the national teacher and principal survey*. https://nces.ed.gov/pubsearch/pubsinfo.asp?pubid=2022113

U.S. Department of Education. (2022b). *ED facts data warehouse: IDEA Section 618 Part B child count and educational environments collection 2020–21*. https://www2.ed.gov/programs/osepidea/618-data/state-level-data-files/index.html

Walker, V. S. (2009). Second-class integration: A historical perspective for a contemporary agenda. *Harvard Educational Review*, *79*(2), 269–284.

Washington, E. F. (2022). Recognizing and responding to microaggressions at work. *Harvard Business Review*. https://hbr.org/

EMBRACING DISCONTENT AND RESISTANCE: STRIVING FOR AGENCY AND PROMISE

Gwendolyn Cartledge

The Ohio State University, USA

ABSTRACT

Education is essential, reading is fundamental, and education is freedom. These are not just hollow clichés, but truisms, probably more so today than ever. Education is freedom, in author's opinion, genuinely reflects the lives of Blacks in this society. The author believes there is no more noble profession than being a dedicated educator but given its current relatively modest status, lives such as Douglass' can emphasize to present and future educators how important their dedication is to the liberation of our youth, particularly youth who are subjugated and possibly experience special needs. The structural obstructions in this society are very real, but the author found the greatest obstacles were psychological, e.g., learning to reject the stereotypes and to pursue her goals, despite the subtle as well as explicit efforts to sabotage. The author shares her early development, which helped shape some personal strategies especially helpful for remaining on course. The author learned the important role of love and passion to enhance her work. The author learned to minimize the negativity, to recruit assistance as needed, to enjoy her students, and to grasp opportunities that presented itself. The author also learned to seek and appreciate the many valuable sources of goodness. Most of the author's battles were within rather than against perceived adversaries, but author did learn to take a stand when external forces appeared to jeopardize the essence of her educational purpose and the constituency, the author was most committed to serve.

Keywords: Higher education; Black educators; stereotype threat; mentoring; teaching; writing; special education; student diversity; writer's Block

Journeys of Black Women in Academe
Diversity in Higher Education, Volume 26, 49–71

Published under exclusive licence by Emerald Publishing Limited
ISSN: 1479-3644/doi:10.1108/S1479-364420240000026003

HONORING THE SHOULDERS WHERE WE STAND

Frederick Douglass, the great 19th-century orator whom David Blight (2018) called the "prophet of freedom," was a fierce abolitionist whose impassioned speeches and advocacy had an enormous impact on the country. As a matter of fact, the United States Library of Congress (n.d.) has included the Douglass (1845, 2021) memoir of his life in slavery as one of 100 books that shaped the course of American life. Douglass highlighted the brutal conditions of the institution with many cringe-worthy, disturbing events, but perhaps the most salient and defining time of his life occurred about the age of seven or eight when he was sent to a new slaveowner in Baltimore. The mistress, an initially kind, caring woman without previous experience in the institution of slavery, began to teach Frederick how to read. When her husband learned what she was doing, he reprimanded her severely, and Douglass reports the slaver's statements as follows:

> "...if you teach that n... (speaking of myself) how to read, there would be no keeping him. It would forever unfit him to be a slave. He would at once become unmanageable and of no value to his master. ... It would make him **discontented** and unhappy." These words sank deep into my heart, stirred up sentiments within that lay slumbering, and called into existence an entirely new train of thought. (Douglass, 2021, pp. 52–53)

Although sad to lose this instruction, Douglass was emboldened with the revelations of ignorance is to slavery as reading or education is to freedom. According to Douglass (2021),

> From that moment, I understood the pathway from slavery to freedom. ... Though conscious of the difficulty of learning without a teacher, I set out with high hopes and a fixed purpose, at whatever cost of trouble, to learn how to read. (p. 53)

And Frederick did just that. During the 7 years he remained with this slaveholder, he used various strategies such as bribing poor white boys in Baltimore with biscuits to teach him words, copying the lessons from the schoolbooks of the son of his slaveholder, and copying letters from work equipment to teach himself to write so that he could write his own passport when he attempted to escape slavery.

I share the story about Frederick Douglass for at least three reasons relevant to the purpose of this chapter. First, African Americans are the only group of people in this country for whom it was against the law to teach to read and the struggle for quality education continues to the present time. Second, despite the tremendous effort to maintain the illiteracy of enslaved persons, there were unwitting (e.g., the wife of Frederick's enslaver) as well as willing (e.g. free persons in Black churches) resources for possible teachings. Third, to seek out or take advantage of these learning opportunities, we need to prepare ourselves psychologically to be *discontent* with the way things are and to resist efforts to maintain the status quo that prevent us from achieving our *agency* and *promise*. Douglass hated being enslaved, he reviled the notion that he would be enslaved and uneducated for the rest of his life. He permitted himself to be greatly disturbed with this notion and therefore, worked steadily and systematically to educate and emancipate himself and others. He had a set purpose from which he would not waiver. The harder he worked toward this end, the more support and encouragement he received.

Frederick was not alone in his discontent. This sentiment was widespread among the enslaved as evidenced in organized and unorganized revolts or uprisings (e.g., Jones, 2021; Smith, 2021) early attempts to promote Black literacy in churches and other small gatherings, and constant reports of enslaved runaways (e.g., Douglass, 2021; Jones). Following emancipation, one of the first undertakings of the formerly enslaved was to pursue education, which meant economic and social freedom. In South Carolina, for example, with the aid of the Freedman's Bureau and sympathetic Whites, Blacks were able to pass progressive legislation through the 1868 state constitution guaranteeing free public education for Blacks and Whites (Low Country Digital Library, LCDL, n.d.a). Pushback from Whites following the period of reconstruction; however, managed to gut this legislation so that the schools would be segregated and schooling for Blacks would be consistently underfunded, ensuring that Black education would be separate and unequal (LCDL-2, n.d.b).

These policies, in various forms, existed throughout the South and were still in practice 40–50 years later when my parents were students in a small town in McCormick South Carolina. My parents shared precious little with their children about their developing years in the South, but through eavesdropping and conversations with older family members, the difficulties of their youth were learned. Both of my grandmothers died in childbirth when my parents were either at or approaching puberty. My father was the oldest of 12 children, six of whom were half-siblings from when my grandfather, John Cartledge, remarried after the death of his first wife, my paternal grandmother, Susie Cartledge. My mother was the seventh of 12 children born to her parents Peter Martin and Isabel Harmon Martin. Her father remarried twice after my grandmother's death, resulting in an additional sister and four step-siblings for my mother.

My maternal grandfather, "Poppa," was a Methodist minister, but the primary means of support for both of my grandfathers was farming, or as stated by my parents, "working in the fields." I subsequently realized that my grandfathers essentially engaged in subsistence farming or sharecropping. My paternal grandfather, John, did accumulate some land and wealth, which mysteriously was confiscated by local authorities at his death. My parents, Estelle Martin and Samuel Cartledge, were married at the ages of 20 and 27, respectively, and had their first child, Barbara Jean Cartledge, during their seventh year of marriage. Six years later, in the late 1930s, they joined the "great migration" from the South to eventually settle in a small steel mill town southeast of Pittsburgh, PA, where they had three additional children: Samuel John, Stella Mae, and myself, Gwendolyn, in that order. By the time I was born, my parents were in or approaching their middle years. My paternal grandfather died before I was born and my maternal grandfather, "Poppa," who I did get to see, died when I was 7 years of age. I did, however, have a "village" made up of lots of aunts, uncles, cousins, and good neighbors, who also made the great migration to our small steel mill town. I especially relished the warmth of those who were a part of our small church family.

Although I knew little of my parents' early years, one of the most important and often repeated stories came from my mother. Daddy was also victimized by this problem, which he acknowledged on occasion, but for mother it was like a festering sore that would not heal. Schooling in McCormick was inadequate in many ways, such as shortened school years, limited resources, teacher shortages, and so forth, but mother loved learning. She was a good student, but schooling in her town for Black students stopped at eighth grade. Mother often talked about how painful it was that she couldn't continue in school, how she stood in front of the school door crying because there were no other options. Her teachers were arranging for her to go to the next town where there was a high school for Blacks, but Poppa felt that he could not afford to send her. She had to remain home and help him with the farming. Mother was devastated. Her dreams of finishing school and becoming a teacher were dashed. She continued to read and engage in self-study, mainly the study of the Bible, which was one of the most available books. She often told us that by the end of her teen years, she had read the Bible three times. There was little questioning that fact because Mother knew the Bible better than anyone I knew, including the various ministers who had the temerity to try to pastor our little church while Mother was the head of Christian education.

Like Douglass, Mother refused to be thwarted by an inhumane system. She became a Bible scholar, which enabled her to teach hundreds of children, youth, and adults for nearly 40 years until her final days. Mother combined her fervent religiosity with her passion for learning to transfer her dream to her four children. She constantly encouraged us to read and study, quoting scripture such as verses from St. Paul's letter to his protégé Timothy: *Study to show thyself approved unto God a workman that need not to be ashamed, rightly dividing the word of truth* (II Timothy, *2:15 KJ*). Mother had a full repertoire of mainly Biblical quotes that she used to guide her children's behavior. Some, such as the one above, I had memorized and, to some extent, internalized by adulthood. Mother also had a dry sense of humor and a bunch of secular witticisms such as, "he's just a lost ball in high weeds," when referring to someone who consistently seemed to be missing the point.

Although the youngest, I was the first of my mother's children to fully embrace her dream, partly because I was so greatly pained by her lost schooling. How could that happen? Why would anyone keep a child from going to school? After hearing her story, I remember saying to myself that I would go to school for Mother. I later realized, as did Douglass and my mother, that depriving knowledge is a sure way of keeping an individual subjugated and disempowered. The second reason was that, in many respects, I was like my mother. I loved to read, I enjoyed school, and I was quite content to sequester myself in my room with a book, affectionately earning the family nicknames of "bookworm" and "housecat." My siblings did eventually also fulfill mother's dream, obtaining their own higher education associate, master's, and doctoral degrees.

NAMING MY PASSION AND PURPOSE

We are often encouraged to pursue that which we "love," which, although debated, this advice does have merit. bell hooks (2001) in her book, *all about* love, discusses the importance of love to work. Bringing love to our work, according to hooks, can contribute to a loving environment and this love can lead to an enhanced sense of self as well as increase the quality of our work. I am particularly attracted to her notion of purposeful work and that doing what you love "may be more important than making money" (p. 63). I like what hooks has to say about love relative to work, but I prefer the words passion and purpose. The words, love and passion, are often used interchangeably. Even in the dictionary there is an overlapping. For example, one definition of passion is: any powerful or compelling emotion or feeling such as love or hate (Dictionary.com, n.d.a). A definition of love is: to have a profoundly tender, passionate affection, often mingled with sexual desire for another person (Dictionary.com, n.d.b).

I prefer the word passion because love tends to have an element of reciprocity, which often sustains and increases it. But passion, to me, has a somewhat stronger connotation. It will persist even if there are minimal or no returns. If we are passionate about teaching children to read, for instance, we are likely to persist even if the gains are not great, even if we must work under less-than-ideal circumstances, and even if we are poorly compensated. If passionate, with an obvious purpose or goal in mind, we are less inclined to wallow in martyrdom and give up, but, instead, keep working to achieve greater gains for our students, to find the best, evidence-based instructional approaches, to increase needed resources, to improve learning conditions, and to receive satisfactory compensation. Love, in my opinion, is likely to fade if the conditions are not rewarding to you. In the professional or work world, we often refer to that state as "burnout." I'm also encouraged by the words of Ella Baker, the great civil rights worker, who was quoted as saying, "We who believe in freedom cannot quit until it comes." Her words were put into a song by "Sweet Honey in the Rock," one of my favorite musical artists. Like Frederick, I equated education with freedom. Education, particularly reading, was the mark of freedom for me and the students I taught. That was my purpose, my life's work.

From my earliest memory, I wanted to teach. When playing with my sister and cousin, I always wanted to play school, and I always wanted to be the teacher, even though I was the youngest. As I got older, I loved it when my mother, the superintendent of our Sunday School, let me teach stories to the younger children. I fantasized about gathering all the little children in my neighborhood to be my students. I would build my own school, and it would be full of books. Of course, I should be a teacher. I never thought of teaching in higher education, I just wanted to teach children how to read. Reading was so much fun; listening to stories was so much fun. Everyone should enjoy reading and stories. My conviction to teach was further driven by the observation that some of my classmates had difficulty learning to read and that the teachers were not sufficiently generous to those students. I went to predominately White schools, and I often felt that much of this harshness was reserved for Black or poor White students. In retrospect and fairness, I realized that these classrooms of 40 plus, mostly low-income or working-class students were more than a challenge in those low-resourced schools. Nevertheless, many of us went on and excelled often despite the questionable schooling. Throughout my public schooling, my passion for teaching the hard-to-teach never waned, despite some disturbing events.

In the 1950s, when I was in the fifth grade, I decided to make my declaration that I wanted to become a teacher. It was a non-instructional time. The other students and I had just finished helping Ms Conner, our teacher, celebrate her birthday. We were all in a good mood. I was the only student in my class that looked like me but that had not been consequential in terms of my peers. I quietly went to Ms Conner and said, "I enjoy school; I want to be a teacher when I grow up." I expected my announcement to make Ms Conner very happy. Instead, she hesitated for a minute and then said, "Well that's great, Gwen, in the South they really could use a good teacher like you." "Thank you," I said and walked away. I was heartbroken.

Why did I have to leave my family to become a teacher? Ironically, my parents left their home and families in South Carolina partly due to the impact of racism on their educational and employment opportunities. Now, they would have to send me back there to realize my professional dreams. All the teachers in my school district were White; I felt like I didn't belong in this school, and I didn't have the right to become a teacher. I felt like an imposter, although I didn't use that word until much later in my life. I use the term "imposter" because of its current broader usage, but the more applicable term for me is stereotype threat, as Claude Steele (2010) defined and researched. That is, cultural stereotypes such as Blacks should not pursue academics, or females are inadequate in math and science, or even White boys cannot jump, can have emotional and psychological effects, damaging, for example, our performance under certain conditions as well as our relationships. Females and racial minorities are often viewed the most vulnerable for stereotype threats or the imposter syndrome. My schooling wasn't all negative; quite the contrary, on more than a few cases, teachers singled me out for special roles such as being on the school newspaper or future teachers club, or academic distinction, but true to imposter form, I always resisted for fear I didn't belong. On the other hand, I had my teaching passion, I had my parents' encouragement, and I had my parents' stories. I had to persevere for them as well as myself. I suppose I emerged doubleminded: positioning myself as the resistant discontent, striving to take my rightful place, while simultaneously struggling to defeat the imposter image lurking in my head threatening my agency and promise.

CONFRONTING THE IMPOSTER AND STEREOTYPE THREAT SYNDROMES

Three rather transformative events occurred during my teenage and early career years. As I approached high school, I wasn't pleased with my course selection, but I didn't ask my parents to intervene because they were already over extended and school personnel had subtle ways of punishing you if you complained. A Black male friend in the same situation from my neighborhood agreed that we would have to up our game if we wanted the rigorous courses needed for college. He suggested that we assert ourselves, all that we had to do was to tell the guidance counselor what we wanted, which we did, and we got it. That was a valuable lesson in assertion, although we did not use that word at that time. I learned I needed to pursue what I needed and wanted. You can be severely short-changed waiting for others to meet your needs regardless of how deserving you are. For example, I had been advised previously by other teachers to upgrade my course of study, but assuming the administration would correct it, I never acted on it until I became desperate and was prompted by another student. Later in my university career, I had a similar awakening about seeking promotion. The message is that advancement is not always automatically or benevolently bestowed; rather, one has to recognize one's own worth and be deliberate in purpose.

A second event occurred during the first or second week of high school. I had been in bed the whole week with the flu. When I returned to my geometry class, Mr A. was giving in-class assignments for some problems in our book. I was totally lost and twice approached Mr A to explain what we were doing, but he kept saying to me that I obviously was not mathematically minded, even though I kept trying to explain that I had been out ill. Mr A. was not budging. I looked around the room; I knew none of the other students, but fortunately, sitting in front of me was the only other Black student in the class. I could tell he was a very good student from his demeanor and his approach to his work. I shyly asked him to show me what we were to do, and he quickly explained to me how to prove the theorems. I was off to the races. I was surprised that Mr A. never commented on the fact that I was excelling in my assignments. I wasn't offended, I always saw him as a nice, nerdy, clueless guy. I did wonder, however, whether he was basing his assumption of "my limited math mindedness" on my race or my gender or both. Nevertheless, this was the beginning of my "T Principle" (named after the student that assisted me with the assignment) I would begin to use to counter my imposter syndrome. Simply stated: *Don't succumb to the negativity that others want to superimpose upon you, look for successful associates or models who will enable you directly or indirectly to achieve your goals.* Recently I read a quote from Warren Buffet who was giving a talk to a young audience and one young man asked for advice on becoming successful. Buffett (n.d.) told him, "It is better to hang out with people better than you are. Pick out associates whose behavior is better than yours and you'll drift in that direction."

A third brief story is from my home-town school district. Fast forward, I graduated from high school on the academic track, commuted to the University of Pittsburg with a few paltry scholarships, National Defense Loans, and an extremely hardworking mother (widowed when my father died the year I started college); finished undergraduate school in 3 ½ years; spent a summer in Europe, supported by the American Friends Service Committee; and then embarked on my teaching career. It was either karma or irony that my first teaching position was in the same school system and across the street from the school where my fifth-grade teacher, Ms Conner, advised me to go South to pursue my teaching dreams.

The previous year, this system hired its first Black teacher at the secondary level, and I was the first Black in the elementary schools. The year began with administrative meetings and the time to meet new faculty. Ms Conner had retired but my ninth-grade math teacher was still there. I did not expect him to remember me even though I had done well in his class. He was always fun and friendly, albeit less than rigorous in his teaching, at least that was the case for my class. As I approached him to speak, he frowned and quickly walked away. For a brief second, I was really puzzled, I had gotten A's in his class. But then I remembered Ms Conner; I wasn't supposed to be there. Instead of succumbing to the stereotype, I affirmed myself in saying, "I can do this." I especially like a quote from Shirley Chisholm: "We must reject not only the stereotypes that others hold of us but also, the stereotypes that we hold of ourselves."

I employed the T principle as needed throughout my university studies, but my doctoral studies provide the best and most beneficial example. I pursued graduate study primarily for one reason: to identify fool-proof strategies for teaching struggling learners, particularly low-income learners of color. There were other incentives, such as teacher tenure or pay increases, but these were of minor concern compared to my need to be successful with my students. The least of all was an interest in the status of another degree or teaching in higher education. As a matter of fact, I never aspired to be a university professor; it just happened because of my quest for knowledge. I eventually realized the search for the perfect learning or teaching formula was complicated because no one really had a silver bullet that could be easily applied successfully for all conditions. Rather, the problem of academic progress for low-income diverse learners was multidimensional, with many key factors beyond teaching per se. I did come to realize, however, that higher education is a primary arena for asking questions where one could find small clues to the larger puzzle, and I could possibly play a small role in that quest. To become a seeker was very attractive and I was on board.

I switched from general education to special education for my master's degree, again due to my fierce interest in educating the most vulnerable. In many ways my master's program was transformative. There I began to learn about the technology of teaching and many principles derived from behavioral psychology. I learned to be more "direct" in my instruction, to target specific skills, to analyze goals and objectives into instructional sequences, and to determine when and how the skill is mastered. Further, what to do if not mastered. This was in great contrast to my general education training, which focused on "covering the curriculum" rather than teaching the skill and child. That is, with the hope and expectation that all the learners would acquire the skills and concepts embedded in the lesson covered. For my special education teaching, I moved from the predominately White suburbs of my initial teaching position to the inner city of predominately Black classrooms. As a result of my master's study, I felt more confident in my ability to help the hard to teach, but it was not enough. I had not factored into this equation the compounding effects of poverty or racism. Although all the parents of my students were responsive, some did not have the economic or physical resources to travel across town to meet with their child's teacher, for example. Other major setbacks included under resourced classrooms, a questionable instructional curriculum, and the low expectations of the school personnel for the students. In contrast to my previous suburban assignment, where personnel frequently raved about or complimented student achievements, in this school, the constant refrain was, "Oh, these kids can't do anything."

The level of instruction was commensurate with this belief system. It was a major battle, for example, to get end-of-year achievement tests to assess formally my students' progress. The administration feared my students' scores would further depress those of the school. I got tests only by promising to hand score my tests and not include them with the schools', but it revealed to me how children in special education could go through their entire formal schooling without anyone taking stock of these learners' progress. My hopes for enlightened teaching and learning were dashed further as I moved into supervisory responsibilities and noticed the number of children languishing in special education classrooms, often receiving little or no useful instruction, and failing to make academic progress. The issue then became not only how do we teach the students but also how do we engage all stakeholders – educators at all levels, politicians, parents, and the general citizenry to recognize the gravity of the situation and take action. My passions again went into high gear, and I returned to graduate school. Initially, it was just to take a few courses to get more information but soon I was convinced to return full time to do intensive study and to get the accompanying degree.

INTENSIFYING THE T PRINCIPLE

During doctoral study, competence in writing for publication emerged as a priority, something well beyond my previous expectations of simply mastering my coursework. I was comfortable in writing class research papers but writing something that others would read was quite intimidating. Although our program emphasized research and publishing, there was little or no hands-on modeling or mentoring for publication, at least for me. At one point, I had a particularly painful writing experience. The department had hired an adjunct professor to conduct a doctoral seminar on writing for publication. I, along with the other students welcomed the class and looked forward to instructional pointers on effective writing. The affable, low-key professor talked extensively about the various journals in our field and the type of articles that most likely would be published, but there was little concrete information on actual writing such as organizing a paper, taking a position, supporting an opinion, writing an introduction, choosing a topic, and so forth. Instead, we were told to write and submit a paper. This was early in my program, and I was lost for a topic and how to develop it. Nevertheless, I dutifully submitted something. I knew it wasn't good, but I had to do something to meet the expectations of the course. To my dismay, the following class, the professor used my paper as a model for many of the things one should avoid doing when writing for publication. It was a small class, and I was the only student of color. He didn't identify me with the paper, but I was certain everyone knew he was referring to me. I was crushed. I was looking for helpful feedback useful in making me a better writer, but, instead, I felt belittled and discouraged. Fortunately, I did not let that experience define me. Along with the comfort of knowing that the course was an outlier in my graduate performance, I was prepared to put my "T" principle into high gear.

One of my doctoral classmates was JoAnne Fellows Milburn. Clearly the strongest student in our class, JoAnne had the added advantage of marriage to a distinguished professor in the psychology department with whom she wrote and occasionally published. JoAnne and I studied the same research topic of social skills, and she delighted me by suggesting that we work together on a few publications. JoAnne perfectly filled this T principle role for me. We not only worked well together but also became very good friends and continued as such until her death in 2016. Because our social skill topic was so aligned with psychology, JoAnne and I went to the annual psychology conferences to get the most current research to use in our studies and writing (e.g., American Psychological Association {APA}), Association of Applied Behavior Therapy {AABT}, and Applied Behavior Analysis {ABA}. We also attended major educational conferences (e.g., American Educational Research Association {AERA} and Council for Exceptional Children {CEC}) for the same purpose. I learned the importance of obtaining original sources for teaching, researching, or writing. At these conferences I learned to identify persons on the cutting edge of topics of my interest. It was of value to attend their sessions as well as, on occasion, to interact personally with them. Perhaps most importantly, I learned the considerable investment associated with being a professional in higher education. The time commitment and expectations were endless. We took copious notes, collected hundreds of handouts (days before electronic transmissions), scoured through these notes and handouts meticulously, and found about 30% of the information valuable to our work. Although we could not use all the information we gathered, the process was invaluable, enabling us to conduct our graduate research and writing, which launched both of our careers, albeit in slightly different directions.

Our first successful publication helped to earn us a book contract that enabled us to continue our writing well into our subsequent careers in the university. I thoroughly enjoyed our time together, whether we were traveling to major cities around the country or simply driving up and down route 71 in Ohio to meet for a 2- or 3-hour writing session at the Mansfield Inn or spending the weekend at our respective homes. While not as much fun, technology in the form of the Internet eased things considerably by the end of the first edition of the first book. In addition to our collaborations, I also wrote independently, soliciting feedback from JoAnne and other colleagues as boosters.

By the time we were writing our second book, I had gained so much confidence in writing for publication that I wrote nearly the entire book, co-authoring chapters with current or former students, while JoAnne traveled with her husband on fellowship in New Zealand. JoAnne protested about including her name on the second book, but I insisted. Our writing together had been such a good working relationship, which she viewed as a student friendship, but I experienced it as a mentoring friendship. In my opinion, writing with an experienced writer is far better than listening to a lecture on writing or even reviewing good models. Parallel writing is both instructive and motivating. The best of all worlds is to have a good writing partner/mentor who also follows through. A partner who is an outstanding writer but fails to follow through is of little or no value. By the time of our second book, I had long transitioned from mentee to independence, but my lessons of partnering with JoAnne would guide me for the rest of my career, particularly in mentoring my students as well as some of my colleagues. Reflecting on my doctoral writing class, I know I was not prepared to write for publication at that time and I might concede having been the least skilled within that class, but I am certain that my current record would compare quite favorably and exceed most of those classmates. This is not to boast, quite the contrary, it is simply to illustrate that a plan of action is far superior to prematurely succumbing to defeat. One of my professors in graduate study related to me and some other students how he developed his writing skill. He obtained a writing tutor/coach and submitted writing paragraphs weekly until they determined he had the skill for professional writing. I realize there are many naturally gifted writers, but I contend that most writers, especially within the professions who write for publication are largely made, not born.

MAKING NO CONCESSIONS TO WRITER'S BLOCK

The "publish or perish" adage continues to rein throughout academia, in some institutions more so than others. It is a real, and often major expectation of these positions, certainly for mine. I was regularly told during university studies that writing is the highest form of communication, and that statement alone can be intimidating. Many of us dread writing due to the preparation, research, and the overall time commitment involved in the process. Rarely is the first draft a final product. Instead, papers are written and rewritten with multiple drafts before considered a final product. In my opinion, the hardest part of writing for publication is getting started, the beginning. We are inclined to revise, rethink, overthink, and postpone the project until we finally convince ourselves that we are having a writer's block and need to put it aside until this moment passes. Fairly early in my career I was on the verge of drawing such a conclusion about a major writing commitment. I had a contract with a publisher with a deadline and what I considered to be a good outline, but nothing seemed to come together as I sat and stared at my computer. My mind was racing about a couple of events that impacted me emotionally, and I was about to capitulate to this state of nothingness until two productive thoughts or memories emerged. First was a saying from my mother, who never accepted "I can't" from any of her four children. She would just quietly and casually say, "You can do anything you want to do if you want to do it bad enough." Of course, we knew that was within limits, but we also knew that was her way of dismissing our whining. This statement reminded me of the many times Mother seemingly worked miracles for our family and others out of sheer determination and grit. I had that model to live up to. The other memory came from directions a doctoral classmate gave her daughter who was procrastinating and not making any progress on her graduate thesis. She told her daughter to get into the home office and start writing, "Write anything; Mary had a little lamb if you want, but just write." Her daughter did begin to write, complete her thesis, get her degree, and become a highly successful professional.

These two thoughts may seem simplistic, but they were useful to me because what I subsequently realized is that what you need is momentum, not for all the problems of everyday living to go away. You must create your momentum. In my case, I was clear-headed enough to know what I could do to just engage in the act of writing, not necessarily produce a first draft. I needed to write. I selected one attractive topic from my outline, along with six or seven articles related to that topic. I then just summarized the articles on my computer, giving little thought to what I wanted to get from the article. This was the easiest and least demanding thing I could do to remain in the state of writing. Eventually, however, as I got to the sixth or seventh article certain themes appeared, leading me to be more analytical about the content and begin to form a narrative for the project. More important, these small successes led to increasingly greater excitement about this writing project, and soon, I was wondering how I let some of these relatively minor issues delay my progress. This turned out to be one of my most successful writing projects.

In addition to creating your own momentum, a second recommendation for making no concessions to writer's block is to get a good writing partner. This is especially true as a beginning professional. A writing partner may help to ignite or augment the momentum you need for writing and publishing success. We are more likely to get something done, for instance, if we know someone else is depending on us. Other advantages are that we have less to write if we have a co-author, ideas from partners help to strengthen a paper, and partners can provide initial editing and reinforcement. Writing with others can be a tremendous learning experience. That certainly was my experience. I was fortunate to have some excellent writing partners early in my career who helped in many key ways, ranging from writing mechanics to writing style. You are fortunate if you can write with your major advisor; she is likely to be skilled, experienced, and knowledgeable about your topic. If not, I suggest you look for someone who is an able writer and is "hungry." Hungry is important because that means that your partner(s) needs to write as much as you do and, therefore, is likely to follow through.

An additional advantage of writing partners, especially experienced partners, is that you get to observe and model effective writing styles. A simple example I learned, for instance, is to write the introduction last. For example, start with the methods section when writing research studies for publication. It is not only the easiest section to write because you are simply telling what you did, you only need to determine how to organize it. This starts you writing. Writing begats writing, this is reinforcing and motivating, likely moving you on to the results section, which, like the methods, is relatively easy to write and will foster additional momentum. For the more open-ended sections such as the discussion and the introduction, experienced, mentoring partners are there to help us think through and answer some of the typical expectations of these sections. In the discussion, for example, you want to answer whether and why findings are consistent or inconsistent with expectations and the various ways to explain outcomes. Avoid writing partners that do little more than write their assigned parts and then abandon you to finish your sections on your own. They need to work with you closely on each aspect of the project, helping you to think through what is needed and why it is needed to produce the desired product.

REFLECTING ON SOME WRITING FAUX PAS

I want to caution the reader against some of my early writing career mistakes. First, refrain from being devastated by rigorous reviews. Thorough, extensive reviews are good for you and your paper, if not good to you. Our personal identity is closely aligned with our writing, and it is rather painful if others do not share our sense of personal perfection. I remember the feedback from one of my first submissions consisted of several pages of corrections and suggestions. I was distraught. This was before the days of email submissions and because I was the first author, they sent the feedback only to me. I remember calling my co-author practically in tears. We had worked so hard on that paper, it was a combination of both of our dissertations, it was a very good journal, and I greatly wanted this publication. I was so fortunate to have my co-author. She was the more experienced and sophisticated one. She calmed me down and pointed out that the editors wanted us to rewrite and resubmit, which we could get together and do in a coming weekend. In the process of rewriting, I realized that the reviewers made some excellent suggestions that considerably improved that paper. It was published and substantially helped my career. An important understanding was realizing and appreciating the phrase, *revise and resubmit*. Having served as an associate editor for two professional journals and reviewer of numerous papers, I am aware that acceptances of initial submissions are extremely rare. I am reminded of a funny encounter with one of my university colleagues. One day she came into my office, announcing in a loud voice that she no longer had any respect for one of the journals in her field. This was a highly regarded journal, and they accepted her initial submission without requesting any revisions or corrections. We had a hearty laugh; although my colleague was an outstanding writer and quite deserving of this acceptance, we both knew how unusual this was, even for those most distinguished in the field. Another of my colleagues was fond of saying, “Good papers are not written but rewritten.”

I would love to say that I was cured of my feedback anxiety after my initial experience. My anxiety did ease, and I learned to appreciate the phrase *revise and resubmit*, but I must admit that I continued to struggle with the process well into my career. I frequently put the feedback aside for a week or two before I could bring myself to read it. Often, I discovered that the suggestions were rather minor, and then I had to scramble to make the changes before the editor’s deadline. Even now, I’m ashamed to confess that I completely missed two publications because I failed to react in time for the deadline. In one case, it was an application for a federal grant that I was convinced they would not fund, so I refused to read the feedback. Later, well past the deadline, when I looked at the feedback, I realized how easily I might have gotten it funded based on the minor and easily amenable recommendations. I share this not to embarrass myself, but simply to say because academe is so insular, we often suffer in silence or alone over trivia that could have made a positive difference if we acted more wisely or assertively.

Despite my preceding comments, I wish to emphasize that I greatly value the writing and publishing process. It is especially important for Black educators because we are more likely than those from other racial or ethnic groups to study problems and possibilities specific to Black children, who make up the most vulnerable learners in our schools. Our teaching and lectures are essential but may be ephemeral. Our writings, however, are permanent, easily resourced products with the potential of more lasting effects. Furthermore, this society places greater value on written documents and it is essential that we validate and document conditions, procedures, and philosophies most beneficial for Black as well as all other learners. We must not only write but also make every effort to maximize our writing. To illustrate, findings from early studies, including dissertations, can be submitted for journal publications, which also can be presented at national conferences and used in grant applications for local, state, or federal funds. Successfully obtained grants can help to fund additional research whose studies are published, and the cycle continues. Assuming an established line of study, other important documents such as books, curricula, and monographs could emerge.

THINKING ABOUT TEACHING

If I am to thrive in this career while simultaneously feeding my passion, I must produce a wholesome and mutually fulfilling teaching experience. I reflected on my own life as a student and realized I had many teachers that I liked, some I admired, but, except for one graduate assistant when I was an undergraduate at the University of Pittsburgh, I never had a Black teacher. I surprised myself when I concluded that my mother, who sometimes permitted me to sit in her adult Sunday School class, was my favorite teacher. I especially enjoyed it when she and my father served as a tag teaching team in these classes. I realized that I enjoyed the classes because they not only thoroughly knew the content but could make practical applications into everyday living. They were the embodiment of my mother's constant admonishments to study to be approved and not be ashamed. Mother's teaching and Biblical charges served as my north star. It meant a lot of work, particularly with constantly changing teaching assignments and increasing amounts of knowledge to absorb within each subject area. Nevertheless, the standard that mother set was the challenge I steadily strove to meet, with varying degrees of success.

My students proved to be one of my greatest pleasures at the university. My undergraduates were nice and interesting; the master's level students were easy to teach, but the doctoral students were delightful and intellectually stimulating. For the most part, they were serious about their studies and spent hours with me discussing education issues and effective ways to study them. No question I learned as much, if not more, from them as the reverse. I promised myself to mentor each of my graduate students to publication, mainly my doctoral students, but often this included master's students, as well as a couple of undergraduate honors students. I envisioned the process as (1) I lead; you follow; (2) we construct together; and (3) you lead; I follow. The amount of writing and publishing varied among the students, but I always followed the process. This is a win-win association with no accompanying exploitation. Student research always informs your knowledge base, no matter how small the research, and students invariably gain much from their own research and your guidance and expertise. I continue to write with some of my former students, not as mentees or as student-learners, but as peers, co-authors, and mutual beneficiaries.

The graduate teaching model that I acquired from my program colleagues at OSU was especially beneficial for teaching and learning. Each year a series of seminars (approximately three or four) were held on Friday evenings at the home of one of the faculty. Along with the faculty, attendees included all the program master and doctoral students. Master students learned how to conduct research in their classrooms and doctoral students assisted their respective advisors in supervising the master students' research from the point of conceptualizing the study to the final written thesis. On a weekly basis, my doctoral advisees would meet with me and my master advisees. Doctoral advisees would be matched with one or two master advisees. This worked quite well because the master students had additional help with developing and implementing the study while the doctoral student gained more knowledge about conducting research. On occasion, the doctoral student would also advise the master student in challenging coursework such as statistics. At these meetings we assembled at a table in my office to discuss as a group each person's research study. These studies often would be an offshoot of my major research, or the replication of a previous student's study so there was a common theme familiar to everyone. Students also were encouraged to investigate novel problems specific to their classrooms. These were extremely worthwhile sessions. If well done, students were encouraged and assisted in submitting their studies for presentations at our state or national conferences, which frequently was the case. I tried to model my research and writing during these sessions. I typically hired my doctoral students and some master students on my research projects as graduate assistants. We used these sessions to discuss the research and writing.

In addition to being competent and personable, my students were diverse according to race, ethnicity, and gender. Much has been said about recruiting diverse populations in higher education, but among other things, it is understood that a diverse faculty facilitates recruiting diverse students. On more than one occasion, for example, a student from a diverse background expressed interest in graduate study because of my presence on the faculty. Many of our students, especially at the doctoral level, were international students and I was pleased to learn that international and many domestic White students appreciated a diverse faculty. On one occasion, one of my students from Taiwan told me that after meeting me, her mother now felt comfortable her daughter was in safe hands.

University faculty often lose sight of the fact that students from different lands and from underrepresented groups in this country are easily intimidated by the large, impersonal US universities. This also may be true for many domestic White students but is more likely to be the case for those from diverse backgrounds. Students need to know they will have the opportunity to meet established expectations within a supportive, rather than an indifferent or hostile, environment.

One story I like to share took place in the spring of 2003 when five of my graduate students and I went to our annual conference in Seattle to present some of our research. Our pattern was to make our presentations, attend other sessions independently, and then meet together for dinner. The first evening, we found a very nice and very crowded restaurant with mostly conventioneers. We had a good meal and conversation about the day's events but didn't take much note of the other diners. The following day after our presentations, one of my doctoral students had another commitment and could not join us for dinner at the Eye of the Needle restaurant. Again, we had a nice meal at the restaurant, which also was full of conventioneers. As we were leaving, another group approached us saying, "Where is your blond?" We were all surprised by the question and it took a moment to understand the question, which they repeated by saying, "Your blond," they said, "the one that was with you last evening." I then understood, smiled, and said, "You mean Amanda, she had another engagement this evening, but she'll be back with us tomorrow." "Oh, ok, just wondering," they said as they walked away.

After they left, my students and I laughed and realized that this group had been at the same restaurant we had the first night and apparently took special notice of our composition, which, up until then, we had never thought about. With me was one Muslim student from Jordan who wore a hijab, one female from India, a White blond female from Ohio, a White male from Oregon, a female from Taiwan and me, an African American female from Pennsylvania. I chuckled to myself wondering what that group would have said if my African American and Hispanic students had joined me on that trip, which they did on later trips. We were so used to and so fond of each other that we never thought of our diversity. This is one of the many reasons why I loved teaching, especially at the graduate level. They were eager, dedicated students and they taught me volumes. My students have gone on to distinguish themselves in universities and school systems all over the world. They greatly enriched my life. I remain close to most of them and they to each other.

The common wisdom, I believe, is that every institution needs to reflect the makeup of the country, particularly institutions of higher education (Brooks, 2023). When I was an undergraduate student at the University of Pittsburgh, I had the pleasure of serving as a hostess for the nationality rooms, which were a series of small classrooms designed and decorated by the ethnic groups populating the city. I was unusually drawn to the Chinese room, which had a large black round teak wood seminar table in the center of the room with matching chairs positioned around the table. One of the underlying themes of this classroom design was that the professor or teacher would sit at the same level with the students because the professor could learn from the students as well as the reverse. This contrasted with most of the other nationality rooms, which had designated and/or elevated locations for the professor. There is mutual learning at every level of formal education, especially in higher education. This sharing of knowledge is circular (i.e., among students) as well as linear (between student and faculty). My international and domestic students made tremendous contributions to my research and writing on cultural diversity and social development. Hua Feng, for example, co-authored with me several very enlightening documents about the upbringing and social development of Asian children (e.g., Cartledge & Feng, 1996). Furthermore, we conducted studies in US schools to study their social skills relative to Black and White children (Feng & Cartledge, 1996). I should note that except for the chapter written with JoAnne Milburn, every chapter in the Cartledge and Milburn (1996) book was co-authored with a current or former student. Teaching in a pluralistic society such as the United States makes learning about other cultures essential. These understandings help us to realize that no group is a monolith, all cultural systems are dynamic, and all cultures are valid, with no one culture superior.

Healthy, close relationships between faculty and students, especially graduate students, are commonplace, and sometimes program policies help to foster those bonds. One such policy in our OSU program was to admit only full-time doctoral students. That meant 3 to 4 years of full-time doctoral study while living sparingly on a 20-hour-per-week graduate assistant stipend. Although a financial sacrifice, it did mean that students had a greater opportunity to work closely with faculty and prepare more adequately for a career in academe. It also meant that students were much more likely to graduate. I supported this practice because I observed other programs in our department that admitted numerous students on a part-time basis. Often, the students rarely saw their advisor and failed to receive the assistance needed to complete their program. Too often, these were students of color who, even if they passed their generals, were never guided in completing their dissertation and eventually disappeared among the large mass of ABDs (all but dissertation). The problem was exacerbated in many cases by the absence of Black faculty committed to their successful program completion. I had a strong need to support my students regardless of background. Support for me started at the point of admission.

MENTORING IS GOOD TEACHING

Mentoring is critical to university teaching, especially at the graduate level. I am not certain what facilitates a good mentoring relationship, but we all know when it happens. I shared earlier in this chapter my good fortune of securing a mentoring relationship while still in graduate school and continuing with that relationship during the first few years of my college teaching career. One obvious important feature of good mentoring is mutual interest and common goals. Likeability is helpful, but most important is working together toward some end. Faculty-student products are ideal for this purpose. In addition to ensuring my students completed their graduate program, I vowed to publish with each of my doctoral students because most of them were bound for positions in academe or administration where professional writing would be expected or required. Many individuals with tremendous potential for publishing and having an impact on the field fail to do so because of missed mentoring opportunities. This is often the case for Blacks in academe. Lisa is a case in point.

When I was at midcareer, a young Black doctoral student, who I will call Lisa from a different department, requested to interview me because a new Black male faculty member in my program designated me as one of his mentors. Lisa was doing a dissertation on mentoring Black faculty in higher education. I answered her questions, and we talked extensively about mentoring in academe. Before long, we began to talk about her graduate program. Lisa shared that she was successful in her coursework and supported by her advisor, who was well known in the field and a prolific writer. She spoke positively about his support. I asked her why he wasn't writing with her. She had no answer. At the time of the interview, I was embarking on a paper that was tangentially related to her topic. I asked her and the Black male whom I was informally mentoring to join me in writing this paper.

This was a great collaboration. The paper was favorably reviewed and published. We continued with a couple of additional small projects, but that publication helped to set Lisa on a trajectory to become an excellent professor widely recognized and revered in her field. Approximately 30 years later, while writing this chapter, Lisa contacted me to invite me to the ceremony where she was being honored on the Hall of Fame of the university of her doctorate studies. Lisa wanted me to come to this ceremony because, although not her advisor, I was the first to invite her to write for publication. I had long forgotten that conversation, but I was honored she remembered it and viewed me as one of many persons who helped to jettison her impressive career. In addition to writing extensively and establishing herself as an authority in her discipline, Lisa distinguished herself in many other ways such as being the first Black promoted to full professor in her large highly rated and predominately White university, being honored by the largest education professional organization, and being honored by her mentees with a book about her impact on them.

FINDING PERSONAL AGENCY

Prior to writing my second book, OSU appointed me to a faculty position where the expectation for research and publishing increased considerably. The move from my first relatively small teaching university to Ohio State compared to a transfer from a one-way country road to a seven-lane Los Angeles highway. To be quite honest and fair both are good, reputable institutions. OSU was much larger with many more resources, and a widely noted faculty. The faculty greeted me warmly and remained friendly throughout my tenure there. No one was out to get me, nor were they going to coddle or do anything special for me, I had to demonstrate that I could stay afloat and that I was more than window dressing. I was on my own and I had to upgrade my T Principle and all other strategies in my toolbox.

Shirley Chisholm is noted for having said, "If they don't give you a seat at the table, bring a folding chair." Another quote from Shirley is – "You don't make progress by standing on the sidelines, whimpering, and complaining. You make progress by implementing ideas." Not long after my appointment, I realized that I did not get a seat at the table for a major funded faculty project, nor was anyone going to make amends. I decided not to whine but to upgrade my strategies. As previously noted, my colleagues had an excellent model for research and publishing. Rather than distance myself, I remained collegial, collaborated appropriately, and studied them closely, noting how they engaged students and implemented research. I paid especially close attention to their time management (e.g., no time wasted on non-essential college committees) and how most undertakings did double or triple duty leading to presentations and publications.

I learned to streamline my work life, cut out the fat, religiously adhere to my students, my research and writing. Although I had my own research agenda, a significant problem for me was not being at the table when graduate students, particularly doctoral students were assigned. Ironically, although I did not get to select, many of my doctoral students often proved to be the best students in our program. Again, my faculty served as models and I aggressively pursued and obtained federal grants, which greatly liberated me and enabled me to expand further my research agenda and recruit my own students. I even supported some of my faculty's students. I had the best of all worlds, collegiality, and independence until 1 day they invited me to the table. Although sanguine and somewhat duplicitous, I sent a dead pan but humorous response saying, "I'll join you but keep in mind, you'll never tame this shrew."

TAKING A STAND

Universities, like all other major institutions are political: schools, churches, families as well as the government. A former colleague used to joke that the university was the most political because the egos were so great and the resources so small. From my experience, the most contentious faculty politics tended to center on what they called "turf" battles, i.e., impinging on another faculty's academic discipline. For example, someone outside the math faculty proposes a theory course based on math concepts, raising the math faculty's ire along with a declaration of war. I assiduously avoided those and other battles partly because I was concerned about misperceptions, especially of me. I just kept my head down and did my work; there is no joy in making work enemies. Eventually, however, as special education program coordinator, I found myself entangled in a conflict I could not avoid. It was a gut punch; it was the place where my faculty and I lived, and I couldn't understand why my esteemed program colleagues, rated among the top in the country, had just capitulated year after year.

It was a David and Goliath battle, and we were David without even a slingshot. My special education faculty espoused expertise on teaching the hard to teach. Most of these children had problems in reading and we strongly advocated for early interventions in phonemic awareness and phonics. Phonics and related skills are not the essence of reading, they are needed to "launch" reading and could be a reading death knell for the most vulnerable, if not adequately learned. The problem: to include this course in our curriculum meant bumping one of the courses our students currently took from another faculty. The other faculty was not only livid, but dug in. It was bad enough that they would be losing students for one of their key courses, but we were salting the wound by replacing it with a course they philosophically opposed. Troubled waters, indeed. Although, some of my faculty began to show soft signs of retreat, for me, the stakes were too high, this was a righteous battle that warranted going to the virtual carpet, if necessary.

Higher administration would not take sides or render a solution; this was a faculty-to-faculty issue. The other faculty was more than twice our size, and the meetings and memos were eternal. I tangled with individual faculty, with college curriculum committees, with program chairs, and with department chairs. I quietly sat through faculty meetings with the occasional opposing faculty meltdown, with misunderstandings and extremely tense environments, but I continued to assure them that our faculty genuinely wanted to collaborate without relinquishing the phonics course. Even my department chair advised me to give in, but I persisted. I knew the right side of this issue. I battled not just for my college students but, more importantly, for all the students languishing in our schools for lack of critical early reading interventions. My early teaching career and my research undergirded my convictions. My research, for example, showed phonemic awareness interventions put low-income beginning readers on a better reading trajectory than their non-intervention peers who initially showed little or no risk. More than well-prepared beginning teachers, I fought for countless potentially marginalized children. How does that weigh against a questionable, non-essential course? Please know that I had, and continue to have, tremendous respect and appreciation for the opposing faculty, most of whom were recognized nationally and internationally. These were very good people with no malicious intent. Unfortunately, they were ignoring or opposing an approach critical for our students, an astronomical price I refused to pay just for collegial comfort.

Without too much bloodshed, we finally got that phonics course into our curriculum, which my colleagues are still teaching. Further, at my last observation, the two faculties had forged a working relationship, and one of the most distinguished members of their faculty provided valuable consultation on one of my grants. Recently, various media sources provided reports of scientific, educational, parental, and political support for the position my faculty took (e.g., Yurick et al., in press). These multiple documents have, for me, iced the cake. Doubtless the squabbles will continue, but it is hoped we will not continue shortchanging children as in the past. Although I am now emerita, I am still monitoring the process and writing about this issue, and continuing to press for the learning, i.e., freedom of our children.

Not all just battles end in triumph but some may be worth fighting even if you know you're going to lose. Nobody seeks pariahdom, such as Margaret Chase

Smith, who singly confronted Joe McCarthy (U.S. Senate: A Declaration of Conscience, 2003), or worse yet, martyrdom, as in Fannie Lou Hamer, who nearly died for voting rights (Hamer, Fannie Lou, n.d.). Both women eventually achieved their goals and tremendous admiration. In no way do I compare myself with the women of that stature, but they are models of hope. As we educators know, not all rewards are immediate, and some are extremely delayed, even posthumously. I often worried, for example, about my student advocacy – had I been too outspoken? But my students informed me in so many ways they greatly appreciated my support when their backs were against the wall.

I share this not because I believe in warfare or to display my warrior prowess; quite the contrary. I think of myself as a practicing coward. Nor was I always right or successful in my advocacy. I wasn't. I stubbed my toe more than a few times. I share it because there are times in various arenas our voices need to be heard, especially in the interest of the neediest or simply because it is the right thing to do. I share this because this battle reflected my lifelong pursuit, my purpose in academe to find some nugget contributing to greater learning success for our most vulnerable learners. Throughout my struggles, and there have been a few, I always heard my father telling my 13-year-old self, "Baby, make sure you are right, then stand even if you have to stand alone." I've repeated those words many times over the years for even though I felt very alone I could not afford to remain silent.

CONCLUDING THOUGHTS

I realized early in my career there is no silver bullet or magical elixir in achieving success in academe, just as there is no simple formula for success with the hard to teach. I did, however, envision a multidimensional goal-directed figure with certain essential components such as *passion, purpose, principles, supports, and perseverance*. Early on I determined that I needed to be purposeful in my career pursuits. Our society offers many options, some of which are highly attractive, but my strivings needed to be based on a genuine desire to know or do. Drifting into an area of work because someone else is doing it or because it appears lucrative could be formulas for disaster. This doesn't mean that I rigidly refused to change course. Changing course can be quite beneficial, especially if the change is toward a more meaningful or useful endeavor. When I realized, for example, that improving social behaviors would not automatically have the desired effect on reading, I broadened my research and writing to study both domains with their respective interactions. Having a solid purpose is a stabilizer, keeping you focused and intentional. This purpose fed my passion, which, I believe, kept me going even when encountering the inevitable disappointments, frustrations, and even failures. My passions motivated me to persist and employ principles and practices enabling me to mitigate or circumvent potentially derailing obstacles. I found no fool proof mitigation strategies. I just know that I was most comfortable and successful if I stayed true to the purposes, passions, and principles I outlined and described earlier in this chapter.

There are some paths, however, I would not recommend. When things are going south, it is often tempting to retreat within ourselves and declare defeat. That is my basic nature, but I learned over the years that just the opposite is required during those down periods. Instead, that is the time to put forth more, not less effort. When denied a grant or publication, for instance, use the feedback to revise and submit two more documents. Others are attracted to you when you are attempting to be productive (even if not successful) but are likely to ignore or avoid you if you are sequestered and inactive. Another caution is to avoid declaring war on perceived antagonists, especially if your position is precarious. I have typically advised junior colleagues in these circumstances to get off the battlefield and focus on increasing their productivity. I observed very quick exits for those who chose to ignore that advice. (Note: if you find yourself in a "lion's den," make a quick exit and don't look back. Find more promising surroundings.) Otherwise, high levels of activity consistent with your institutions' goals almost automatically recruits supports, which help you to persevere and, in turn, reciprocate the support. It is a cyclical, potentially sustaining process.

REFERENCES

Bible. (n.d.). *II Timothy*, 2:15 KJ. https://www.biblestudytools.com/kjv/2-timothy/2-15.html

Blight, D. W. (2018). *Frederick Douglass, prophet of freedom*. Simon & Schuster.

Brooks, D. (2023, November 17). Universities are failing at inclusion. *The New York Times*. https://www.nytimes.com/2023/11/16/opinion/college-university-antisemitism-crt.html?campaign_id=39&emc=edit_ty_20231117&instance_id=107966&nl=opinion-today®i_id=30421208&segment_id=150308&te=1&user_id=d124616e7ec8d35d888b2c33fcc93d67

Buffett, W. (n.d.). It's better to hang out with people better than you. Pick out associates whose behavior is better than yours and you'll drift in that direction. https://www.brainyquote.com/quotes/warren_buffett_398945

Cartledge, G., & Feng, H. (1996). Asian Americans. In G. Cartledge & J. F. Milburn (Eds.), *Cultural diversity and social skill instruction: Understanding ethnic and gender differences* (pp. 87–131). Research Press.

Cartledge, G., & Milburn, J. F. (1996). *Cultural diversity and social skill instruction: Understanding ethnic and gender differences*. Research Press.

Dictionary.com. (n.d.a). https://www.dictionary.com/browse/passion

Dictionary.com. (n.d.b). https://www.dictionary.com/browse/love

Douglass, F. (1845). *The narrative of the life of Frederick Douglass*. https://www.loc.gov/item/prn-13-005/books-that-shaped-america-on-amazon/2013-01-22/

Douglass, F. (2021). *Narrative of the life of Frederick Douglass*. Independent Publishers.

Feng, H., & Cartledge, G. (1996). Social skill assessment of inner city Asian, African, and European American students. *School Psychology Review*, *25*, 227–238.

Hamer, Fannie Lou. (n.d.). The Martin Luther King, Jr. Research and Education Institute. https://kinginstitute.stanford.edu/hamer-fannie-lou

Hooks, b. (2001). *All about love*. Harper Collins.

Jones, R., Jr. (2021). Denmark Vesey. In I. X. Kendi & K. N. Blain (Eds.), *Four hundred souls: A community history of African America, 1619–2019* (pp. 187–190). Penguin Random House LLC.

Low Country Digital Library (LCDL). (n.d.a). *Origins of public education in South Carolina*. https://ldhi.library.cofc.edu/exhibits/show/history_burke_high_school/origins_public_education

Low Country Digital Library (LCDL). (n.d.b). *Developing public in South Carolina*. https://ldhi.library.cofc.edu/exhibits/show/somebody_had_to_do_it/struggle_for_equal_ed/devloping_education
Smith, C. (2021). The Louisiana Rebellion. In I. X. Kendi & K. N. Blain (Eds.), *Four hundred souls: A community history of African America, 1619–2019* (pp. 173–176). Penguin Random House LLC.
Steele, C. M. (2010). *Whistling Vivaldi: And other clues to how stereotypes affect us*. W.W. Norton & Co.
United States Library of Congress. (n.d.). *Books that shaped America*. https://www.loc.gov/item/prn-13-005/books-that-shaped-america-on-amazon/2013-01-22/
U.S. Senate. (2003, August 7). *A declaration of conscience*. https://www.senate.gov/about/powers-procedures/investigations/mccarthy-hearings/a-declaration-of-conscience.htm
Yurick, A. L., Council, M., Telesman, A. O., Musti, S., Gardner, R., & Cartledge, G. (in press). On the science of reading: How social justice, behavior analysis, and literacy instruction converge. *Behavior and Social Issues*. https://doi.org/10.1007/s42822-023-00154-1

MAKING OUR ANCESTORS PROUD: AFRICAN AMERICAN WOMEN ACHIEVING SUCCESS IN THE ACADEMY

Lillian B. Poats

Texas Southern University, USA

ABSTRACT

The article focuses on the challenges and issues which African American females encounter in navigating the Academy as faculty and doctoral students. The literature is replete with discussions of African American female scholars and the feelings of isolation, marginalization, and invisibility which they experience. The same would be true for African American female doctoral students. The author provides a discussion of the concerns which African American females encounter while navigating the tenure process. It is suggested that critical factors include understanding the environment while focusing on ensuing expectations of the academy are met. The importance of effective communication in the academy is highlighted. The context of the meaning of teaching, research and service and the need to balance work in these areas are delineated as this becomes critical for a new faculty member navigating the process. It is replete with key points to consider and personal experiences which highlight effective behaviors. The second part of the discussion focuses on the issues which African American females have in navigating the academy as doctoral students. It provides insight into issues of understanding the environment and the expectations of the academy along with the benefits of establishing effective communication with faculty and peers. Within the discussion are key points designed to assist female doctoral students in being successful. Advisors working with doctoral students are encouraged to establish relationships while at the same time requiring excellence as a means of assisting students in their process and professional life.

Journeys of Black Women in Academe
Diversity in Higher Education, Volume 26, 73–83

Published under exclusive licence by Emerald Publishing Limited
ISSN: 1479-3644/doi:10.1108/S1479-364420240000026004

Keywords: African American faculty; tenure process for African American faculty; African American female doctoral students; doctoral study for African American females; navigating the tenure process

INTRODUCTION

Working in the Academy is a labor of love. It's the kind of work that creates a schism as you enjoy teaching and learning, but you also have the stress of assuring that you have the publications required to be successful and remain in the academy. It is this framework which causes many female faculty to depart the academy. The literature is replete with discussions of African American female scholars and the feelings of isolation, marginalization, and invisibility which they experience. The same would be true for African American female doctoral students; however, I would suggest that they have more to lose in this power play. Observing this phenomenon for over 30 years has led to questioning how to navigate the academy to achieve the doctorate and/or tenure and promotion. In fall 2021, of the 1.5 million faculty at degree-granting postsecondary institutions, 56% were full time and 44% were part time. Considering full-time faculty in fall, 2021:

- 73% of faculty were White, specifically 35% white female and 38% white male
- 23% of faculty were Asian, specifically 5% Asian female and 7% Asian male
- 6% of faculty were Black, specifically 4% Black female and 3% Black male
- 6% of faculty were Hispanic, specifically 3% of each Hispanic female and Hispanic male (retrieved from https://nces.ed.gov/fastfacts/display.asp?id=61)

Hinton (2009) suggests that African American female faculty have been historically marginalized within most Predominantly White Institutions (PWIs), and historically, this has been viewed in a negative light. She suggests that Black women in academe might view this position as one of power that can be used to propel them toward the goals of tenure and promotion. It has been argued that meaningful change in the representation, equity, and prestige of women faculty of color will require validating their experiences, supporting and valuing their research, creating opportunities for their professional recognition and advancement, and implementing corrective action for unjust assessment practices (Fox Tree & Vaid, 2022). There are some basic rules that might assist in navigating the field for African American female faculty and students.

ACHIEVING SUCCESS IN THE FACULTY RANKS

At the outset, it can be established that there may be little support for a young faculty member navigating the tenure process. Racial disparities in tenure and promotion outcomes are well-known in the existing research literature. Scholarship establishes that Black and Brown faculty experience unique challenges when navigating the tenure and promotion process, such as a lack of diverse mentorship, biased student/peer evaluations, and disproportionately high service demands (Carter & Craig, 2022). Even in an environment that might not be hostile, there is often a lack of camaraderie and mentoring. Young female faculty often find themselves navigating the path alone. New faculty may find themselves struggling to understand the unwritten rules of the game.

Nationally, we need to clearly understand some of the issues surrounding tenure:

- The guarantee of a lifetime job may be seen as a means of protecting ineffective faculty members.
- There is an institutional desire to have more flexibility in faculty negotiations and budgetary concerns.
- Minorities and women are not highly represented in tenure-track positions.

Because of these issues, a large number of positions are currently being posted as non-tenure track. Unfortunately, African American women are adversely affected by these concerns.

There are some basic principles that might guide us in achieving success in the academy.

- Understanding is critical. It is imperative that a young faculty member have a great understanding from the outset of employment at the institutions. There will often be mounds of hearsay regarding this process, which proliferates the environment; however, it will be necessary to obtain the official documents that outline the time frame and requirements at the institution. It is not uncommon for these to be hidden documents from some minority groups. I will tell you that it is written in some document, faculty manual, guidelines for tenure and promotion, or a specific publication which outlines what is expected of an individual who is applying for tenure and promotion. Faculty should pay specific attention to the expectations – number of publications, types of publications, and authorship requirements. One university or department may require five publications, whereas another may require nine. Their number is specific to the institution and/or department. The new faculty member will need to conform to what is published. There is often the tendency to compare the work of seasoned colleagues; however, it should be noted that the expectations may have changed. I recall upon my first employment one of my mentors from another university continuously asked me what the requirements were. It was literally a scavenger hunt to locate the appropriate document which outlined the specifics.
- On a personal note, there is a need to outline the expectations so that you are clear. Also, be alert for changes to the process, timelines, etc. Institutions often make changes over time. Success is obtained when you are committed to the process. A new faculty member can ill afford to have doubts regarding their success. Junior faculty members will often feel ambivalent and vulnerable. After all, your ability to survive depends on how well you balance. It has been

suggested that "To not make it now may be considered intellectual death." Unfortunately, this sentiment remains today.

- Communication is key for new faculty members meaning that you can ill afford to make enemies. Not to compromise your beliefs but to be tactful. Make sure that the lines of communication are open. You will want to speak up for yourself; however, you will find that there is a way to do it. I'm reminded of a situation during my young faculty days when I entered the building on my way to give the Dean a "piece of my mind." One of the senior faculty members stopped me and cautioned me to calm down. I think my emotions kept me from remembering that this administrator provided a copy of a book focusing on the leadership acumen of Atilla the Hun as suggested reading for the leadership team. Little did I understand that this was probably NOT the person to approach in this manner. This administrator later became a true mentor during my career. It was about understanding how and when to approach an individual.

We are all clear that evaluation for tenure and promotion is based on teaching, research, and service. Many institutions have added other requirements which might include community engagement and service learning. Most additions can be broadly categorized in the service arena.

Teaching. The questions we must ask as it relates to teaching include:

- What is included in the evaluation of teaching? It is often measured by
  - Student Evaluations
  - Peer review
  - Administrative review
  - Self-documentation
  - Student performance (accountability)
- Teaching effectiveness may be measured by
  - Department Chair Evaluations
  - Recognition given by peers for having made substantial contributions to your academic specialty in teaching
  - Awards for excellence in teaching
  - Development of instructional materials and methods (i.e. instructional manuals, workbooks, visual media, software)

This author contends that teaching is an art. The longer you function in the classroom, you will find that your pedagogy skills improve. Effective teachers always prepare for the classroom; they identify additional resources that might assist students. Our students arrive at the university at varying levels, and it is the job of the faculty member to attempt to meet them where they are. There was a time when we expected students to arrive prepared to be successful; however, that is not always the case today. As a young faculty member, know that it is okay to ask for assistance if you need assistance with teaching strategies and/or subject matter adaptation. Many institutions have Teaching and Learning Excellence centers that have resources to assist. You will also need to evaluate the course materials from previous offerings of the class so that you can review current information and infuse it into the class. Making your classes relevant will assist with student learning. Now for the caveat that all new faculty must remember – Teaching can be one of the most rewarding aspects of being a college professor. Be careful not to get overwhelmed with teaching. We often find that female faculty get overwhelmed with teaching and life activities at the expense of their research agenda.

Research is often the most important aspect of navigating the tenure process. Many have arrived at the end of the probationary period with inadequate research, only to find that they are not successful in this journey. Scholarly inquiry is the foundation of research. It is often regarded as the most critical component in the tenure process.

It includes Research, Publications and Grantsmanship.

As a new faculty member, there are some major considerations in assuring that you meet research goals. You will want to spend time developing a clear research agenda so that you can be focused. It is important that you prioritize research. This will assist you in setting aside a specific time to work on projects. It is always helpful when you become guarded about the time that you dedicate to research. It works if you select a set date/time to work on your research without interruption. I say be guarded so that you do not allow other activities to take the place of this time. Lastly, I would encourage you to take advantage of released time to conduct research. Again, be careful to utilize any released time to focus on your research.

You can maximize your research efforts by being clear about what you would like to publish. Identify target journals and review their requirements. Seek input and review the publications of colleagues in the department and university.

We would urge you to prepare for well-respected publications in your field by identifying those publications that are respected in your environment. A focused and targeted approach will benefit you throughout this process.

If your focus is on publications, you will need to identify journals where you want to publish. We suggest that you be realistic in this selection. You might focus on articles, book chapters, reviews, and other materials rather than having your first goal focus on publishing a book. You may want to target regional and state journals which may be more accepting initially. We cannot emphasize the need to develop alliances with other professionals in the field. These alliances will identify individuals – on and off campus – who can assist you in meeting your goal.

Please be sure to seek out refereed and/or peer-reviewed journals for submission of materials. The guidelines may require that you publish in refereed publications, and you should be sure to meet this requirement. Another idea is to develop relationships with professionals in the field. This will facilitate your ability to get published as well as assist you in getting invited to publish in various publications. On another note, we suggest that you review current writings of faculty in your department to determine the kinds of materials which are respected. To facilitate review of your work, it is helpful to develop professional relationships with colleagues and/or mentors who will provide preliminary reviews of your materials. Remember that the emphasis on research and publications is critical to your survival.

Service. Service is broadly defined as those activities which provide leadership and enhance the professional community. This is generally evidenced in service at the college or university level and includes activities such as serving on committees which function to benefit the institution. Also included are those activities within the community which focus on dissemination of scholarly information and broaden the impact of the university. Again, we encourage you to review carefully any specific requirements outlined in this area. Faculty service might include involvement in university services such as departmental committees, college committees, accreditation studies, leadership in faculty governance, leadership of a department center or institute, and advisement of students, including student organizations.

Aspects of service that might also be found in the realm of professional service include involvement in Professional Societies, holding leadership positions in professional organizations at the State, Regional, or National level, planning and management of a conference, and involvement in external agencies that review programs and/or accrediting entities.

Service may also include leadership within the community, which is measured by serving on committees and as consultants to entities related to the discipline. There are ample opportunities that focus on involvement with the community to share your expertise based on work in your academic discipline.

We GUARANTEE that you will be asked to do more than you have time for!! Be alert for the informal rules of service which might suggest that you:

- Select those activities which benefit you as a junior faculty member and allow you to build relationships with senior colleagues
- Select those activities that are considered power committees
- Be careful to balance those activities that stereotype you in terms of ethnicity or gender. Tierney and Bensimon (1996) refer to some activities as "Mom work" or "smile work" and suggest that women may often be asked to do maternal things and relate to students on a different level.
- Be careful of those things that are "time burners" or waste time.

Guillaume and Apodaca (2022) reviewed how faculty of color navigated service demands at their institutions. Three commonalities were found among participants: (1) being strategic about commitments to students and promotion and tenure efforts; (2) making connections between faculty workloads and motivation for pursuing promotion and tenure; and (3) believing relationships with students were a benefit during the promotion and tenure process. Wright-Kim and Perna (2023) suggest that inequities in faculty representation and support have long been documented, though a potentially key contributor to these inequities – negotiation behavior – remains underexplored. Their research suggests that significant differences are found in the likelihood of seeking and receiving external offers and negotiating employment. Men of color are less likely to engage in many behaviors, though women of color may be less successful in receiving changes to their employment context.

You will be called upon to balance the three areas: teaching, research, and service. Be careful of the political pitfalls. Higher education is full of political pitfalls, and you want to make sure you do not inadvertently create a problem. This is even more important today with all of the discussion and focus on diversity, equity, and inclusion. Please know that there is a formal and informal process, and it is incumbent upon you to become aware of both of these networks. Your success depends on it.

Organize your process to include keeping documentation for all your activities. Please do not wait until the end of the probationary period to collect materials. You should create a file where you place this information. Organize your material based on the primary areas of teaching, research, and service. Make sure that you are clear on the process used to submit materials –electronic, portfolio, etc.

A proactive approach was used at one institution where new faculty were provided a seminar focusing on how to navigate the tenure track. It provided an opportunity for individuals to come together to share and discuss some of their challenges. It required faculty to review their process on an annual basis and be cognizant of their progress. It ultimately provided an esprit de corps for individuals while providing accurate information, which is often not understood for the novice. During this time frame, we are pleased to say that only one faculty member did not earn tenure. Any tenured faculty member could provide a discussion of the lessons learned (good and bad) as they navigated the process.

AFRICAN AMERICAN FEMALE STUDENTS – NAVIGATING THE PATH TO THE DOCTORATE

Doctoral students also find themselves in a schism also as it relates to achieving the terminal degree. Data for the Annual *Survey of Earned Doctorates* show that universities in the United States conferred 52,250 research doctorates in 2021, down 5.5% from 2020. Of the 2,431 African Americans who earned doctorates from US universities in 2021, 1,552 were women. Thus, women earned 63.8% of all doctorates awarded to African Americans in 2021. This is up from 62.3% in 2020. The number of African American men who earned doctorates in 2021 was the lowest number since 2017. African Americans earned 7.7% of all doctorates awarded to US citizens or permanent residents of this country (Journal of Blacks in Higher Education, October 2022). These numbers reflect the college going rates for African Americans with females having higher numbers. Many have been successful individuals who find themselves in a classroom where there is a need to conform as they progress. This is not much unlike African American female faculty members. The academic requirements are often easier to navigate even though they may find themselves the target of uncaring behavior from faculty members. If we refer to the various forms of bias, we can clearly see that often, students are treated differently in doctoral programs. There is often the feeling on the part of the professor that they do not belong in a doctoral program, and thus, they become a target. The literature is replete of stories of how students were treated in a manner that made them question their worth and their ability to succeed. They are often isolated and made to feel invisible in programs. We might open the discussion of how this treatment differs at PWIs and Historically Black College and University (HBCU); however, there is an element of the same behavior in both arenas. Having spent over 30 years of my career working with doctoral students in an HBCU, we see the same behaviors. In some instances, it is just clear to us that it is not based on race. In other instances, some non-minority faculty members use the environment and their power status to question the worth of students. To begin with, doctoral study is different. It requires the ability to conceptualize information along with engage in independent thinking.

Understanding is critical in this arena also. It is imperative that female doctoral students understand the expectations and the environment at the outset. Many students are the first to obtain a bachelor's degree, and even more, students are the first among their family and friends to obtain a doctorate. The process is foreign, and there is a need to seek out individuals – faculty, advisors, and others in the environment who can assist in clarifying what the expectations are. Academic curricula, as well as other program requirements, should be reviewed. Students must re-acquaint themselves with degree plans, catalogs, and other publications designed to outline them with the process. McCallum (2013) summarizes her findings to suggest that despite the attainment of a bachelor's degree, and sometimes even a master's degree, students are still unsure of the pathway to pursue the doctorate. In response to this factor, institutions might begin introducing students to the idea of pursuing doctoral education early in their academic careers. There must be a clear understanding of the program and what is expected. For example, some doctoral programs require publications as a measure of graduation. This should be noted. Developing a relationship with doctoral faculty and advisors is critical to the success of the student.

On a personal note, again, there is a need to outline the expectations so that the student is clear on what they will need to complete to be successful. Because earning the doctorate primarily has intrinsic value, students will need to be clear that this is their goal. It is even more important for female doctoral students because they often find the need to balance their academic studies, life activities, and family. Females who have a family have a special burden as they must work to balance their lives. It is often suggested that they require support which allows them to focus on their studies. It is easy to get overwhelmed and remove doctoral study from the many life activities that they must engage in. Commitment to completing the program of study is critical. In my work with female doctoral students, they sometimes become discouraged because of the conflict with academic requirements and other life activities. As an advisor, you will find that you need to be there for them. They have not seen anyone go through doctoral study and may not be familiar with the rigors that they will go through. We all can recall those long nights of completing the work that is required. I'm often enlightened by the students who think if I can just get to the dissertation stage, I'm through. I quietly have to let them know that the dissertation is often the hardest part of the process. There are often no timelines that must be met. Students can literally disappear back into their lives. As an advisor, you really do have to be willing to reach out and encourage them to move forward. McCallum (2020) defines the concept of "Othermothering" and suggests that African American students are influenced to pursue and enroll in doctoral degree programs by faculty whom they consider to be trusting, caring, and supportive. These faculty members have high academic expectations, and they typically share a marginalized identity with these students. The ways in which students described these relationships align with the concept of Othermothering. Thus, it is concluded that relationships with individuals who exhibit the characteristics of Othermothering will influence African American students to pursue and enroll in doctoral study programs.

Reaching the dissertation stage is a major accomplishment. We always say to students that they will begin to wonder how they ever had the time to attend classes when they have difficulty finding time to write. We find that if students are not totally committed, they begin to lag behind in this phase, with some never finishing the degree. As I remind my students, ABD is NOT a credential. Communication is extremely key for all doctoral students – and certainly, African American female doctoral students cannot afford to make enemies in this process.

As you interact with faculty and administrators, there will be times when you will need to speak up; however, you should always remember what you were taught growing up. From an old family proverb, I often tell my students "You can catch more flies with honey than with vinegar." In other words, it is easier to persuade others with polite requests and a positive attitude rather than with rude demands and negativity. We often say that your attitude determines your altitude. This should be a cardinal belief for doctoral students. This also entails keeping your emotions intact so that you don't alienate those who might be called to assist you in the process. These are often lessons learned for all students, especially doctoral students. During a period of service as Interim Provost and Senior Vice President for Academic Affairs, I received several letters requesting that a faculty member be terminated because the students didn't like her teaching methodology. That was a teaching moment for students to come to understand that the academy does not work in that manner. There are certain processes and protocols which must take place. Even more important was the lesson that without a faculty member doing something that violated the rules and regulations, an individual student cannot get fired because they don't like the way they teach.

Doctoral students come to the academy from two perspectives – one ready and willing to engage and learn new content and ways of doing things and seeking support for this effort. The other perspective is those students who think they only need to go through the motions to get the degree. Some are, after all, the first to enter doctoral study and are convinced that makes them smarter than everyone else. There are students who will seek you out for discussion and clarification, as well as those who already know everything and plan to do it their way. As a faculty member, you need to bridge the gap and help them to understand the academic arena. Curry (2011) examined the impact mentoring relationships between African American women doctoral students and faculty members have on the students' professional identity development. The findings indicate that

"African American female doctoral students involved in mentoring relationships are more engaged in professional development activities that address their professional identity or feel more supported in their efforts to explore and solidify their professional identity and career trajectory." Mentoring is highly regarded as a means of improving success.

In instances where students are required to complete a comprehensive examination and/or a dissertation, we could do well by having them to understand the nature of these requirements. Just as with tenure a failing score on a comprehensive examination may signal the end of the academic career for them. Oftentimes, they are extremely bright students who have never failed at anything, and this presents a unique challenge for them. Faculty advisors have a duty to work with students to understand this process and be clear that they can be successful. We find on our campus that many times, students fail to put in the focused study time that is required to be successful.

We do want to say a word about the dissertation process. Every person who has obtained a doctorate has a story to tell. Some of them may have been horror stories, while sometimes they were lessons learned. In my day, we sometimes considered it a hazing activity – although we know that faculty would never haze their students. I've heard stories of faculty being abducted overseas during the process, faculty leaving the institution in the middle of the process, and faculty quitting the project because of the negative interaction with the student. Doctoral students have little ability to do anything about any of these; thus, there is a need to build relationships within departmental faculty. I spoke with a student the other day who has changed dissertation chairs two times since he began the process. I politely reminded him that he was in a small department and at risk of running out of faculty to select as chair. The student's goal should be to graduate; not engage in warfare with the chair. A calm mind will take them a long way. We also encourage students to select the chair (if your institution allows you to select) who you work well with. In my quiet voice I caution them to select a chair who they can trust to get them through because they will surely be at odds with that person before the dissertation is completed. This allows the student to graduate and tell your story. One of my former students who currently serves as a dean at a small private university often tells the story that she brought the first draft of the dissertation to me, and I threw it back at her and told her I knew she could do better. That clearly doesn't sound like me; however, I knew that it was not written as well as she could have done. She politely took it back and returned with a stellar document that she could be proud of. It's the relationship that matters in this process, and students have to trust that the advisor has their best interest.

It is an expectation that earning the doctorate will provide some challenges and require an additional amount of effort. It is, after all, the terminal degree in an academic discipline. While challenging, there is a sense of accomplishment as we work to increase the number of African American female scholars in the academy. Female scholars who can serve as role models and mentors for other women in the environment. The work is challenging but well worth the effort. Working with doctoral students is actually a highlight of my career. Establishing a relationship while at the same time requiring excellence assists them in their professional life. When we look back at the students we have worked with, it is an honor to have been a part of their academic journey.

REFERENCES

Carter, T. J., & Craig, M. O. (2022). It could be us: Black faculty as "threats" on the path to tenure. *Race and Justice*, *12*(3), 569–587. https://doi.org/10.1177/21533687221087366

Curry, N. D. (2011). *Mentoring and professional identity development for African American female doctoral students: An exploratory study* (Order No. 3469636). ProQuest Dissertations & Theses Global. (893651987). http://tsu.idm.oclc.org/login?url=https://www.proquest.com/dissertations-theses/mentoringprofessional-identity-development/docview/893651987/se-2

ED.gov, Fast facts race/ethnicity of college faculty. https://nces.ed.gov/fastfacts/display.asp?id=61. Accessed on January 31, 2024.

Fox Tree, J. E., & Vaid, J. (2022). Why so few, still? Challenges to attracting, advancing, and keeping women faculty of color in academia. *Frontiers in Sociology*, *6*. https://doi.org/10.3389/fsoc.2021.792198

Guillaume, R. O., & Apodaca, E. C. (2022). Early career faculty of color and promotion and tenure: The intersection of advancement in the academy and cultural taxation. *Race, Ethnicity and Education*, *25*(4), 546–563. https://doi.org/10.1080/13613324.2020.1718084

Hinton, D. (2009). Creating community on the margins: The successful Black female academician. *The Urban Review*, *42*(5), 394–402. https://doi.org/10.1007/s11256-009-0140-3

McCallum, C. M. (2013). *Examining African American female students decision to pursue the doctorate.* Michigan State University Press.

McCallum, C. M. (2020). Othermothering: Exploring African American graduate students' decision to pursue the doctorate. *The Journal of Higher Education*, *91*(6), 953–976. https://doi.org/10.1080/00221546.2020.1731262

Tierney, W. G., & Bensimon, E. M. (1996). *Promotion and tenure: Community and socialization in academe*. State University of New York Press.

Wright-Kim, J., & Perna, L. W. (2023). Gender and race-based differences in negotiating behavior among tenured and tenure-track faculty at four-year institutions. *The Review of Higher Education*, *47*(1), 61–91. https://doi.org/10.1353/rhe.2023.a907271

IF I CAN HELP SOMEBODY AS I PASS ALONG

Patricia J. Larke

Texas A & M University, USA

ABSTRACT

As the author reflects on her journey of becoming the first African American female to receive tenure and promotion to the rank of full professor beginning at the rank of lecturer, to assistant professor, associate professor and then to full professor and retired as Professor Emerita, she is amazed at the stamina that she used to achieve such milestones. "If I can help somebody, as I pass along," has been the author's mantra for helping others. Therefore, this chapter begins with a synopsis of the author's career goal that was set early in life as an educator. The chapter continues by sharing stories that are embedded in: (a) the author's personal story at Texas A&M University; (b) a mentoring framework; (c) advantages of mentoring, and (d) lastly, her 4 Cs (communicate, create, collaborate and change) and 4 Ps (politics, power, policies, and prayer) to encourage the next generation of African American faculty members.

Keywords: Journey of an African American faculty; tenure and promotion (T&P); stories of African American faculty; navigating the T & P process; working and staying in higher education

As I reflect on my journey of becoming the first African American female to receive tenure and promotion at Texas A&M University to the rank of full professor beginning at the rank of lecturer, to assistant professor, associate professor and then to full professor and retired as Professor Emerita, I am amazed at the stamina that I used to achieved such milestones. It is with much pleasure, that I am provided an opportunity to share my journey to help somebody who may feel they cannot endure the intellectual and emotional hardships of the academy to achieve tenure and be promoted to the rank of full professor. Getting through the dissertation and fulfilling requirements necessary for hiring

Journeys of Black Women in Academe
Diversity in Higher Education, Volume 26, 85–102

Published under exclusive licence by Emerald Publishing Limited
ISSN: 1479-3644/doi:10.1108/S1479-364420240000026005

should provide faculty members the necessary stamina needed to seek the next level of their career—tenure and promotion.

Let me be clear. While there were several African Americans at my university who received full professor status during my tenure at Texas A&M, however none began at the lecturer rank. Some received tenure at other institutions and were able to negotiate tenure upon arrival. My tenure at Texas A&M University began in 1984 when I was hired as a Lecturer in the Department of Educational Curriculum and Instruction (EDCI). EDCI was the name of the department and as a part of my leadership, the name later changed to the Department of Teaching, Learning and Culture (TLAC). My office number was 339 Harrington and I stayed in that office until my retirement in 2017 with the title of Professor Emerita. When I was hired in 1984, there were no African American faculty members in the Department. One was hired later in the Department but left after a few years. And, for many years, I was the only African American professor in a tenure line track. When I retired in 2017, there was one tenured African American female at the rank of Associate Professor and one non-tenured African American male at the rank of Assistant Professor in the Department.

"If I can help somebody as I pass along" was and is my mantra. This mantra began early in life while playing school with my cousins and neighbors. My mother taught me how to read before coming to school. The spirit of helping/teaching was nurtured early in my life by my African American first through 12th grade teachers, Sunday School teachers and, of course, my first teachers, my mother and grandmothers. Therefore, my career goal was set early in life as an educator.

It was during my first grade, that I learned the value of helping others. I had "my own reading group." My African American first-grade teacher allowed me to use my instructional skills to teach several of my classmates how to read. My teacher, Ms. Will, understood the value of students teaching each other and today scholars identify it as the tutor–tutee model of instruction. This instructional strategy enhances the learning of both students, tutor and tutee. My experiences in first grade boosted my self-confidence and self-esteem that I have used throughout my life experiences. My self-confidence heightened my belief in myself and in my abilities and my self-esteem enabled me to appreciate and value myself. It was my self-confidence and self-esteem along with my intellectual ability that enabled me to persist in the academy.

Graduating from a Historically Black University (HBCU), South Carolina State College, Orangeburg, South Carolina with my Bachelor of Science degree (1974) and Master of Education degree (1977), I got my first teaching job as a first-grade teacher, in Cameron, South Carolina, in August 1974. I was rifted the next year through what was called reduction in force (RIF). While RIF is often used in companies for layoff, mine was due to a disagreement with my principal regarding an educational issue. In October 1974, the principal asked me to give my first-grade students a state standardized test that required reading. I rejected and said that I was not going to give the test, because my students were not reading. I explained that as a first-grade teacher, I was still teaching the fundamentals, alphabets, letter recognition, sounds, and sight words. We had a heated discussion but, I did not give the test. In fact, he had the wrong grade in which the test was to be given, but never apologized for his error. The next year, I was sent to another school and the principal at my new school said that I was a reduction in force. In August 1975, I was reassigned the next year to teach sixth- and seventh-grade mathematics in St. Matthews, South Carolina where I taught for 5 years. My total years of teaching in South Carolina was 6 years. In 1980, I moved to Columbia, Missouri, teaching seventh- and eighth-grade mathematics for 4 years while attending graduate school at the University of Missouri-Columbia (UMC). I taught a total of 10 years in the public elementary and secondary schools.

I was in culture shock when I took my first doctoral class at the UMC, in Columbia, Missouri in Fall 1980. While an undergraduate and graduate student at SCSU, I had only one European American professor, but then as a graduate student at UMC, I had no African American professors, nor students who looked like me in the program. I recall only one African American female student in a school law class during my entire doctoral process. However, one professor in my curriculum and instruction class, asked me to do a project on multicultural education, and that provided the tools and skillset for the foundation of my life-work at Texas A&M University. This was where, I began the journey of teaching in higher education and participated in experiences that have crystalized my mantra, "If I can help somebody, as I pass along." Therefore, this chapter shares my: (a) personal story at Texas A&M University; (b) mentoring framework; (c) advantages of mentoring, and (d) lastly, 4 Cs (communicate, create, collaborate, and change) and 4 Ps (politics, power, policies, and prayer) to encourage the next generation of African American faculty members.

MY PERSONAL STORY AT TAMU

Chocolate Block # 1. When I arrived in the fall 1984, and was assigned to room 339, little did I know the value of the Chocolate Block. The Chocolate Block consisted of three people—two African American graduate students and one African American, Lecturer, me. Since I was 34 years old at the time, many of my colleagues thought I, too, was a TAMU graduate student. Our offices in the section of that hallway became known as the Chocolate Block. We were close to each other and talked frequently, many times giggling and laughing as many graduate students do. In reality, I was a graduate student, not at Texas A&M, but at the UMC. During my first year at Texas A&M, 1984–1985, I was writing the final chapters of my dissertation and graduated in May 1985 from the UMC with a degree in Educational Administration with a support area in Curriculum and Instruction. We spent many long hours on campus during the first years and the support that I obtained from the Chocolate Blocks #1 and #2 helped to pave the way for me to continue to work at Texas A&M for 34 years.

My Chocolate Block #1 enlightened me on the writing, publishing and conference presentation process. In fact, it was the Chocolate Block who showed me how to write an article for publication from my dissertation and how to write a conference proposal. With the help of the Chocolate Block #1, I got my first article published, presented the findings of my dissertation at my first conference and the rest is history. Over my academic career, I had over 125 publications from articles, books, book chapters and other publications and over 350 conference presentations and workshops. I passed the skills of publishing and presenting to my graduate students. As a part of my class requirements, my graduate students were taught to write a conference proposal, and seek to present at a conference, if the proposal was accepted.

My first conference presentations were with the Chocolate Block#1. Also, my husband and I would share information since he did not have a faculty mentor in his department. Between my Chocolate Block#1 and my husband, Dr. Alvin Larke, Jr, and I mentoring each other, we made history at Texas A&M. He was the first African American male to received tenure in his department and I was the first to move from the rank of lecturer to full professor. In my husband's department, there were no tenure packets for him to review when he prepared his papers for tenure. He had to develop the first tenure packet for his department in 1988. Our common research interest in educating teachers for diversity paved the way for collaborating on writing projects and conference presentations, since we both were teacher educators. During the years, we continued to publish articles and presented papers at conferences. Chocolate Block #1, in particular, was the impetus that inspired and supported my moving from Lecturer to Full Professor.

Chocolate Block #2. Knowing the value of a Chocolate Block, I did not want to continue to be the only African American Professor in the department where I was often referred to as the "only lonely." I wanted to have colleagues on tenure track lines. There were two openings in the department—one with emphasis in foundations and one with emphasis in curriculum and instruction. My European American colleague recruited an African American male, Professor R, in foundations and I recruited an African American female, Professor W, in curriculum and instruction. Their offices were located on my hall—one in room 341, next door to me and one in room 345. Each of them was newly graduated from institutions in Illinois, and Texas A&M University was their first tenure-line positions. Now, I had professors who looked like me and shared some of my research interests. I was able to use my skills from Chocolate Block #1 to mentor Chocolate Block#2 in their teaching, publishing, and presenting at conferences. Of course, they did not stay at Texas A&M, for they were recruited to other universities. Yet, we continued to present at conferences and publish papers. One returned to Texas A&M University and currently is a tenured Associate Professor in another Department in the School of Education while the other is currently in his fourth year as a College President in Indiana. We continue to communicate throughout the years.

From Lecturer to Full Professor to Professor Emerita. I was hired in the Department of Curriculum and Instruction as a Lecturer to supervise student teachers. My hire was a spousal hire, since my husband was hired as an Assistant Professor in the Department of Agricultural Education. However, after receiving my degree in May 1985, I advocated for my myself to be placed on the next rank. I wrote a letter to the Department Head and the Dean and made the request for the promotion. The request was granted, and I was promoted to Visiting Assistant Professor in 1985. However, this was not a tenured track rank. The next year, I continued to advocate for myself and was awarded the Assistant Professor tenure track position in 1986. The Dean played an important role in my receiving the position. Dean D was an advocate for diversity and when I would share my research interest with him, he found money to support the project. In fact, he provided the Multicultural Mentoring Project with a graduate student and over $20,000 to support the project activities during the years. To him, no idea about diversity issues in teacher education was a bad idea, and he wanted me to succeed at Texas A&M. Even after his retirement, he still contacted me by email.

After receiving the title of Assistant Professor, I was unaware that it did not automatically provide graduate teaching status. I learned this the hard way. Having an identity in the department became apparent and I did not realize the importance until a graduate student asked if I would become a member of her master's committee. I responded yes, but when she came back, she said that I did not have graduate status, and I was unable to become a committee member. I thought that my rank automatically provided graduate status. Here again, I had to advocate for myself to obtain graduate status. Making the request and understanding the process were shared with me by Chocolate Block #1. I had to learn this process without the support of a faculty mentor but with the advice of Graduate Student V. Graduate Student V shared that I needed to find the department's policy and to write a letter to the department head requesting graduate teaching status. I received graduate teaching status and during my tenure, I chaired or served as a member of 84 doctoral committees and 114 masters committees. I was tenured and promoted to Associate Professor in 1992 and received Full Professor in 1998.

However, presenting my papers for promotion to full professor was met with a challenge. As a part of the process, your fellow colleagues have to present your body of work and advocate on your behalf. Well, to that avail, 3 days before it was time to present my body of work, the full professor who said he would present my papers to the tenure and promotion committee informed me that he could not present my papers. There were politics in the department, and some members of the committee did not like him. He shared with me that he suspected that some members would vote against me because of a conflict with him. There was only a few days before the meeting, scrambling to decide about who would present my papers and advocate on my behalf. I asked another faculty member to present my papers. I developed a notebook with information about my packet and explained to him the nature of my scholarship. He was likable among the faculty members and was respected in the department. My vote was unanimous. Having to endure this process was difficult for me to accept and I promised that I would become a beacon of light for other faculty members and it further supported the role of the need for a true mentor.

Moving Through the Tenure Process. To move through the tenure process ranks required maintaining a research/scholarship, teaching and service record. I excelled in all three. My research/scholarship record was centered around tenants of multicultural education, more specifically, educating teachers and other professionals for diverse environments with the last focus on education of African American girls. While I had no on-campus mentor to steer me in this direction, I found national and international scholars to mentor me. With the help of a colleague, we developed the Multicultural Mentorship Project (MMP) that was piloted in three universities located in California, Illinois, and Virginia. I integrated my teaching and service projects and activities under my research area. I developed and taught undergraduate and graduate multicultural education courses and developed a master's and doctoral emphasis in multicultural education. All of this was achieved without having an on-campus mentor. I sought positions in my professional organizations, was on the board of our national organization, National Association for Multicultural Education and was a 1990 charter member. I was also a charter member of Texas Chapter of National Association of Multicultural Education and served as the second President. I affiliated with committees in the American Educational Research Association and with the Association of Teacher Educators and served in capacities of member and/or chair. Such national, state and local visibility and service records enhanced my body of work to received tenure and promotion.

Seeking Mentors from Afar. Faculty members who seek tenure and promotion in the academy understand the role of a faculty mentor and the relationship built with your colleagues. Therefore, there were no faculty members who shared my research interest. As a consequence, I sought our national leaders in the field at conferences and asked them to share how to navigate the process. We became acquaintances and some became dear friends. When I had ideas and needed someone with whom to discuss issues, they provided the mentoring that I needed. When I needed letters of support for grants, awards, or other activities, they were familiar with my research and could provide information. These relationships provided the support I needed on campus and even after retirement, we still keep in touch.

Turning My Pain into Gain. Throughout the beginning of my journey, I was alone in the academy. I often referred to myself as the "only lonely." I promised and worked diligently to insure that others would not be the "only lonely" in their respective institutions. It is very painful when you are the only African American female among a majority of European American faculty members who are mostly male. That is why the Chocolate Block#1 was so important during my initial years. After 1988, I had no more Chocolate Block#1. Their graduation was bittersweet for me. My Chocolate Block #1 graduated and took positions at other Predominately White Institutions. One went to the Louisiana State University and the other to the University of Georgia. Instead of feeling sorry, I decided to enhance my recruitment efforts, and to that avail, Chocolate Block #2 was the result.

I continued to recruit African American faculty and faculty of color in the department and to serve as a mentor to faculty on and off campuses around the country. Recruiting and mentoring graduate students of color, more specifically African American students, became by mission. While, I had the desire and understood the need, I wanted to improve the experiences of others through quality mentoring. Therefore, my mentoring approach was guided by research that evolved from the Multicultural Mentoring Project (MMP). Thus, mentoring became one of the most beneficial ways to continue my mantra, "If I can help somebody as I pass along."

THE MENTORING FRAMEWORK

Mentoring is a highly complex process that involves people developing relationships that are both professional and personal. In many instances, the relationships become life-long relationships. A mentor often is called a friend, a teacher, a counselor, a role model, or someone who has a genuine care for another. The mentor encourages this special person to pursue life's goals to the fullest of his or her capacity (Larke et al., 2011).

My framework for mentoring was crystalized with a co-developed project entitled, Minority Mentorship Project (MMP), which was later changed to Multicultural Mentorship Project (MMP). This model incorporated three stages of the mentoring relationship as shown in Fig. 1. The first stage is identified as *M p/me* in which the Mentor (Faculty Mentor/Graduate Advisor) does most of the giving in the relationship, sharing information about themselves, finding out likes and dislikes, and discovering basic knowledge that enhances the relationship, helping the protégée/mentee (faculty member/graduate student or *p/me*) navigate the academy. In this stage, the Mentor institutes most of the activities as identified by the role of the capital M and small *p/me* for the protegee/mentee (faculty member/graduate student). In the second stage, both the Mentor and Protégée/Mentee have equal roles. Each brings something of value to the relationship in which the mentor and faculty member/graduate student share information, such as presenting together at conferences, writing for publication, etc.

The last stage denotes significant changes in the relationship in which the Mentor takes a lesser role, and the Protégée/Mentee takes on greater roles in the relationship. During this stage, the Mentor appreciates and acknowledges the professional and academic development of the Protégée/Mentee. As a faculty mentor/graduate advisor, understanding and participating in the last role can be difficult or easy, depending on how relationships have developed during the previous two stages. The Protégée/Mentee (Faculty Member/Graduate Student) takes more ownership in the relationship and is moving to become your colleague. The Protégée/Mentee has the skillset to help others on their journey within the academy. This framework (Fig. 1) was enhanced by my ability to mentor new faculty and graduate students and what I wanted as a new faculty member and as a graduate student.

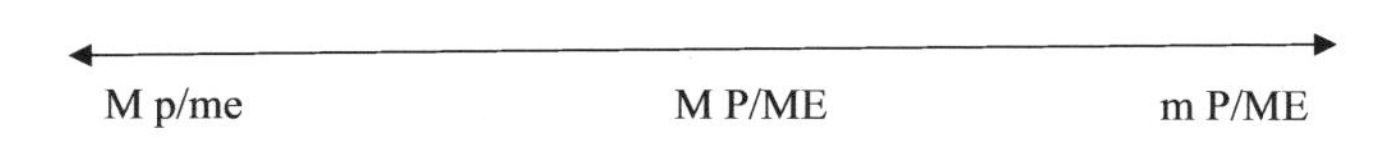

Fig. 1. Protégée/Mentee Framework. *Source:* Larke, Wiseman & Bradley adaptation of Gray & Gray model (1990).

ADVANTAGES OF MENTORING

After reflecting over my years in higher education, I believe that there are there many advantages that will benefit new faculty members and graduate students when they can participate in formalized mentoring relationships in the academy. I will share two of the advantages and examples. These advantages include self-worth and opportunities to know professionals.

Self-Worth. A quality mentoring relationship will strengthen new faculty members/graduate students' feelings of self-worth. It is not that faculty/graduate students are not academically capable, but many find themselves having to second guess their self-worth that is sometimes operationalized through systemic racist practices and stereotypical beliefs held by many within the academy. When faculty and graduate students are recruited, they come to a department with a required skillset of academic credentials. Often, failure is not the result of academics, but a work environment that does not value them as a person. African Americans often are viewed through the lens of double consciousness. According to W.E.B. DuBois (1903) double consciousness is defined as a struggle that African Americans endure when trying to remain true to the African American culture while conforming to issues of the White society. Always know that participating in double consciousness will cause conflict and question your self-worth.

At one of my faculty meetings, I presented an overview of a teacher education project from a departmental grant. One of my colleagues had the audacity to ask in the faculty meeting, during my presentation. "Pat did YOU developed this framework?" I replied, "I have a brain and I can think." After my response to her, I did not "blink," I just proceeded to continue my presentation. If I did not have the scripture, 2 Timothy 1:7 (KJV) embedded in my mind: "For God did not give us the spirit of fear, but of power, and of love and of a sound mind..." (Holy Bible, 1985), I would have begun to ask questions about my own self-worth. Over the years, I have seen too many African American faculty members denied tenure and promotion because other faculty members did not value them nor their scholarship. Often, failure in the academy is equated to "I am not good enough; therefore, I must be a bad person or I must be a failure" rather than "I am a good person, but my ability was not recognized nor valued." Self-worth can be enhanced by understanding the systematic practices of the academy and by providing encouragement and support to the faculty mentee/graduate student.

Opportunity to Know Professionals. When you are hired in the academy or selected for a graduate program, your knowledge of professionals in your field of study is sometimes limited. The mentoring relationship will provide many opportunities to know scholars in your field. The mentor can introduce the mentee to scholars in the field at conferences or professional meetings. This introduction is valuable for the mentee and such acquaintance is needed for letters of support for tenue and promotion or future employment opportunities. When a mentor is unavailable, the mentee may have to initiate the contact. Let me share one story. I was in the field of multicultural education with no fellow faculty members in my department. I had to initiate my own opportunities to know professionals/scholars in my field. I would review the list of presenters at conferences and attend sessions where scholars presented papers/talks. Afterward, I would dialog with or invite them to talk with me over lunch or ask for a designated time to meet to discuss my research or issues within the discipline or how to navigate the academy. Sometimes, I would be either rejected or accepted. I would recite the scripture found in Matthew 7:7 (KJV), "...Ask and it shall be given you; seek, and ye shall find; knock, and it shall be opened unto you..." (Holy Bible, 1985) This scripture helped me to accept rejection or acceptance. It was exhilarating talking to a scholar whom you had read about in classes, and now, talking to them in person and most importantly, the scholar later becomes a life-long friend.

4 Cs AND 4 Ps

My concluding thoughts on If I can help somebody as I pass along are embodied in these 4 Cs and 4 Ps. While I had to navigate the professional ranks in the academy often by myself which began with knowledge from the Chocolate Block#1 and my husband, I did not want others after me to go through the same isolation. Therefore, I conclude this chapter by providing some suggestions that I call the 4 Cs and 4 Ps. I want to leave some tips for the next generation of professionals from my lessons learned. The four Cs are: communicate, create, collaborate, and change. The four Ps are politics, power, policies, and prayer.

Communicate. Learning how to communicate effectively within the academy is paramount to your success as a faculty member. To communicate is to share information that involves a sender and a receiver. There are four types of communication that are expressed in the academy. They are verbal, non-verbal, written, and visual. Having competency in all four are necessary. For African Americans, these communitive expressions can be perceived differently for us than for other faculty members.

Verbal. There is much bias surrounding the way African Americans talk. Often, we are burdened with "talking White," using Ebonics, slow-talking with southern accents, or "she or he is so articulate. I have been accused of all the above. I grew up in the South and was taught during my formative years the importance of 'speaking correctly' and expressing myself." Like many African Americans, I learn those skills from experiences from reciting Easter speeches, participating in junior and senior drama club and school plays and keynote speaking at church programs or conferences. There were some African Americans who participated in the debate club. These experiences provided opportunities to understand the power of speaking and to know how to code switch once back into your home environment or among your kinfolk celebrations.

Historical bias perceptions about verbal communications are alive and well in the academy. I remember during the interviews of the Chocolate Block#2 candidates who grew up in the Chicago area. My colleagues had the audacity to say while discussing the candidates, "They were so articulate." I had to ask, "What does that mean?" as if I did not know. And the usual response, "Well Pat you know," and I responded, "No, please explain." Confronting bias statements like this is necessary, but often it becomes the discussion in the search committee meeting. As with these Chocolate Block candidates, nothing was mentioned about their intellect and how deep their discussions were about the educational issue. I had to intervene and redirect the committee back to their strengths and academic credentials. Sadly, sometimes this bias caused excellent candidates to find their "dream job" because the committee did not focus on their intellect but rather on their verbal expression.

Non-verbal. Often times, African Americans non-verbal facial expressions can carry different messages. For example, when your grandmother or mother gave you "the look" or should I say "eyeology" in church to sit properly on the pew and all that she did was move her eyes, you understood the task. Or your mother or grandmother gave you the "neckology, a movement with her neck and you knew exactly what it meant." The "eyeology" and "neckology" non-verbal movements occur when the eyes or neck express from the sender to the receiver a message that a person's behavior or verbal statements are inappropriate for the situation. For example, I remembered in faculty meeting when I was making a statement to one of my faculty members about getting students to understand a multicultural education concept. I used one of my grandmother's saying: "Well, you know sometimes, Faculty member X, you can bring a horse to the water, but you cannot make him drink." He replied adamantly, "I am not a horse." I looked using my "eyeology" and gave a slight neckology twist and the room was silent. Then I proceeded to share that I did not call him a horse, but was saying sometimes, you can teach students multicultural concepts and they make a choice not to understand or refuse to accept the concept. I used a saying to explain a point, but the faculty member thought that I called him out of his name and became defensive.

Be aware that sometimes non-verbal expression can be perceived as "the angry Black woman." I have a difficult time, trying to understand that eyeology and neckology perceptions denote anger when my mother and grandmother loved me enough to express their displeasure with my behavior, in ways of showing love that did not require harsh words. As African American faculty members expressing yourself in non-verbal ways is necessary, but know there maybe consequences when you have prejudiced faculty members who feel that you are not worthy to be a part of their department and judge you harshly for your non-verbal behaviors.

Written. Written communication is one of the most important tools in the academy for faculty and graduate students. When there are issues to be addressed, written communication is necessary. Writing is an integral part of everyday experiences for faculty. Faculty members writing responsibilities include reports, proposals, articles/books, letters or responding to emails or texts. Unfortunately, the writings of many African Americans are scrutinized more than other faculty members. For example, an incorrect subject/verb or spelling mistake by some faculty are perceived as just making a simple mistake. However, when the same incorrect subject/verb or spelling mistake is made by some African

American faculty member, then their writing is viewed from a deficit perspective indicating that there is a writing problem. While the next example is an event involved my graduate student, it happens often, but there is silence in the academy.

Graduate Student L. In February 2000, when I returned home from my Grandmother's funeral, I called four committee members to get the results of my doctoral student proposal she had given her committee. The proposal hearing was to be held the next day. Three members of the committee said the errors were minor, but they supported her defending her proposal the next day since her research design, review of literature, and concept were good. When I called Faculty Member F for his results, he said the student was not ready to defend the proposal and the writing was terrible. I responded yes, there were a few errors, but overall, three members on her committee felt the writing was good and her research design, review of literature and concept were good. and that she could defend her proposal. I shared with him that my Grandmother had passed and her errors were minor and that we could continue. He stated, I don't care about your grandmother passing, I will not approve her proposal. Well, I said, "Faculty Member F, you are one person on the committee, and we will have the hearing tomorrow. Then I responded, how dare you talk about the death of my grandmother, when you did not know her. You will not deny this student a chance to defend her proposal because of a few minor writing errors when others have agreed to have her defend. Given his history in the department, he had bullied many other African American graduate students and often used their writing as excuses to keep them from the proposal stage. As chair, I exercised my authority and dismissed him from the committee and informed him that he was replaced."

The next day, as we began Graduate Student L proposal hearing. Faculty member F showed up anyway. I excused the graduate student, and said politely in a calm voice, "Faculty Member F please excuse yourself because you have been replaced and no longer a member of the committee. I told you yesterday that you were replaced on the committee. Yet, you are here today." He said that I did not tell him that he was misplaced as a member of the committee yesterday. I showed him the new paperwork where he was replaced. Then I called him a "habitual liar." He was known in the department for lying about students. After a few quiet moments, he proceeded to leave. Graduate Student L was asked to return to the hearing and she proceed with her proposal. The committee passed her and she continued working on her dissertation.

As readers, I know you are wondering what happened to Faculty Member F and me regarding this incident. I asked for a meeting with the Department Head and Faculty Member F. He denied that he said, "who cares about your grandmother passing" to the department head and I again called him a "habitual liar." He was known also to bully faculty members as well and deny that he did or said anything. I told him in front of the Department Head that I was not afraid of him nor any other faculty member in the department. Then I went old school. I said: "I put my pants on just like he did and I was not afraid of HIM nor any man in this department." After that day, Faculty Member F and I became cordial and he did not disrespect me anymore.

Visual. While visual includes color, graphics, and layouts, I am using visual representation to address, skin color, hair, and dress of African American faculty. The statement "I don't see color" is a bias statement for many African Americans. African Americans are a range of hues, from lighter complexion to darker complexion. Some research indicates that the lighter the skin tone, the more preferential treatment people receive. Regardless of what others may think, people do see color. Within the African American community, hair styles are increasingly changing. Hair styles range from braids to natural from locks, to weaves and wigs. Even, shaved heads are a part of the look. At the date of this writing, one point of clarification, locks are no longer called dread locks. Hair colors have changed from blonds to reds and other colors. These changes can have an impact on faculty hires. Judging the look by outside appearances can cause job offers to diminish, rather than looking at the body of work or making decisions on their intellectual contribution. Dress is another significant visual for African American faculty. Many like bold colors with matching accessories and often will receive comments about their dress but receive very little, if any, comments regarding their intellectual capabilities.

Create. To create means to bring something into existence. You were hired because of your academic skills set; therefore, use it to your advantage. As an upcoming scholar, keep up with the latest research or create a new line of research and develop graduate programs in the area of multicultural education. I was charged with creating the first undergraduate multicultural education course entitled, EDCI 322, Foundations of Education in a Multicultural Society. I was at the right place at the right time. In 1986, the State of Texas' Coordinating Board had a requirement that all elementary education students needed to have a course in multicultural education as they were preparing teachers to work with its diverse population of students. I was approached by one of my colleagues about if I was interested in developing such a course. I always had a desire to prepare teachers to work in diverse classrooms, and this was an answer to my calling. I shared with my colleague that while completing my doctoral studies, I was asked by my Educational Curriculum professor to do a class project on multicultural education. Therefore, I had some knowledge of the subject matter. I used the concepts in my doctoral project as the foundation of the course. I began to review multicultural texts from scholars in the field such as Geneva Gay Carl Grant, Donna Gollnick, Phil Chin and James Banks. This allowed me to increase my dept of the discipline of multicultural education. I used my knowledge to develop research projects, undergraduate class projects and a program of study at the master's and doctoral level. My work is still continuing in the Department today. However, I am somewhat disappointed at the lack of emphasis the State of Texas has taken toward diversity programs in higher education and how critical race theory (CRT) is misunderstood when many of my doctoral students have used CRT as a part of their research studies.

As a faculty member, you can create knowledge. Never underestimate this important skill as you refute or support past research. Use your ability to create areas of study or research that contribute to your department and can also make you marketable, not only in your department but at other institutions. Always be mindful of the question: "What contribution describe your role in your department?"

Collaborate. Collaborating means working jointly together as faculty members to create or produce something. Working together allows faculty members to design research projects, to seek external funding and to share knowledge and experiences. Responsibilities of the academy require working together with other faculty members; therefore, no one works alone in the academy. Assignments within departments such as course development, student recruitment or retention, study abroad, or accreditation renewals require faculty members to work together as a unit. Collaboration provides opportunities for the development of mentoring relationships with junior and senior level faculty members. In many instances, when faculty members are working together on projects or department activities, they begin to build both a professional relationship and share personal stories about families. Often the invisible faculty member becomes visible within the department. Discussions become centered on personal information such as "Oh, I didn't know you like basketball," or "You play spades" or "You went to High School X, why that was near my grandparents' house." The invisible Black Professor is now becoming visible.

I remember faculty members would call me the wrong name so many times. There was another African American in a different department, but we were in the same college. When other faculty members saw me, they would call me her name. Somehow many faculty members thought all African Americans looked alike. I was 5 feet and 1 inch tall and she was 5 feet and 5 inches tall. We did not have the same complexion nor the same physical size. I just corrected them and said my name is Pat and not LaWanda. Sometimes, they would be polite and say, I am so sorry, but each time they met me again it was the same thing, wrong name and I had to do my usual correction.

Change. Change means to do something different or to modify an existing condition to receive a different outcome. There are times when change is necessary in the academy, especially when you are the only African American female in a department and without a mentor or when your working environment is toxic.

In my 34 years of teaching at Texas A&M, I had no mentor in my department nor college. However, I found ways to develop mentoring relationships with other faculty members away from my campus. When I got my job at Texas A&M as a part of the spousal hire, I was new to higher education. While I was a doctoral student at the UMC, I was a part-time doctoral student. I was enrolled in 12 hours, four 3-hour courses a semester. I took two classes at night, twice a week, while teaching seventh- and eighth-grade mathematics at the local junior high school. I was never a full-time doctoral student on campus and did not receive higher education experiences as a graduate student. Being hired as a lecturer and supervising student teachers allowed me the time to complete my school law dissertation entitled "Legal Requirements Concerning the Teacher as An Exemplar." I had to figure out, with the help of my Chocolate Block #1 and my husband, how to navigate working higher education. I needed help. I needed a mentor. Clue number 1. Always know when you need help, and don't be too proud to ask for help.

Developing and teaching the undergraduate and graduate multicultural education courses allowed me to meet scholars in the field and to establish relationships. I talked with them at conferences, worked with them on national committees, invited them to be keynote speakers when I was chair of the program committee, and sought their suggestions when writing manuscripts for publication or editing books. I built relationships with scholars in the field who became my mentors. For one mentor in particular, I will share our story.

Mentor G. I met Mentor G on a yacht in San Diego when I attended a multicultural education workshop that was hosted by another multicultural scholar. My mentor was one of the keynote speakers for the workshop and for the closing activities, we had dinner on the yacht. While I was familiar with her work, I wanted to know more about her as a person. That night, I found out that we were southern girls, had many of the same upbringings and talked about stories we had in common. We communicated after the visit and started sharing rooms at conferences such as the National Association for Multicultural Education (NAME) and American Educational Research Association (AREA). I visited her university, and she visited my university. We always called on holidays, Thanksgiving, Christmas, and New Year and have continued that today. In fact, when we talk, it is always an hour. She mentored me through the full professor tenure process and assisted me with research ideas and how to navigate higher education.

Always know that change is necessary in the academy. Learn how to network with faculty who are in your field by joining your professional organizations. Don't take no for an answer, and don't get discouraged when you ask others to help. No matter the discipline, there are scholars/leaders who will help and have a kind spirit. Senior professionals all started out as new faculty members and understand the professorial process. They will help you if you ask them.

Change is necessary, especially when situations are not working to your advantage. It's important to know when change is necessary. Sometimes, the climate in the department is not conducive to enhancing your skillset. The work environment is toxic, and colleagues do not "value your contributions." While faculty members tend to think that jealousy, deceitfulness, and divisiveness do not exist in the academy, many are surprised and unprepared to deal with such divisions in the department. Therefore, change is necessary, and sometimes it's important to seek positions in other departments or change institutions. Don't allow the environment to slowly erode your identity or cause doubts about your self-worth. Therefore, as a precaution, always keep your vita up-to-date and "move on to a better place." There are institutions that will welcome and support your work. While I had no mentors on campus, I vowed that I would become a mentor to others and would not be the only lonely in my department. So, I began to participate on search committees to look for candidates to support my discipline. The story of Professor N is an example.

Professor N. To my surprise, I went to one of my professional conferences and a young scholar name Professor N, came to me and asked if she could talk with me about her career and to get some advice. I politely said yes and I found out that she was working in an environment that was not supportive of her work and she wanted to learn more about my discipline, multicultural education and how it could be used in urban education. We talked and I shared that I was teaching a 2-week intensive graduate class during the summer and would love to have her attend. She agreed and came for the summer and stayed with me. I also shared that my colleague and I had developed the Multicultural Mentoring Project and she indicated that she wanted to pilot it at her university. We began to present at conferences, published and conduct research together. In fact, we visited schools in London and in the surrounding areas to see how they addressed diversity issues among their population. When an opening became available, I recruited Professor N and she was hired at Texas A&M and later became the first African American female to have an endowed chair in Urban Education. We retired together in 2017.

Politics. Within the academy are politics. They are the governing activities of unwritten rules, behaviors that can be supportive or unsupportive in a department, college, or university. These behaviors can help with tenure or cause your dismissal. They can be found in the department, college, and in the administrative levels. As much as possible stay out of the politics. As a new faulty member, say less than you think, because you do not know the past relationship other faculty members have with each other. Some are married but have different last names, some are relatives and some are partners. Listening is an important tool to apply when not knowing the background of the situation. Professor M story is an example of politics.

Professor M. At the same conference in San Diego in which I met my mentor, I also met another African American female, Professor M. Professor M's background was in special education, and she was participating in the multicultural workshop to learn how to integrate principles of multicultural education into special education. We were office suite mates, staying in the dorm and at night sharing stories. Professor M was very vocal and spoke with such depth and insight into the usefulness of special education and multicultural education. She was working at a Predominately White Institution on the east coast and was the only African American female in her department. She asked me to mentor her on the tenure process and to help her prepare her packet for tenure. During the next summer, Professor M stayed with me for a few days as she prepared her packet. While Professor M had the required publications, had good teaching evaluations and outside letters of support, her department failed to support her for tenure. Professor M was a gifted scholar and critical thinker and often found herself having to speak up for equity and inclusion issues regarding students and the biases she found within her discipline. She would not allow equity issues that she felt strongly about to go unchallenged. That was to her detriment when her tenure committee said that she was not a team player and would not support her promotion to Associate Professor with tenure. She left and was sought employment at another university.

Power. Within the academy power can be defined as the ability to direct or influence the behavior over events or activities such as decisions regarding the tenure and promotion process. The faculty members, department head and other tenure and promotion committees can exert power over non-tenure faculty. To receive tenure your fellow faculty members must vote. Don't alienate the members who will have to vote for you. Often in the academy, faculty will say nice things to you, but will not vote for you to become a tenured faculty member. Many times, African American faculty are hired, but not tenured. They become members of the revolving door, like Professor S.

Professor S. Professor S was an assistant professor at a private liberal arts college on the east coast. This was her first job after receiving her doctorate degree. She was in the area of reading and had developed a unique type of reading program for elementary students. She was the only African American professor in her department. Her classes consisted of 98% European American students. For most of her students, she was their first AA professor at the university or the first in their entire elementary or secondary school years.

Professor S worked relentlessly trying to get her students to share her compassion for reading. As a part of her course requirements, she had students to develop reading kits that were used to assist students of color with reading instruction. For many of her students, this was their first time working with diverse students. On her teaching evaluations many students noted the creative ways she taught her classes and were thankful for the diverse experiences. Yet, several said it was too much work and they felt uneasy being taught by a "Black" professor and noted such comments on her evaluation. While the majority of her evaluations were positive, her department chair continued to focus on her negative ones, although over the next years, the number of negative evaluations decreased.

While the majority of her students liked her class, a few students disliked her class. Several students wrote letters to the dean and department chair, indicating that they felt uncomfortable with some of her assignments, especially the ones working with students of color. The department head sent her an email requesting that she meet with her to discuss the issues in the students' letters. It was a raining the day that Professor S met with her department chair. When she arrived to the meeting, her clothes were wet and hair was in disarray. The chair focused on her appearance without giving her the opportunity to explain. The chair insinuated that she needed some professional help and assumed that this was her normal appearance. The department continued to discuss the students' letters and did not provide her an opportunity to provide an explanation. Professor S was devastated and powerless. She could not understand why she was not given an opportunity to explain her situation regarding her appearance nor explain why the students would make such comments. After that meeting, her relationship with the department chair became unfavorable. She was denied tenure and left the university and was told that she was not a good fit for the department. She left the university.

Policies. Policies are written rules that govern the college or university. These set of rules have been voted on and adopted by the institution. As faculty members, take time to become familiar with the policies. Often, the policy manual is read during times of crisis. That is too late. Know what is expected of non-tenured faculty and tenured faculty seeking the next rank. As untenured

Assistant Professors do not wait until the fourth year to find out about the procedures. Ask recently tenured faculty to share their experiences of the process. When you are hired, the first thing you want to read is the policy manual. While spending time negotiating salary and work responsibilities, the policy manual will guide you. Remember that policies change over time. The story of Professor G describes a painful lesson about policies.

Professor G. I mentored Professor G at another university. While I met her as a graduate student, I continued to keep in touch with her at this university. Professor G was in a special education department. Unlike many other African American professors, Professor G was not the only African American in her department. She was always kind and helpful to all of her colleagues. She published and presented at conferences, served on committees in her national, local and state organizations and received good ratings on teaching evaluations. However, Professor G did not have a mentor nor advocate for her tenure and promotion hearing. She did not know the policies. In October the committee met, and papers were forwarded to the college. The college met in November and the recommendations and papers were forward to the University.

In December, the university committee met, and recommendations were sent to the Dean, who prepares recommendations for confirmation by the governing board or shares the recommendations for approval or not approval. A few days before Christmas, Professor G gets a call from the Dean of Faculty that she was not approved for tenure nor promotion and therefore, will need to seek employment at another institution. Professor G was devastated. How could she not know at her department level that she was not approved? No one told her anything. She relied on the notion that no news is good news. She was not aware of the policy to note that, at each juncture, the faculty member should have been notified. If she had known the policy, she could have inquired. It was when she received the call from the Dean of Faculty in which he informed her of the policy that she could have inquired. While I and others assisted her in writing a letter to the Dean of Faculty to get him to overturn the decision, he did not. She left the university and is now a tenured Associate Professor at another institution.

Prayer. Without prayer, I would not have been able to stay at Texas A&M University for 34 years. I found that prayer assisted me in so many ways when I was facing racism and discrimination. When I was at the crossroads with difficulties, I prayed and used scriptures to provide me calmness. One day when I was leaving one of my many faculty meetings in which there was a heated discussion about an issue, I walked out frustrated and ran into one of my doctoral students. She looked at my face and knew that I was upset. Before I could say anything, she asked me: "Dr. Larke did you pray in the meeting?" That was an awakening moment for me. So, I began to make sure I said a silent prayer not only in faculty meetings, at conferences, or any places when I had to present workshops. While I am not advocating a particular religion or spiritual activity, I know that prayer worked for me. Prayer provided relief when I faced impossibilities. I often use the scripture found in Psalm 94:19 (TLB)... "When my heart is in turmoil, quiet me Lord and give me renewed hope and cheer..." (Holy Bible, 1985).

Reflecting on my journey, I feel that African American faculty will continue to increase in the academy and that my lessons learned will help somebody to achieve their professional goal in higher education. In conclusion, to my future African American professors, embrace your Blackness, but know the journey will not be easy. Contrary to a misguided belief, many African American faculty members still have to carry a systemic burden of racism and gender inequality. Although many baby boomers, my generation, understand the double standards, there is a concern about the next generation, who were not products of segregation, to have a spirit of stick-to-it-ness or tenacity when "life is not fair" or when they are not "treated fairly." It is important to know how to bounce back from negative evaluations or negative letters for tenure. You focus on the good letters and review the negative ones to see if the statements are true. Students would write on my evaluations that I talked about Black people too much or people of color. They failed to realize that it was a multicultural education class and students of color were the topics of discussion.

While many African American faculty members get frustrated, do not quit your job! No one has the power to make you miserable. Find your place of positivity and not negativity. Remember the scripture: weeping may endure for the night, but joy comes in the morning. As with Professors N and G, they found other jobs and continued their careers, you can do the same.

While this is painful to write, sometimes your own African American faculty members can be your worst enemy, especially when there is a "crabs in the bucket mentality" or microaggression. You can have microaggression within your own cultural group. While I will not define crabs in a bucket, I am giving you an assignment to look it up and apply it to your situation. That concept is a teachable moment for you. This mentality is alive and well in the academy.

Lastly, use your tools of writing to express yourself and keep accurate records of behaviors that support or devalue you. Always know, the pen is mightier than the sword and be aware of the digital footprint. At the time of this writing, the digital footprint does not go away.

I often quoted during my years at Texas A&M University that: "Maybe I was hired because I was Black (Affirmative Action), but I stayed there because I was excellent at my work." As such, retiring as Professor Emerita demonstrated the noteworthiness of my body of work. Yes, I believed that I have helped somebody as I passed along, through the campus of Texas A&M University and in helping other faculty members across the country.

REFERENCES

DuBois, W. E. B. (1903). *The souls of Black folk*. Oxford University Press.

Larke, P. J., Larke, A., Jones, W., & Lea, J. (2011). Mentorship programs: Essentials for today's urban African American youth. *Journal of Education and Social Justice*, *1*(1), 140–145.

Larke, P. J., Wiseman, D., & Bradley, C. (1990). The minority mentorship project: Changing attitudes of preservice teachers for diverse classrooms. *Action in Teacher Education*, *12*(3), 5–11.

The Holy Bible: Authorized King James Version. (1985). Holman Bible Publishers.

IF THEY DON'T GIVE YOU A SEAT AT THE TABLE, BRING A FOLDING CHAIR: MY HBCU FACULTY EXPERIENCES

Veronica G. Thomas

Howard University, USA

ABSTRACT

The author reflects on her journey to becoming a Black female full professor at a Historically Black College and University (HBCU). Additionally, she summarizes the research on the successes and challenges for women professors, Black professors more broadly, and Black female professors, more specifically, to contribute to a deeper understanding of the positionality and stance of Black women professors. Although HBCUs are higher education institutions where Black female professors achieve tenure in the greatest percentages, the author highlights the intersection of race and gender and the unfortunate gendered power dynamics in these spaces that frequently place Black female faculty at a disadvantage. The chapter concludes with strategies for Black women professors to survive and thrive in academia, in general, and at HBCUs, more specifically.

Keywords: Black women professor; HBCUs; intersectionality; positionality; research

INTRODUCTION

The main title of this chapter, "If they don't give you a seat at the table, bring a folding chair" (cited in Williams & Ziobro, 2023, p. iii) is an assertion made over 50 years ago by political icon and New York Congresswoman Shirley Chisholm. She was the first Black woman elected to the US Congress, serving seven terms from 1969 to 1983, and the first Black candidate (in 1972) to seek a major party

Journeys of Black Women in Academe
Diversity in Higher Education, Volume 26, 103–120

ISSN: 1479-3644/doi:10.1108/S1479-364420240000026006

nomination for US president. Chisholm was a trailblazer and a staunch advocate for women's rights, civil rights, and poverty amelioration. As an adolescent girl "coming of age" in the 1970s, Chisholm inspired me to think beyond the limited expectations that my White teachers, school counselors, and administrators had for me as a Black girl growing up in rural South Carolina. Chisholm's inspiring philosophy, along with the support of two loving parents, siblings, extended family, and "my village," shaped my worldview about being Black, female, and a university professor, and it has been a guiding principle in both my professional and personal life.

To date, most voices of Black women professors include the perspectives of Black women working at predominately White institutions (PWIs). Indeed, these women have much to say about their experiences and need to be heard. There is ample research documenting a chilly and, sometimes, hostile climate at PWIs for Black faculty that is created through their experiences of racial and gendered microaggressions (Kelly et al., 2017; Louis et al., 2016), social isolation, tokenization on faculty committees (Edwards & Ross, 2018), being othered by gender and race (Kelly & Winkle-Wagner, 2017) and the devaluing of their research (Edwards & Ross, 2018; Harley, 2008). Undoubtedly, many Black women faculty at PWIs continue to endure trauma stemming from being discredited, scrutinized, and blamed for their circumstances, all while holding innocent those who target and treat them as a threat (Gayle, 2022).

Limited attention continues to be paid to the voices of Black women professors in the historically Black colleges and universities (HBCU) context. As a result, little is known about the experiences of Black women faculty at HBCUs (Del Priore, 2022). The HBCU academic context, where race often "recedes" into the background, is indeed different than the context of our counterparts at PWIs. As HBCU Black women professors, we, too, are worthy of having a space to tell our stories, present our realities, and share our experiences, triumphs, and challenges. In this chapter, it is within the spirit of sharing my story as a Black woman (full) professor at an HBCU, reflecting on this continuing journey and summarizing the research in this area that I hope to contribute to a deeper understanding of our standpoint as Black women professors at HBCUs and, most importantly, to inspire other Black women and girls to pursue the professoriate.

I do not dare claim to speak for the countless numbers of Black women professors working at HBCUs across the country. My story is my own, so it may not reflect the journey and perspectives of other Black women professors. The type and culture of one's university are integral elements in understanding how Black women faculty perceive and experience the academy. Reflecting over 30+ years in academia, I can unequivocally conclude, for me, the benefits of being a Black woman professor at an HBCU, most notably the intellectual stimulation, teaching and mentoring of majority students of color, research opportunities, collaborations, and ability to engage diverse communities on a range of issues without judgment, far outweigh the challenges. The last part of the chapter concludes with strategies for Black women professors to survive and thrive in academia, in general, and at HBCUs more specifically.

MY POSITIONALITY AND INTERSECTIONALITY AS AN HBCU PROFESSOR

First, I want to point out that my perspective as an HBCU Black woman professor is shaped by my race (African American), generation (Baby Boomer), political affiliation (registered Democrat), social class (upbringing in a working-class community) and other factors (e.g., temperament, work values). I was born in Florence, South Carolina, the youngest of six children of working-class parents. As a 10-year-old sixth grader, my parents enrolled me in an elementary school consisting of only White students. A recurring incident that has left an indelible impression on me was one White teacher who would go down each row of students in the class requiring them to read a passage. However, every time she got to me, she would skip over. She never called on me to read aloud, answer questions, or demonstrate my knowledge. Essentially, I was invisible to her, not worthy of being in a class or a school with White students. I often wondered, as a young child, how could a teacher, someone so revered, especially in the Black community, treat a child that way in public view for other students in the class to see, ridicule, and model. While the school's principal and other White teachers at the school did not explicitly replicate or even seemingly condone that teacher's behavior, there were no policies put in place either to protect me or sanction the teacher.

Although I did not have the vocabulary to articulate it clearly, during that year as the only Black student in an all-White elementary school in the South, I began to understand discrimination, prejudice and racism at both individual and systemic levels. Subsequently, during my junior and senior high school years, I was not the sole Black student in the school but still attended a school that was roughly 80–90% White. I preserved and, at times, even thrived. Through my parents' encouragement, I joined the school band, participated in school plays, and engaged in other extracurricular activities in each school environment. Even at that young age, I was already being groomed by my parents to "bring a folder chair when not invited to sit at the table." My parents endured isolation when attending parent–teacher meetings and sometimes experienced subtle threats that I did not learn about until I was much older. Concepts such as self-efficacy, persistence, confidence, motivation, resilience and racial identity were not part of my vocabulary or that of my parents during that time. However, through the guidance of humble parents, who were my first educators, these important (then unnamed) traits were instilled in me and became an enduring part of my life. These early experiences laid the foundation for how I sought to be someone who could make a positive difference and make the people I interacted with feel seen, heard and respected.

Later, searching for my place (and voice) in the world, I, very intentionally, 1 month after my 17th birthday, landed at an HBCU for my undergraduate studies (South Carolina State), then subsequently to another HBCU (Howard University) for graduate studies and now where I have been employed as a faculty member since completion of my doctorate in social psychology. Consistent with my values, the overarching mission of HBCUs is to be part of the "resistance" in confronting racism in this country, serving as pillars for civic discourse, activism, and community engagement, as well as safe places that provide an educational experience of exceptional quality for its students. It was at my chosen HBCUs, particularly at the graduate level, that I was introduced to theoretical perspectives and research that brought the intersection of race, gender, and other issues to the forefront of psychology, my academic discipline. At the HBCU, I began to conduct research that "centered" the experiences of Black people, particularly Black women, to contribute to filling some gaps in our knowledge and understanding.

HBCUs have been an integral part of my life for most of my life! In this space, I continue to do the work through the lens of a scholar and a well-defined worldview that continues to shape me. As an HBCU Black woman professor, I see my role as a culturally responsive teacher and mentor, an engaged and reflective researcher, and an advocate for a more just society. All my work (teaching, research, service) is filtered through a social justice lens, guided by my own lived experiences and intersecting identities, including but not limited to race, gender, age, and socioeconomic class.

THE LANDSCAPE FOR BLACK WOMEN PROFESSORS: HBCUS AND BEYOND

Women in the academy. In some respects, the landscape for women, Black men, and Black women professors has improved over the past several decades, but in other ways, inequities persist or even worsen. On the positive side, colleges and universities employ more female faculty than in previous decades. In 2003, women comprised up to 31% of full-time faculty members; by 2019, that percentage had increased to 45%. However, much of this growth is attributed to women faculty working in untenured ranks (Turner, 2019). Among tenured professors at public institutions, women comprise only 27% of the faculty. Relatedly, women are less likely to be full professors at research/doctoral institutions, making up 47% of all faculty at these institutions but slightly less than one-third (or 32%) of full professors at public research/doctoral-granting institutions (Clery, 2022).

Women professors are paid less than their male counterparts. Rather than narrowing, this pay gap has persisted for years and grows wider at higher faculty ranks (American Association of University Professors, 2023). Data reported for fall 2018 indicate that among full professors, women, on average, earn approximately 85% of what men earn (i.e., $114,919 for women vs $134,997 for men), while among associate and assistant professors, women earn 93% and 91%, respectively, of what men earn (Colby & Fowler, 2020). The argument that the pay disparities faced by women faculty and faculty members of color can be explained by "market factors" and the tendency for women and people of color to be clustered in low-paying disciplines has been disproven as the sole explanation for pay inequities. Findings of a recent study of more than 2,300 STEM (science, technology, engineering, and math) faculty illustrate that women professors are underpaid relative to their male colleagues with similar publication records (Samaniego et al., 2023).

Black women in the academy. Consistently, studies show that individuals in two underprivileged classes (e.g., women and persons of color) face more significant inequities than individuals in only one such class. In academia, Black women face unique barriers concerning employment, advancement, salary, and job security (Bonner, 2001; Colby & Fowler, 2020; Ogbe, 2022). They are among the smallest demographics of the faculty workforce. Furthermore, Black women are more likely to be hired in the non-tenure track ranks of instructor and lecturer, which partially explains the pay gap and job insecurity (Boss et al., 2019; Lin & Kennette, 2022). Statistics indicate that Black women make up only 6.5% of tenure-track faculty, and this percentage decreases as faculty rank increases. They occupy only 2% of full professor positions, 3% of associate professors, and 4% of assistant professors across degree-granting postsecondary institutions (U.S. Department of Education, National Center for Education Statistics 2020, 2023).

HBCUs context, funding, and HBCU Black women faculty. Faculty members at HBCUs are much more diverse relative to race and ethnicity than those at PWIs. National Center for Educational Statistics (NCES) data show that HBCU faculties are 56% African American or Black, 24% White, 9.5% Asian, 2.5% Hispanic, 0.7% Indigenous, and 0.7% two or more races. On the other hand, PWI faculties are 69% White, with very low percentages of Black and Hispanic faculty.

Faculty, both men and women, at HBCUs are at a financial disadvantage compared to their PWI counterparts (Clery, 2021, 2022). In AY (academic year) 2021–2022, HBCU faculty earned approximately $24,000 less (or 74 cents to the dollar), on average, than their colleagues at other institutions (Clery, 2022). A significant contributor to this disparity is that HBCUs have long been underfunded. For example, it was only after a 15-year federal legal battle with the state, arguing that Maryland HBCUs were being purposely underfunded compared with PWIs in the state, that Coppin State, Bowie State, University Maryland Eastern Shore, and Morgan State were awarded $577 million from the state legislature, starting in July 2022, that will be disbursed over the 10 years (Broady et al., 2021). Decades of underfunding HBCUs have, in turn, prevented these institutions from offering more competitive faculty salaries and scholarships for top students. Undoubtedly, HBCU faculty should be paid similarly to PWI faculty doing comparable work. However, for me, as is the case for many other HBCU professors, particularly Black women professors, working at an HBCU is not about the money. Instead, many Black professors at HBCUs are willing to settle for less pay since they see themselves at these culturally affirming institutions on a mission to both "give back" and "pay it forward." In some respects, it is a "calling" to work at an HBCU and be a place without enduring racial microaggressions and ongoing battles to prove that you belong there and have earned (not given) the status of your position.

HBCUs are the places where Black women faculty achieve tenure in the highest percentages out of all institutions of higher education in the country (U.S. Department of Education, National Center for Education Statistics, 2017). Additionally, while a gender pay gap exists at HBCUs, it is smaller in comparison to the gender gap at PWIs (Renzulli et al., 2006). Within the HBCU context, Black women faculty generally do not feel isolated, hypervisible, or over-scrutinized because of simple, everyday decisions such as how they dress, how they wear their hair, their vernacular, or appearing too "Afrocentric." For example, as a junior faculty member during the 1990s, I freely wore my hair in braids while teaching classes and attending meetings. Interestingly, however, I was advised by a more seasoned Black female mentor to remove the braids when I was invited to interview for a position at Wellesley College in Boston, Massachusetts. Fighting hair discrimination and prejudice remain issues for Black women, even within certain academic circles. The New Crown 2023 Workplace study results, including over 2,000 female-identifying respondents, highlight the systemic social and economic impact of hair bias and discrimination against Black women (Dove & LinkedIn, 2023). The findings indicated that Black women's hair is 2.5 times as likely as white women's hair to be perceived as unprofessional and that Black women with coily or textured hair are twice as likely to experience microaggressions at work than Black women with straighter hair.

Even with the positives and the opportunities for Black women professors at HBCUs, there exist unfortunate gendered power dynamics in these spaces that frequently place Black women faculty at a disadvantage (e.g., Davis & Brown, 2017; Gasman, 2007). Blackshear and Hollis (2021) point out that despite the profound academic and professional achievements among Black women, the intersection of race and gender in higher education remains inescapable. Gender issues at HBCUs exist, but often, they are not explicitly addressed and are confounded by and in conflict with issues of race (Bonner, 2001). As Blackshear and Hollis (2021) further noted, ". . .. Black women continue to come to terms with the undeniable reality that the shadow of sexism falls even here at the HBCU. . .." (p. 30). In their qualitative study of Black women faculty at PWIs and HBCUs, Blackshear and Hollis found that the while the HBCU women professors did not feel silenced along racial lines, however, they voiced feelings of "being diminished due to gender," "having to produce more," and that "men's opinions and projects were taken more seriously while they were ignored" and they were "more often assigned additional work or tougher work than men" (p. 36). Gender gaps are particularly pronounced when it comes to leadership positions at HBCUs with data indicating significant limits to the upward mobility of Black women in top leadership (i.e., the presidency) at HBCUs (e.g., Horton, 2020). This has led some scholars to conclude that Black men gain immensely from the HBCUs' racial fairness while Black women grapple with gender equality (Blackshear & Hollis, 2021; Bonner, 2001; Hills, 2019).

GETTING A SEAT AT THE TABLE: WHAT IT DOES AND DOES NOT MEAN

The main title for this chapter, "If they don't give you a seat at the table, bring a folding chair," is not intended to put the burden of success entirely on the actions (or inactions) of individual Black women faculty. It is not intended to deny, ignore, or dismiss the pressing need for systemic and institutional change to address complex and multifaceted ways that racism, sexism, and their intersection manifest within the professoriate—even at HBCUs. As evident in the data cited in the previous sections of this chapter, decades of intentionally inadequate legal protections, discriminatory employment practices, and persistent racial stereotypes and biases contribute to disparities faced by Black professors, in general, and Black women professors more specifically.

Considering the pivotal role that Black women can serve in academia through supporting an agenda of equity and inclusion across disciplines, university administrators must understand better how to recruit, develop, and retain Black women professors and integrate their perspectives into educational development processes and practices (Priddie et al., 2022). Solving these systemic issues is undoubtedly beyond the control of an individual faculty member. Collective action is required to improve campus climate, change institutional and departmental structures, and implement more equitable institutional policies and practices. In an ideal world, all faculty would have "a seat at the table [in academia]," that is, everyone within the professoriate would receive the same opportunities as everyone else to listen, share, influence, and advance.

"If they don't give you a seat at the table, bring a folding chair" conveys having a voice and speaking out as a Black woman, particularly when feeling unwelcomed at the table, displaced at the table, or not even invited to sit. Black women professors differ in experiences, backgrounds, values, and beliefs. We are not a "one size fits all." As such, the way a Black woman professor chooses to "speak out" and the battles she chooses to "fight" or "ignore" varies. Some may not want a seat at the table and may not want to bring in a folding chair; in fact, some Black women may want to "blow up the table." As Black women professors across the higher education spectrum, we are not a monolith even at HBCUs; however, we are connected and unified in our struggle to be accepted, respected, and treated fairly and have a voice in our diverse institutions.

DEFINING ONESELF: DARING TO BE BRAVE AND AUTHENTIC

With her iconic words, "If they don't give you a seat at the table, bring a folding chair," Chisholm encouraged us not to wait for an invitation but to pull up a chair with all that we bring to the table and make our own space in the conversation. As Black women professors, we sometimes are (implicitly or explicitly) exposed to attacks on our identity, in part due to historical stereotypes. A significant part of Black women professors being at the table and having agency in this space is knowing their worth and having confidence in the value they bring to the table (i.e., the institution). It is crucial for Black women to self-define and express who they are and to define their existence within the institution (Del Priore, 2022). Self-definition can be achieved through self-awareness, self-acceptance, and living a life that aligns with one's needs and values.

Furthermore, self-definition calls for authenticity and embracing one's intersectionality as a person of color, a woman, and incorporating other valued parts of one's sense of self (e.g., partner/wife, mother, caregiver, friend).

The intersection of gender and race results in Black women experiencing unique forms of oppression, including stereotypes they seek to distance themselves from in the workplace. To avoid being labeled with the "angry Black woman" trope, Black women professors at HBCUs and other places frequently fail to express legitimate concerns about discrimination and bias (Davis & Brown, 2017). Obge (2022, p. 681) recounts a conversation with a Black woman professor who stated that "her good works.... were never credited to her without her 'making a fuss.' This fuss, the Black woman professor goes on to say, however, gets noticed very quickly, and then she becomes 'that angry Black woman.' She says her fear of reinforcing the 'angry Black woman' stereotype has kept her from taking credit for some of her work." Unfortunately, many Black women too often feel and act this way.

The mythical image of the "strong Black woman" (SBW), often given as a compliment but enacted to mask the unfair work burden placed on Black women (hooks, 1993), is another concern of many Black women professors. Trying to live up to this SBW persona can further marginalize and create ill health and other negative consequences for Black women (Watson-Singleton, 2017). In a February 5, 2020 blog posting in *The Professor Is In*, written by a Black-tenured HBCU woman professor who preferred to remain anonymous, the author referred to Black women as "the mules" of HBCUs, stating that "we are expected to pull our academic workload, along with more than our share of service and advising, while remaining collegial and ensuring there are refreshments available for faculty meetings. Black women faculty are the mules of HBCUs, working from the bottom and bearing the weight of the challenges encumbering these institutions. I understand that women at PWIs are enduring a similar struggle with inequitable expectations of teaching, research, and service. However, I do not see these same expectations of White women faculty at HBCUs" (https://theprofessorisin.com/2020/02/05/black-women-faculty-at-hbcus-woc-guest-post/).

The loyalty that many Black women professors have toward "racial uplift" results in them being apprehensive in taking steps, either legally or otherwise, to address the "isms" that affect them at HBCUs. As Black women professors at HBCUs, particularly from the Baby Boomer generation, we often remained silent, ignored, set aside, or at least not prioritize issues related to gender equality, instead focusing our social justice lens on racial equality issues. As a Black woman professor, I have experienced all these situations in some form, and over the years, I have been challenged with finding ways to navigate these real and perceived realities. On a positive note, over the past 10–15 years, I have witnessed Black HBCU millennial women professors (those born roughly between 1981 and 1994), especially, be more unapologetically outspoken about real or perceived gender discrimination and racialized gender inequities within the department and university. Within the evolving context of faculty life, as Black women HBCU professors, we must continuously find ways to innovate and navigate gendered, racialized, and other dynamics even in spaces we perceive as culturally affirming and safe places whose mission we support and strive to uphold.

ADVANCING IN ACADEMIA

As I move toward the latter part of my journey as an HBCU Black woman professor, I reflect on my many years in academia, my successes, challenges, lessons learned, and connections made along the way. First, I cannot understate the role of mentors throughout this journey. Fortunately, I had multiple mentors simultaneously at various points during my academic career. Some of my mentors were women, some were men, some were Black professors, and some were White professors. Some were within my academic department, while others were outside my department, School/College, or academic institution. Each mentor provided me with valuable yet varying perspectives and expertise. Most times, I followed my mentor's guidance. However, in some instances, my course of action did not align with the advice of my mentor because it was inconsistent with my value system and how I wished to be represented within the academy. Some mentors assisted me with focusing more broadly on my professional goals, whereas others provided mentorship and collaborations on research, grants, and publications. Yet, still, I had other mentors who provided advice regarding teaching and managing coursework. Some of my mentoring relationships included the traditional, hierarchical relationships with a senior-level professor or administrator, while others were peer mentoring relationships with colleagues at the same faculty rank as myself. Moreover, some mentors became lifelong friends, whereas others transitioned out of my life for various reasons.

Through great support systems and trial and error, I was able to deploy strategies that helped me not only survive but thrive and build a sustainable career in academia. These strategies, which I summarize below, include some of my own, some I learned from mentors and colleagues along the way, and some found in the abundant literature. None of these strategies are likely to be successful if the Black woman professor is not confident in her ability as a professor and scholar. Further, any strategy for success that Black women professors adopt or adapt must be aligned with their values, level of comfort, and ability (and willingness) to follow through.

In the last part of the chapter, I offer suggestions and recommendations for Black women interested in having a successful academic career. Of course, this listing is not exhaustive but is intended to provide some guidance and must be tailored to the specific context.

Have and project confidence in your abilities as an educator and scholar. Confidence is not a fixed trait but a skill that Black women professors must cultivate. Being confident means having a belief in oneself, knowing one's strengths, and having the conviction that one can meet the challenges of the academy and succeed in doing so. As professors, our students look toward us to be both knowledgeable within our discipline and confident within our skin. Research demonstrates a gender gap in confidence and self-promotion. Women generally feel less self-assured or confident in themselves and their abilities than men (Exley & Kessler, 2022). Studies suggest that confidence can matter as much as competence in the workplace (Kay & Shipman, 2014). Individuals with confidence in their abilities tend to have higher aspirations, invest more efforts in endeavors, and persevere longer in the face of difficulties and setbacks (Bandura, 1991, 1997).

Confidence also requires having an awareness of when the problem is not personal but instead is systemic. I hope that younger generations of Black women professors do not, as was the case for many women in the Baby Boomers generation during the earlier parts of their careers, experience what is described as the "imposter syndrome" (Clance & Imes, 1978). Clance and Imes point out that such individuals have intellectual self-doubt, believe others have overestimated their talents and abilities (i.e., "the superwoman"), and feel less competent or less worthy of their positions or achievements, ultimately leaving them feeling like a phony.

Bias and discrimination, being underestimated, receiving less recognition for their work, and encountering biased expectations have been linked to the imposter syndrome in women professors. McGee et al. (2022), however, argued that the impostor syndrome label is sometimes falsely applied and is an incorrect attribution of the underlying cause of Blacks' feeling otherness in educational spaces. Instead, they contend that the imposter syndrome, for most Black scholars, particularly in White spaces, is a synonym for structural and institutional racism that results in these individuals experiencing emotional, mental, academic, and professional distress. Consistent with the conclusions of McGee et al., I stress that Black female faculty who do feel like an imposter in their academic space stop, reflect, and recognize that the source of this is not necessarily an internal psychological shortcoming but instead more likely due to systemic racialized gender biases and messages occurring within the environment.

Black women professors must and can build confidence by recognizing their value while documenting and communicating their accomplishments, contributions, and the distinct perspectives they bring to their discipline, academic program, and university. This is also better accomplished when they do not internalize the negative messages being transmitted, implicitly or explicitly, within the institutional context.

Speak up for yourself at the right place, the right time, and in the right manner. As Black women professors, it is essential for us not to be silent. We must choose our battles and speak up and out at the right time and in the right manner for the educational context in which we work. We must become our strongest advocate (with humility) while simultaneously adding value to the department and university.

How Black women professors speak out and advocate for themselves may look substantially different for Black women professors within the HBCU context than those in the PWI context and is often an individual choice. Some Black women faculty may be more comfortable being "tempered radicals" (Myerson, 2001; Meyerson & Scully, 1995), that is, being insider activists challenging the status quo through gently pushing the existing culture of their university and serving as a catalyst for incremental constructive changes which, over time, can build more socially just and inclusive environments. There may be defining periods in Black women professors' careers that tempered radicalism is most effective; yet, in other instances, Black women professors may need to be unapologetically forceful in pushing for systemic change to readdress inequities. If unsuccessful with the latter, this may require deep reflection about whether your university context is the right fit for you.

Be intentional in charting your academic career path. As discussed throughout this book, it is well documented that Black women experience unique challenges in academia. These include overall challenges navigating the institutional culture, in general, and more specifically in navigating the tenure and promotion process, dealing with biased student/peer evaluations, having disproportionately high service demands, and experiencing other manifestations of gendered racism (e.g., Blackshear & Hollis, 2021; Bonner, 2001; Carter & Craig, 2022; Davis & Brown, 2017; Gayle, 2022; Griffin, 2016; Kelly & Winkle-Wagner, 2017). As such, Black women who desire to have a career in the professoriate must be intentional in charting their career path.

Everyone benefits when more Black women enter the academy and advance to the top rank of full professor. These include benefits for the discipline, the university, students, and faculty. A diverse faculty brings diverse perspectives that ultimately enhance teaching and advising, research and scholarship, clinical practice, and community engagement (Perna, 2023). It also elevates the educational experience of underrepresented students and better prepares all students to successfully interact with the diverse people they will encounter after leaving the university. However, the intersectionality of race and gender undoubtedly affects the progression and experience of Black women as they seek to move through the upper ranks of the professoriate and, as a result, the numbers of Black women are small among the ranks of full professors in US colleges and universities (U.S. Department of Education, National Center for Education Statistics 2020, 2023).

Early in their academic journey, Black women should create a set of outcome objectives that align with their broader academic goals. I found it useful to have a personal set of SMART objectives (specific, measurable, achievable, relevant, and time-framed) to chart one's faculty trajectory. Being specific requires the faculty to identify the type of academic career they want (e.g., faculty vs administrative track), where they want it (e.g., HBCU vs PWI, large vs smaller institution, rural vs urban), and what they hope to accomplish in the short- and longer-term. Having measurable indicators (e.g., implement two community-based projects over the next year; submit three manuscripts for publications per year) aids faculty in tracking their progress. Achievable means setting attainable goals considering one's assets, constraints, and resources. In being intentional about your career path, faculty career objectives must be relevant and align with the university's mission. Lastly, setting a specific timeframe for achieving one's objective is essential, considering the tenure clock may be ticking. Unexpected opportunities (e.g., fellowships, administrative positions, grant awards) and life circumstances, which will indeed happen along the way, may require modifications of these objectives from when they were initially articulated.

Start preparing for the tenure process from the first day of faculty appointment (or even before). Studies characterized the tenure evaluation process as stressful, full of contradictions, and often highly conducive to reproducing racial and gender inequality (Wolf-Wendel & Ward, 2015). Furthermore, in many instances, the tenure evaluation process is strategically ambiguous, governed by criteria that are unclear in ways that benefit the institution but, at the same time, are an essential part of the racialization of higher education organizations (Cate et al., 2022; Ray, 2019). Navigating the tenure process can be incredibly daunting for Black women faculty with less access to informal professional networks and mentoring that provide guidance.

Over two decades ago, research by Allen et al. (2000) found the two key obstacles restricting Black women's faculty advancement in the professoriate. These include (a) the tendency to be overburdened with teaching and service responsibilities and (b) the inflexible expectations relative to research and publications. This still rings true today for Black women pursuing an academic career, particularly at research-intensive institutions. Teaching-heavy faculty report the lowest levels of job satisfaction and the highest turnover intentions, whereas classic (dual research and teaching focus) faculty report higher levels of job satisfaction and low turnover intentions (French et al., 2020). As such, although Black women professors historically experience disproportionate service (mentoring, advising, serving on committees) responsibilities, they must negotiate time to build a strong and consistent research and publication record that contributes to the knowledge base in their discipline (and across disciplines if possible!).

The stark reality is that tenure and promotion decisions at most US universities are often heavily tied to faculty research productivity and grantsmanship; teaching is important but generally given less weight, and service contributions, which are also expected, are generally given even less significance in tenure decisions. Despite HBCU's tradition of student service, the long-term research productivity of HBCU faculty seems to mirror that of faculty at PWIs, suggesting that HBU faculty allocate their time in a way consistent with the expectations of large research institutions (Escobar et al., 2021). Therefore, Black women professors at HBCUs, too, need to prioritize negotiating research-protected time. One successful strategy for junior faculty to pursue to bolster their research capacity and productivity includes negotiating a first-year course reduction to allow time to build a research program and team at the institution. Black women faculty should also renegotiate course reduction in subsequent years or after receiving a major federal grant or award. Other strategies include negotiating for research startup funds, research space, and a research assistant to support their work.

Build and maintain meaningful mentors and allies and create robust professional networks and connections within and across the campus, professional organizations, and other related spaces. The importance of building and maintaining relationships within and across one's university and other professional and personal spaces cannot be overstated. As described earlier in this chapter, I had a diverse mentors, allies, and networks (both within and outside the university) who provided me with support, guidance, and advice on various issues throughout the academic year, especially during the early years. Mentors can help junior faculty better understand and adapt (if that is a goal!) to the existing university culture and navigate those expected and unexpected challenges. Building warm and positive relationships across the campus is especially valuable at HBCUs, with their emphasis on community and a sense of belonging. Mentors can facilitate this relationship building.

Black women professors often need a mentoring network to buffer or cushion (since they cannot eliminate) the negative experiences they endure (Turner Kelly & Fries-Britt, 2022). Mentors and allies can increase Black women faculty's visibility and recognition within the university and the discipline by actively advocating for them, recommending them for leadership roles and research collaborations, and providing opportunities for growth and professional development that align with their faculty career goals. Black women professors should also look outside their university for suitable mentors. Lane and Cobbs-Roberts (2022) highlight how Zoom and other digital platforms have opened options for Black women to access a broader community of support inside and outside the academy and increase their opportunities to have connections and mentoring across institutional context, disciplines, and geographic space.

Lift while you climb. Lifelong educator and champion of civil rights and founder of the National Association of Colored Women (NACW), Mary Church Terrell (1864–1964) adopted the motto "lift as you climb." Lifting as we climb is a phrase often associated with Black communities to describe the strategy of a person pulling someone up the proverbial ladder as they succeed. As Black women faculty, it is essential to "lift while we climb." Doing so builds on our legacy of community through determination and struggle.

Lifting as we climb is accomplished by providing others (i.e., students and faculty) with advice, guidance, and multiple opportunities to collaborate and contribute to the discipline in various ways. Some of my most satisfying experiences as a professor continue to be mentoring and witnessing the growth and professional development of students and faculty with whom I collaborate both within and outside my university. Lifting as I climb through mentoring students and junior colleagues has also significantly contributed to my growth and professional development, giving me new perspectives on old ideas and extending my legacy and accomplishments.

Take care of yourself physically and mentally. For some Black women professors, effectively navigating academia means working 14–16 hour days to meet the high demands placed upon them with pressure to do more work to be viewed as equal to their colleagues (Del Priore, 2022; Jarmon, 2001). In doing so, they may neglect their own health. We often hear about the importance of prioritizing goals related to self-care to ensure our well-being and sustained success. At different phases of Black women's faculty careers, their lives can become overwhelmed with competing personal and professional responsibilities. Black women professors can get so immersed in their work and in assisting others that they neglect their own physical, mental, and social-emotional health.

Furthermore, particularly over the past decade, Black women faculty, like many others, have experienced trauma, outrage, and racial battle with recurring incidences such as the brutal murder of unarmed Black people such as George Floyd (age 46), Breonna Taylor (age 26), Freddie Gray (age 25), Eric Gardner (age 43), and countless others. This is coupled with experiencing the devastating effects of the COVID-19 pandemic. In the spring of 2020, higher education underwent more sweeping changes within a few weeks than in the previous 10 years (Hammoudi et al., 2023). With these changes, all faculty were required to quickly adjust to new circumstances, including making substantial changes to how they teach, collaborate with others, and juggle their personal and professional lives. Zoom fatigue and a lack of boundaries between work and personal are real threats to Black women professors' well-being. It is not surprising that research findings indicate that the high-stress environment of academia may play a role in the adverse mental and physical health outcomes seen among Black women in academia (Journal of Blacks in Higher Education, 2022).

Self-care is vital for Black women faculty. Dorociak et al. (2017) describe self-care as a multidimensional, multifaceted process of purposeful engagement in strategies that promote healthy functioning and enhance well-being. Self-care involves conscious acts of prioritizing, preserving, improving, and maintaining one's overall health and well-being by doing something that individuals genuinely enjoy. Black women faculty cannot be the best version of themselves for their students, research collaborators, family members, and friends if they are over-extended and exhausted.

Most of us understand the concept of self-care quite well; however, putting it into practice and prioritizing it remains a challenge. Numerous health experts remind us to schedule our time wisely and allocate regular time to "unplug" and "recharge." There is no singular approach to self-care. For some Black women professors, religion and faith are essential elements of the self-care practice. Research indicates that Black women professors view religion or faith as providing encouragement, guidance, and strength, ultimately boosting their perseverance in competitive and stressful academic climates (Del Priore, 2022; Gregory, 2001). For other women, self-care includes active engagement in sports, physical activities, regular meet-ups with friends, and connecting with their sororities or other community-based organizations. The specific strategies used to accomplish self-care can vary depending on individuals' personal preferences, resources, and constraints. The key is doing so consistently and with joy!

CONCLUSIONS

In 2024, being a Black woman full professor at an HBCU seems unremarkable. I am in good company as many incredible Black women at our nation's HBCUs hold the rank of full professor. Over my HBCU career, I have assumed varied positions, including professor, department chairperson, interim dean, graduate studies coordinator, research institute director, researcher, mentor, and colleague. Throughout most of my tenure as a professor at an HBCU, I have felt appreciated and as if I truly belong there. This is so far removed from that 10-year-old Black girl thrust into an all-White elementary school in the South.

I am not trying to be "pollyannish here" and minimize real challenges Black women professors may face at HBCUs. Yes, even with the gratitude of finding both "my voice" and "my place" at my HBCU, there were still times along this journey when my feelings were shaken (e.g., being capriciously kicked out of my office, offered a "lowballed" salary for an administrative position that I was being recruited to fulfill, having a male colleague referring to my research as focusing on "that women's stuff"). There were times when my faith was tested. As Biblical scripture (James 1: 2–4) says, "...For you know that when your faith is tested, your endurance has a chance to grow..." and we should enter our hardships as deposits in life, not withdrawals. During times of discord along my journey, I kept my "eyes on the prize," recognizing that the mission of the HBCU is bigger than interpersonal dynamics with any one faculty member, Dean, Department Chair, or even University President.

As Black women enter the professoriate, they must think about what their seat at the table represents, what it looks like, what they bring to the table, and why they want to be there. They sometimes must decide if they want to continue at this table. Black women professors must be thoughtful about crafting their definition(s) of success and remember that this is a continuous journey of balancing teaching, research, and service.

As Black women professors working at HBCUs, we must stand in solidarity with our Black sister professors at PWIs, collaborating and supporting their efforts to challenge dominant racist paradigms and close gender and other inequities on those campuses. Likewise, we need Black women professors at PWIs to stand in solidarity with HBCU Black women professors as we navigate more hospitable environments yet often deal with limited resources, "superwoman" expectations, and gendered and other intersecting dynamics that can make the HBCU context less affirming.

In closing, I add my voice to a growing chorus of Black women professors at HBCUs who are grateful to share our experiences with others in hopes that future generations of Black women faculty can learn from our stories, successes, and struggles. Black women belong in academia, whether they are employed at an HBCU or a PWI, which is a matter of personal choice, preference, or circumstance.

Just as I began this chapter with an assertion made by a powerful Black woman I deeply admired as I was coming into adulthood, Shirley Chisholm, I will close with another quote from her. This quote is one that, for me and many other Black women professors, reflects the spirit behind the career path that we chose. Toward the end of her life, when asked about her legacy, Chisholm stated [National Visionary Leadership Project (2010, February 19)]:

> I want history to remember me... not as the first black woman to have
> made a bid for the presidency of the United States, but as a black
> woman who lived in the 20th century and who dared to be herself.
> I want to be remembered as a catalyst for change in America. –Shirley Chisholm

REFERENCES

Allen, W. R., Epps, E., Guillory, E., Suh, S., & Bonous-Hammarth, M. (2000). The Black academic: Faculty status among African Americans in U.S. higher education. *The Journal of Negro Education*, *69*(1), 112–127.

American Association of University Professors. (2023). *The annual report on the economic status of the profession, 2022–23*. American Association of University Professors.

Bandura, A. (1991). Social cognitive theory of self-regulation. *Organizational Behavior and Human Decision Processes*, *50*, 248–287.

Bandura, A. (1997). *Self-efficacy: The exercise of control*. Freeman.

Blackshear, T., & Hollis, L. P. (2021). Despite the place, can't escape gender and race: Black women's faculty experiences at PWIs and HBCUs. *Taboo: The Journal of Culture and Education*, *20*(1). https://digitalscholarship.unlv.edu/taboo/vol20/iss1/3

Bonner, F. B. (2001). Addressing gender issues in the historically Black college and university community: A challenge and call to action. *The Journal of Negro Education*, *70*, 176–191.

Boss, G. J., Davis, T. J., Porter, C. J., & Moore, C. M. (2019). Second to none: Contingent women of color faculty in the classroom. In R. Jeffries (Ed.), *Diversity, equity, and inclusivity in contemporary higher education* (Vol. 2019, pp. 211–225). IGI Global.

Broady, K., Perry, A. M., & Romer, C. (2021). *Commentary – Underfunding HBCUs leads to an underrepresentation of Black faculty*. Brookings Institute.

Carter, T. J., & Craig, M. O. (2022). It could be us: Black faculty as "threats" on the path to tenure. *Race and Justice*, *12*(3), 569–587. https://doi.org/10.1177/21533687221087366

Cate, L., Ward, L. W. M., & Ford, K. S. (2022). Strategic ambiguity: How pre-tenure faculty negotiate the hidden rules of academia. *Innovative Higher Education*, *47*, 795–812. https://doi.org/10.1007/s10755-022-09604-x

Clance, P. R., & Imes, S. A. (1978). The imposter phenomenon in high achieving women: Dynamics and therapeutic intervention. *Psychotherapy Theory Research and Practice*, *15*(3), 241–247. https://doi.org/10.1037/h0086006

Clery, S. (2021). *"The calm before COVID: The last look at faculty salaries before the tumultuous pandemic" Faculty salary analysis, 2019–20*. National Education Association. https://www.nea.org/resource-library/professional-pay-higher-education. https://www.nea.org/sites/default/files/2021-04/2021%20Higher%20Ed%20 Special%20Salary%20Issue_0.pdf

Clery, S. (2022). *Collateral damage: Effects of the pandemic on academe. Faculty salary analysis: 2020–21*. National Education Association. https://www.nea.org/sites/default/files/2022-03/NEA%20HE%20Salary%20Report%202022_0.pdf

Colby, G., & Fowler, C. (2020). *Data snapshot: IPEDS data on full-time women faculty and faculty of color*. American Association of University Professors.

Davis, S., & Brown, K. (2017). Automatically discounted: Using Black feminist theory to critically analyze the experiences of Black female faculty. *International Journal of Educational Leadership Preparation*, *12*(1), n1.

Del Priore, A. (2022). Strategies for support: Black women faculty career advancement at Historically Black Colleges and Universities. *Journal of Black Studies*, *53*(1), 19–44. https://doi.org/10.1177/00219347211047878

Dorociak, K. E., Rupert, P. A., Bryant, F. B., & Zahniser, E. (2017). Development of a self-care assessment for psychologists. *Journal of Counseling Psychology*, *64*(3), 325–334. https://doi.org/10.1037/cou0000206

Dove & LinkedIn. (2023). *CROWN 2023 workplace research study*. https://www.thecrownact.com/research-studies

Edwards, W. J., & Ross, H. H. (2018). What are they saying? Black faculty at predominantly White institutions of higher education. *Journal of Human Behavior in the Social Environment*, *28*(2), 142–161. https://doi.org/10.1080/10911359.2017.1391731

Escobar, M., Bell, Z. K., Qazi, M., Kotoye, C. O., & Arcediano, F. (2021). Faculty time allocation at Historically Black Universities and its relationship to institutional expectations. *Frontiers in Psychology*, *12*, 734426. https://doi.org/10.3389/fpsyg.2021.734426

Exley, C. L., & Kessler, J. B. (2022). The gender gap in self-promotion. *Quarterly Journal of Economics* (2022), 1345–1381. https://doi.org/10.1093/qje/qjac003

French, K. A., Allen, T. D., Miller, M. H., Kim, E. S., & Centeno, G. (2020). Faculty time allocation in relation to work-family balance, job satisfaction, commitment, and turnover intentions. *Journal of Vocational Behavior*, *120*, 103443. https://doi.org/10.1016/j.jvb.2020.103443

Gasman, M. (2007). Swept under the rug? A historiography of gender and Black colleges. *American Educational Research Journal*, *44*(4), 760–805. https://doi.org/10.3102/0002831207308639

Gayle, J. G. (2022, April 17). Does anyone see us? Disposability of Black women faculty in the academy. *Diverse: Issues in Higher Education*. https://www.diverseeducation.com/opinion/article/15295726/does-anyone-see-us-disposability-of-black-women-faculty-in-the-academy

Gregory, S. T. (2001). Black faculty women in the academy: History, status, and future. *The Journal of Negro Education*, *70*(3), 124–138. https://doi.org/10.2307/3211205

Griffin, R. (2016). Black female faculty, resilient grit, and determined grace or "just because everything is different doesn't mean anything has changed". *The Journal of Negro Education*, *85*(3), 365–379. https://doi.org/10.7709/jnegroeducation.85.3.0365

Hammoudi, H. D., Soltani, A., Dalli, R., Alsarraj, L., & Malki, A. (2023). Understanding and fostering mental health and well-being among university faculty: A narrative review. *Journal of Clinical Medicine*, *12*(13), 4425. https://doi.org/10.3390/jcm12134425

Harley, D. A. (2008). Maids of academe: African American women faculty at predominately white institutions. *Journal of African American Studies*, *12*(1), 19–36.

Hills, D. D. (2019). "Admirable or ridiculous?" The burdens of Black women scholars and dialogue in the work of solidarity. *Journal of Feminist Studies in Religion*, *35*(2), 5–21. https://doi.org/10/2979/jfemistudreli.35.2.02

hooks, b. (1993). *Sisters of the yam: Black women and self-recovery*. South End Press.

Horton, T. W. (2020). *The career advancement narratives of Black women presidents of Historically Black Colleges and Universities (HBCUs)*. University of New Orleans Theses and Dissertations (pp. 2795). https://scholarworks.uno.edu/td/2795

Jarmon, B. (2001). Unwritten rules of the game. In R. O. Mabokela & A. L. Green (Eds.), *Sisters of the academy: Emergent Black women scholars in higher education* (pp. 175–181). Stylus Publishing.

Journal of Blacks in Higher Education. (2022, May 16). *How stress in the academic environment impacts the health of Black women*. https://jbhe.com/2022/05/how-stress-in-the-academic-environment-impacts-the-health-of-black-women/#:~:text=%E2%80%9CIn%20our%20study%2C%20we%20found,they%20are%20good%20or%20bad

Kay, K., & Shipman, C. (2014). *The confidence code: The science and art of self-assurance: What women should know*. Harper Business.

Kelly, B. T., Gayles, J. G., & Williams, C. D. (2017). Recruitment without retention: A critical case of Black faculty unrest. *The Journal of Negro Education*, *86*(3), 305–317. https://doi.org/10.7709/jnegroeducation.86.3.0305

Kelly, B. T., & Winkle-Wagner, R. (2017). Finding a voice in predominantly White institutions: A longitudinal study of Black women faculty members' journeys toward tenure. *Teachers College Record*, *119*(6), 1–6. https://doi.org/10.1177/016146811711900604

Lane, T. B., & Cobbs-Roberts, L. (2022). A critical duoethnographic account of two Black women faculty using co-mentoring to traverse academic life. In B. Turner Kelly & S. Fries-Britt (Eds.), *Building mentorship networks to support Black women: A guide to succeeding in the academy* (pp. 19–22). Routledge.

Lin, P. S., & Kennette, L. N. (2022). Creating an inclusive community for BIPOC faculty: Women of color in academia. *SN Social Sciences*, *2*(11), 246. https://doi.org/10.1007/s43545-022-00555-w

Louis, D. A., Rawls, G. J., Jackson-Smith, D., Chambers, G. A., Phillips, L. L., & Louis, S. L. (2016). Listening to our voices: Experiences of Black faculty at predominantly White research universities with microaggression. *Journal of Black Studies*, *47*(5), 454–474. https://doi.org/10.1177/0021934716632983

McGee, E. O., Botchway, P. T., Naphan-Kingery, D. E., Brockman, A. J., Houston, S., II., & White, D. T. (2022). Racism camouflaged as impostorism and the impact on Black STEM doctoral students. *Race, Ethnicity and Education*, *25*(4), 487–507. https://doi.org/10.1080/13613324.2021.1924137

Meyerson, D. E., & Scully, M. A. (1995). Crossroads tempered radicalism and the politics of ambivalence and change. *Organization Science*, *6*(5), 585–600.

Myerson, D. (2001). *Tempered radicals: How people use difference to inspire change at work*. Harvard Business School Press.

National Visionary Leadership Project. (2010, February 19). Shirley Chisholm: How I want to be remembered. Oral History Video. YouTube. https://www.youtube.com/watch?v=31fzqYfqgGI

Obge, A. (2022). A seat at the table is not enough: A perspective on Black women's representation in academia. *Immunology & Cell Biology*, *100*, 679–682. https://doi.org/10.1111/imcb.12584

Ogbe, A. (2022). A seat at the table is not enough: A perspective on Black women representation in academia. *Immunology & Cell Biology*, *100*(9), 679–682. https://doi.org/10.1111/imcb.12584

Perna, L. W. (2023, January 9). Why we need better data on faculty diversity. *Inside Higher Ed*. https://www.insidehighered.com/views/2023/01/10/why-we-need-better-data-faculty-diversity-opinion

Priddie, C., Palmer, D., Silberstein, S., & BrckaLorenz, A. (2022). Centering Black women faculty: Magnifying powerful voices. *To Improve the Academy: A Journal of Educational Development*, *41*(2), 5. https://doi.org/10.3998/tia.246

Ray, V. (2019). A theory of racialized organizations. *American Sociological Review*, *84*(1), 26–53.

Renzulli, L. A., Grant, L., & Kathuria, S. (2006). Race, gender, and the wage gap: Comparing faculty salaries in predominately White and Historically Black colleges and universities. *Gender & Society*, *20*(4), 491–510. http://doi.org/10.1177/0891243206287130

Samaniego, C., Lindner, P., Kazmi, M. A., Dirr, B. A., Kong, D. K., Jef-Eke, E., & Spitzmueller, C. (2023). Higher research productivity = more pay? Gender pay-for-productivity inequity across disciplines. *Scientometrics*, *128*, 1395–1407. https://doi.org/10.1007/s11192-022-04513-4

Turner, B. T. (2019). *Commentary. Though more women are on college campuses, climbing the professor ladder remains a challenge*. Brookings. https://www.brookings.edu/articles/though-more-women-are-on-college-campuses-climbing-the-professor-ladder-remains-a-challenge/

Turner Kelly, B., & Fries-Britt, S. (Eds.). (2022). *Building mentorship networks to support Black women: A guide to succeeding in the academy*. Routledge.

U.S. Department of Education, National Center for Education Statistics. (2020). *The condition of education 2020 (NCES 2020-144), characteristics of postsecondary faculty*. https://nces.ed.gov/fastfacts/display.asp?id=61

U.S. Department of Education, National Center for Education Statistics. (2023). *Characteristics of postsecondary faculty. Condition of education*. U.S. Department of Education, Institute of Education Sciences. https://nces.ed.gov/programs/coe/indicator/csc

U.S. Department of Education, National Center for Education Statistics. (2017). *Integrated postsecondary education data system*. U.S. Department of Education, Institute of Education Sciences. https://nces.ed.gov/ipeds/datacenter/InstitutionByName.aspx?goToReportId=1

Watson-Singleton, N. N. (2017). Strong Black woman schema and psychological distress: The mediating role of perceived emotional support. *Journal of Black Psychology*, *43*(8), 778–788. https://doi.org/10.1177/0095798417732414

Williams, H. V., & Ziobro, M. (Eds.). (2023). *A seat at the table: Black women public intellectuals in US history and culture*. University Press of Mississippi.

Wolf-Wendel, L., & Ward, K. (2015). Academic mothers: Exploring disciplinary perspectives. *Innovative Higher Education*, *40*(1), 19–35. https://doi.org/10.1007/s10755-014-9293-4

ENTER TO LEARN, DEPART TO SERVE: ACCESSING POWER, WHILE WALKING IN CIRCLES

Gwendolyn C. Webb

Texas A & M University, USA

ABSTRACT

Several African American educators served as an inspiration in the development and scholarship of an African American female who teaches at a Predominantly White Institution (PWI) of higher learning. This chapter shares the author's foundational beginnings and persistence in academe while teaching and leading in a race-conscious society. She shares some of her upbringing, education, and early teaching experiences. She also shares her motivation to learn and serve (Bethune, 1950, 1963), while walking in circles. Sizemore (1973, 2008) to provide a roadmap of her journey to support new and developing African American female professors. She uses poetry and the dimensions of African American culture (Boykin, 1983) to guide her sharing. The author uses her exploration of identity development as an African American womanist who advocates as an African American first, to share how she has developed as a scholar whose renewal of purpose targets becoming a full professor.

Keywords: African American females; African American scholars; culturally responsive mentoring; dimensions of African American culture; predominantly White institutions of higher learning; teaching and learning

Strangely, I *knew* Shakespeare before I *knew* me.
My love for *the* theatre, fueled by a Heston
Disguised by a story, poised as the greatest,
And sprinkles of being Mother Earth at age five,
Easter speeches, then high school roles, and college roles
With peripheral visions of being a *star*,
Yet never good enough in the eyes of those who taught me.

Journeys of Black Women in Academe
Diversity in Higher Education, Volume 26, 121–146

ISSN: 1479-3644/doi:10.1108/S1479-364420240000026007

My desire for stardom was steeped
In someone else's perceptions of me
And who I *should* or *could* be?........ (Webb, 2022)

Identity is a shadow that persists in following me. My identity is my shadow, and she persists in following me. I have learned and continue to learn to be me. I have lived a dynamically blessed life. As an African American female, I have often struggled to be who I am, as I learned how to "live" who I am. I am a teacher, and I wanted to be a star. I found my stage in classrooms as I learned to help my students shine in the glory of their identity as they explored the importance of academic engagement. The struggle was real as I learned to affirm who I was so that I could support and teach my learners how to be "free," and successful.

In my early classrooms during the 1970s, I cried a lot. I had no words for what I witnessed and facilitated in high school and then middle school classrooms as a teacher. Yet, I knew who I wanted to serve. I was not effective in that desire, nor the actions that accompanied that desire. I slowly discovered that without knowing who I was, it would be impossible to optimally expose my students to their wonderful possibilities. As a result, I decided to earn a doctorate in special education.

As I earned my doctorate, the importance of mentoring and support bestowed upon me, placed me on a trajectory that continues to challenge me today. I was blessed with wonderful African American scholars who embraced, loved, taught, and challenged me to do and be my best. They were, and some of them are still my mentors. Many years later, I continue to be blessed because they continue to challenge me. However, I have persisted in a quest for the muse that would lead to my ultimate success to better serve others in the field of education. Amid the pandemic and current assault on diversity, equity, and inclusion, I have found my muse, and this chapter shares the Sankofa of my life, with the hope that I may offer support to new or emerging African American female professors in the field.

This chapter will share my foundational beginnings and persistence in academe while teaching and leading in a race-conscious society (Banks, 1993; Gunzenhauser et al., 2024; Pitts, 1974). My motivation to learn and to serve (Bethune, 1950, 1963), while walking in circles (Sizemore, 1973, 2008) will provide a roadmap of my journey. It also highlights my uncommon journey at Predominantly White Institutions (PWIs) of higher learning, intending to become a full professor, while I contemplate my humble imprint to support new and developing African American female professors. In search of myself, I am not yet fully there. However, two African American women, pioneers in the field of education, have paved the way for me. I continue to learn from these two African American scholars.

THE CHALLENGE OF ENTERING WHILE WALKING TO SERVE

Mary McLeod Bethune

Mary McLeod Bethune was born in 1875; she was the 17th child born in her family. She was also the first free-born person in her family and the first in her family to attend school. In fact, all her siblings helped fund her education. She loved school so much that she decided to become a teacher. She opened her own school with $1.50 as an investment to sell sweet potato pies and fried fish. Her doors opened to five girls and her son in 1904 (Peare, 1951). By 1907 she had raised enough funds to build Faith Hall and serve 250 students. That first building, carried her mantra, "Enter to Learn" at its entrance, and "Depart to Serve," as one exited. Mrs. Bethune wrote the foreword to her biography written by Peare (1951):

> ...because I see young Mary McLeod in all struggling boys and girls, I can never rest while there is something that I can do to make the ground firmer under their feet, to make their efforts more productive, to bring their goals nearer, to make their faith in God and their fellow men a little stronger. (p. 12)

Learning about her life (Blackwell, 1979) and talking about her accomplishments, as I escorted visitors to our nation's Capital to see the Bethune Memorial, in Lincoln Park was empowering. Her memorial was the first to honor an African American on public land in Washington, DC. As tour buses passed the home where she once lived, I was able to share excerpts from her life as those visitors to the city received an African American tour experience. I was also proud to share their reactions and experiences with my new students in DC public schools. I had entered a new teaching arena and I found myself walking in circles as I encountered some of the same teaching issues I experienced in Illinois (to be shared later).

Dr Barbara Sizemore

Dr Barbara Sizemore was born in 1927. She was born in Chicago and raised in Terre Haute, Indiana. She attended segregated schools and arrived knowing how to read because her parents had already taught her. She was continually affirmed in her educational environment and she was quite aware of African American identity development. Her third grade taught her to be proud of being a "Negro" (Sizemore, 2008). Her teacher was the author of the "first book about Negro children in the United States" (p. 19). Ms Shackleford taught Dr Sizemore "Knowledge was power. What you don't know can kill you." (p. 19). If Dr Sizemore misbehaved, this dynamic teacher would tap her with a tree limb. Dr Sizemore noted that while she received many bruises during her third grade, she never learned to stop talking. I was so excited to learn that Dr Sizemore was an avid talker throughout her K-12 education. Her teachers affirmed her and demanded that she do and be her best. She was told, "You must be better than white folks. It is not enough to be as good. You must be so good that it becomes impossible to say otherwise" (p. 21).

This scholar wrote about five teachers who nurtured her spirit. I "met" Dr Sizemore when I began attending the annual conferences of the National Alliance of Black School Educators (NABSE), during my doctoral program. As I sought more purposeful emphasis on working with African American learners, I was exposed to Dr Barbara Sizemore's brilliance. She began as a teacher in Chicago

Public Schools (CPS). She also served as a principal in CPS from 1963–1967. She became the first elected African American superintendent of DC Public Schools in 1973 and she served as the Dean of the School Education at De Paul University in 1992. Dr Sizemore studied African American academic excellence in what we now call Title One Schools. She asserted:

> ...that knowledge of African American heritage and culture is essential to developing positive self-concepts, and that we must affirm ourselves in order to understand, appreciate, and successfully pursue excellence in academics. (p. 250)

Her work spoke to my soul as she encouraged freedom fighters (future educators committed to the education of African American learners) who followed. She said,

> ...any approach which fails to address white supremacy and its counterpart, the imputation of Black inferiority, will force you to walk in circles as I have done. Unless you want to wind up where you came in, seek strong confrontation of white supremacy at every opportunity and keep the glare on it. (p. xxiv)

EARLY FOUNDATIONS COMPELLING ME TO SEEK AND FIND

My elementary and secondary education did little to teach me to keep a glare on White supremacy and the imputation of Black inferiority. Nor did it teach me much about the history of people of African descent in the United States and throughout the diaspora. It did, however, teach me that others thought I was less than, even in kindergarten and first grade. I thank God that I had a mother who countered those voices and actions designed to assert a "less than" mentality.

My Mother and Her "Black Mama Stance"

My mother became a parent at the age of 17, however, I have never referred to her as a teenage mother. She grew up taking care of her younger brothers and she was considered an "old" soul because of what she learned from her grandmother and mother. I have no memories of a teenager raising me. She was a giant of intention and action. My mother taught me to read when I was 3 years old.

When I entered kindergarten at the age of four, I was excited about school. I wanted to answer every question and learn everything. On my first day of school, I was told to obey my teacher and walk home with a neighbor, after the half day of instruction. After raising my hand persistently, I began to shout out answers. My teacher spoke to the entire class to share the importance of following directions and speaking when called upon. I apparently paid no attention to those directions because by 10:30 a.m. on a day that began at 9:00 a.m., I was sitting in a corner, facing the wall, with a one-inch piece of masking tape over my mouth.

My teacher resorted to saying, "Shut up," after trying, "purse your lips, 'shh, shh,' be quiet, and good kindergarteners follow instructions." I listened to none of those requests or imperatives. The tape was removed at noon. I was then to walk home with the neighbor. I, however, returned to the afternoon session. I wanted to learn. The teacher called my mother, who came to escort me home. She did not spank me; she told me I needed to be quiet and do what the teacher said. I remember the incident, but I do not remember my teacher's name.

I discovered acting in first grade. I was cast as Mother Earth in "Mother Earth's New Dress." I was so excited. I wore my burlap dress, adorned with plastic flowers, and assumed I was a star. By second grade, I tried out for the next school play. However, I was not cast in the show because as my school tried to deal with the overcrowding, I was transferred for a few months to another school known to educate children from the "better" projects. I could not be in the play, but I could be made to loan my brand-new sweater to the little girl who was given the part for which I auditioned. My sweater was good enough to be in the play, but I was not. I was relieved when we returned to our home school.

My mother knew I was smart, and she persisted in telling me to be quiet in school. That never happened. A few years ago, we found a report card from my 2 weeks in eighth grade. I received a "U" (unsatisfactory) in conduct. I had something in common with Dr Sizemore. She talked and was reprimanded throughout her early education.

I was consistent in talking, and like Dr Sizemore, I always received good grades. My mother persisted in supporting my love for learning and she truly tried to convince me not to talk so much in school. She raised six children in the housing projects and a suburb of Chicago. For much of that time, she was basically a single mother. Teachers did not "see" my mother, they did not truly care to see "her" with all her power as a parent. She also raised two grandchildren with school experiences in that suburb and the State of Texas, while she assisted me as I began my professional career in academia. Schools made negative assumptions, but often, in surprise, commented on how supportive she was. However, they did threaten to have her arrested for spanking or "whupping" her grandson because he disobeyed her instructions to come straight home from school.

After she disciplined my nephew and was threatened with arrest, she said she was not worried because she was sure no one else wanted her 13-year-old grandson. Because she loved him, she was willing to take the risk. She proudly walked into the principal's office and told him that her grandson being obedient was of the utmost importance. My mother's grandmother stance was like her Mama stance!

Again, because I did well in school and was never suspended because of my behavior, I seldom received physical reprimands. My mother saw "me," and few of my teachers did. Much of my school conversation was about the fact that I wanted to "know" everything. The greatest challenge for some of my teachers was the fact that I wanted to understand what I came to know.

I was very frustrated when teachers did not want to take the time to help me understand my questions of "why." I did not like learning just for the sake of learning if explanations and "history" were not a part of the teaching. I developed interesting habits centered around reading. I read the encyclopedia to learn how to (a) tie a tie, (b) describe the digestive system, or (c) design costumes from different periods. I learned the designated curriculum, but I learned little in school about who I was as a cultural and racial being.

I did not know why my elementary school was chosen for a feature newspaper article as it shared that the children from the projects would be going to camp for a weekend. I did not know why everyone was so surprised that I was excited about taking a shower. The reporter acted like I did not bathe. Our apartment did not have a shower. It had a bathtub. I did not know then I was being objectified as the "poor Black child from the projects." I did not know why adults were so surprised that I loved going to museums and especially loved The Art Institute. I loved learning about the many periods of art history and the styles of artistry used by artists like Monet and Picasso. I did not understand at that time that no artist of African descent was introduced to me. I was fascinated to learn that the college student from a nearby suburban liberal arts college introduced me to The Art Institute because she wanted to teach me something I did not know. Her tutoring was not successful in teaching me to be a better reader or better at my multiplication tables. I already knew that information. My two African American and one Asian American teacher had already done that by the fifth grade. My European American teachers always focused on trying to get me not to talk so much. I have no memories of my teachers of color trying to stop my talking; they tried to redirect my constant chatter.

My tutor from the liberal arts college became more interested in sharing with me her love for learning and she appreciated that I wanted those postcards to study the techniques of so many famous artists of European descent. Few of my teachers did that. When we visited the small liberal arts college, I was enthralled by the fact that college students had a food fight in the cafeteria, and no one was upset by the action.

Middle and High School

By seventh grade, my elementary school, in a large urban school district, was even more overcrowded. My older brother and I were given the option to take a test to skip the last 2 weeks of seventh grade and attend eighth grade for 2 weeks to take the constitution test. My brother did this in 1967 and I followed suit in 1968. I went to high school at age 13 and graduated at age 16.

I discovered acting again in high school when we moved to the suburbs. While I was Mother Earth in a first-grade production, I did not act again until I entered a suburban high school in a predominantly European American environment. I was blessed to have a theater teacher who was very conscious of the social climate of the times. As a result, we did plays that championed multicultural casts and political messages. We earned third place in the state competition for one-act plays with our rendition of "Viet Rock." We proudly traveled from the stage to the audience, challenging the societal status quo at ages 14–18. This play provided chanting and dialog with music, dance, and pantomime while championing satire on attitudes about the Vietnam War. We did another play, *J. B.*, about the character Job in the Bible as told by a modern-day millionaire, with God and the Devil telling their stories in poetic verse, from the top of a Coke can and a Snickers bar.

I do not remember talking about race as part of a group of high school students, but I do remember competitions where students from other suburban school districts did not have a growing number of African American students. We were different, we were controversial, and our Drama teacher, a young and energetic European American female, loved us, and taught us to display our dynamic talent to answer those concerns about our worth through that talent. We won often and we were proud of our controversy and our success. Yet we did not talk about it. At our home school, we did musicals with multicultural casts as lighthearted as *Little Me*, and *Mr. Wonderful*. Our teacher created a safe place where we grew and learned as students.

A Liberal Arts College Experience

College was completely different. By that time, I knew I wanted to major in theater, but the small liberal arts college I attended did not embrace their one African American theater major with integrity and respect. The purpose of a liberal arts education is to prepare learners for intellectual and spiritual experiences so they can learn to take broader learning experiences into real life, as they work with others.

I truly loved theater for theater's sake, but I was often lonely in my classes and while on set for stage productions. I did not see anyone who looked like me daily, in my classes. The plays were about European and French snapshots of life. I played a "Sweet Young Thing," in a play about the French Revolution. My costume was beautiful, but I was a young woman taken advantage of by a man. As a result, I had few chances for laughter or joy in the reflection of my daily experiences. The only time I felt joy in my choice of a major was when I did something to bring African Americans "to the theater." I invited friends to work on production sets with me. When I designed costumes, I recruited friends to assist in making costumes. When I had to direct a one-act play, I recruited an African American upperclassman to perform in "The Slave," written by LeRoi Jones (1964), who later changed his name to Amiri Baraka (1964). My friend reluctantly came, and he was phenomenal in the one-person stage production. My friends I invited to "the theater," loved the fact that the play was about an African American man confronting his White ex-wife and her new White husband during a race war in the 1960s. I also invited my African American friends to try out for my college production of the musical, "The Me Nobody Knows," (Livington et al., 1970). The production was based on the writings of children who grew up in New York City.

My high school drama teacher took a group of us to see a production of this Broadway musical, in Chicago. Because the musical had such a significant impact on me, I decided to direct and design the costumes for my capstone theater experience in college. I received a grade of "C" on that project. My professors felt that my cast did not demonstrate enough knowledge about the project and they did not believe I demonstrated the type of growth one should in a capstone project. My friends enjoyed the experience, I enjoyed the experience. Most important, I learned from the experience, but none of my professors asked me what I learned. More importantly, I did not know how to process the experience as one honoring the original authors of the self-expression experienced in the musical. Yet, each one of us resonated with the experiences of the authentic authors of the text and the music. My professors only shared how the project did not measure up to their "theatrical" standards. None of my professors gave me suggestions as I produced the musical. I had no words in response. I never talked about it with my college theater department. I accepted my grade of "C." I was "The Me Nobody Knows," at a small liberal arts college in the Midwest. I graduated and began my journey as a teacher.

Loved the Idea of Teaching, While Knowing Little About the Purposeful Impact

I entered the field as a young secondary teacher who struggled. At the age of 20, I did not know how to create a line between my role as a teacher, and my role as a "friend" to my students. I did not understand that my job was not to be their friend, but to be their teacher. My first teaching position was at my high school alma mater. I felt uncomfortable calling my former teachers by their first names. As a result, I avoided settings where such expectations existed. I did not go to the teacher's lounge; I did not go to the faculty cafeteria.

I spent most of my time outside of my classrooms with high school students. I walked to school with my younger sister and cousin. I walked home from theater and speech team rehearsals with my students. I knew many of them from church and the suburban neighborhood. I directed plays and forensic competitions. I was the sponsor of the cheerleading squad. I attempted to convince my sister, not to refer to me by my first name as she walked past my classroom door.

I confused my learners. They waited to have fun with me when my department chair came to observe me. For example, on one occasion, one of my students, a popular and talented basketball player, sat in my chair, put his feet up on my desk, and asked, "So what are we going to learn today, Gwen?" Everyone laughed. My department chair was appalled, and he documented what he observed. When asked what I had to say about the behavior of my students, again, I had no words. Yet, my students were never confused about my focus on higher education when it came to discussing their academic future.

I Stressed the Importance of a Higher Education

As I sat with my students during lunch and talked about the importance of going to college, they listened. That basketball player went to college. He became a professional player and then a head coach for the NBA. One young man on the speech team (under my direction) shared many years later that he went to college because I said I knew he would be successful. He attributes my encouragement of him writing an extemporaneous speech about his birth, as the beginning of his personal belief in himself. He felt he lived in the shadow of successful parents and brilliant siblings, with no place for himself. He had little confidence about what he brought to his family arena. He knew he was loved, but did he have what it took to go to college like his parents and his older siblings? His father was a successful insurance salesperson and broker. His mother was a minister and teacher. His brother was a doctor, and his sister was a registered nurse.

That young man said my mentorship (Davis et al., 2022), meant the world to him because he believed I saw him amid the discovery of his promise. He won several speech competitions during his high school career and then majored in theater in college. Many years later, his son entered the university where I taught, and I was able to mentor him over 5 years as he served in a PWI military school experience and earned a teacher certification (Webb, 2021). I circled back to the father and served the son. I worked diligently with him to help him understand the context of teacher development and how he would be perceived as an African American male in a race-conscious society. While he was a successful graduate, he chose not to become a teacher. He chose not to confront the biased racist policies he saw manifested in schools and decided to become a police officer in a large urban area. He chose to serve and protect while confronting societal bias on a different level. He was and is the epitome of what DuBois posited in 1905. He exercised his right to think, know, and aspire.

LEARNING TO BE PURPOSEFUL IN TEACHING AFRICAN AMERICAN LEARNERS

It was not until 1988 that I learned of the life and legacy of Mary McLeod Bethune (Leffall & Sims, 1976). I left Illinois and moved to Washington, DC. At a special education conference, I learned that most of the children served in DC Public schools were African American. I was so excited. After crying for 11 years as I struggled to become an exemplary teacher in the state of Illinois, I was sure that moving to "Chocolate City," Washington, DC would make a difference. I was convinced that this system would help me understand how to better serve African American children.

I was shocked to learn that DC Public schools experienced the same challenges I found in the state of Illinois. All of my experiences pointed to me and what I did not know as I strived to become an excellent teacher. However, I "met" Mary Mcleod Bethune as I studied DC History to be able to teach the subject matter. I knew nothing of the rich "Black" history of Washington DC. A tour company was using the same textbook that I would be using as a teacher in the DC system, so I decided to join the class. The African American owner of the company said I might as well earn the tour guide certification. As a result, I became a licensed tour guide for a company that provided tours on the African American history of the nation's capital. The tour company and my teaching experiences changed my professional life at that time.

When one entered my Washington, DC classrooms for learners who demonstrated severe behavioral challenges, the words, "Enter to Learn," greeted them.

The words "Depart to Serve," offered a farewell as they left. I felt so empowered in my teaching. My teaching experience was affirmed for the 4 years I taught in our nation's capital. I even received a teaching award. Principals, department chairs, and teachers affirmed my teaching and effectiveness with African American learners on two campuses. Yet, I wanted more as it relates to improving my teaching toolkit. While I felt better in a predominantly African American environment, there was still something missing in my consciousness and actions as a teacher. My colleagues thought I was too optimistic in my teaching. Most of my colleagues, who looked just like me, did not appreciate me not referring to my students as troublemakers, or "bad" children. I was often teased, and I also became the object of many jokes. They believed that learners who were unsuccessful in general education environments were "bad." They thought I was confused when I used person-first language to say my students demonstrated behavioral challenges. I did not say they were emotionally disturbed. I struggled to find like-minded colleagues who would listen to ideas about how to more effectively teach learners who experienced challenges. Again, I was walking in circles. I then decided to return to school for my doctorate.

My Doctoral Journey

When I entered my doctoral program, I was faced with fellow doctoral students who were European American and female. They made their opinions very clear, "it is a really good time (1990)" to be African American and female. Their beliefs asserted that I was "lucky," because so many resources were available to me. I had a fellowship. I was the only African American female in special education. I was always happy. Many of the topics in our classes addressed multicultural education. Further, they asserted that the two African American professors (from Special Education and Curriculum and Instruction) acted like they had known me for a very long time. They never said they wished they were African American because they viewed me as "so" lucky. They merely thought I had it made because the system was predicated on providing me assistance in the program.

These women also shared that they were happy we had feminism in common. This was my first introduction to the term and the sentiment. They thought we should be supportive of one another because we were all women. They wanted me to choose to advocate for women first because together we could change the modes of the "old boys" network in the College of Education and the field of education. I made it very clear that I saw no reason to advocate only for the fact that I was a female. I often shared, "I am African American and female." I chose not to put one identity aside for the sake of joining forces with other women. I went on to share that if I was "forced" to make a choice, I would always choose my positionality as an African American first. Being considered a feminist did not rest well in my soul. I rejected the term because I felt forced to take a side. The European American women with whom I interacted in my doctoral program, consistently shared with me that they did not think about their race as they thought about being female. They were feminists, advocating for women. They urged me to join them to get to know each other better. I resisted.

At this time in my educational journey, I knew nothing about Black Feminist Thought and the intersectionality of race, culture, gender, and socioeconomic status (Collins, 1986, 1990, 1996). I did not understand the power of the two terms together. Could I live as a Black Feminist with other African American women in the academy? There was only one other African American doctoral student in the college, and we agreed with one another. It was not until 1990 that I ever read about the term Black Feminist Thought.

My introduction to the scholarship of Patricia Hill Collins remained dormant until I discovered the literary work of Alice Walker and the term she coined, Womanism (Walker, 1988). The term was first used in 1967 and officially coined in 1979. It champions the lived experiences of Black women, their culture, their history, and the term feminism in an African American context. As she shared her literary genius, she contextualized the lived experiences of African American mothers and foremothers who observed and "mothered," their daughters, while reflecting on Black Folklore which often profiled young women who were "womanish beyond your age" (Walker, 1988).

The work of Patricia Hill Collins then caused an explosion of life in me as I worked with other African American women in the Academy. While I continued to remain silent about my advocacy as an African American first, and a woman second, I saw and lived how Womanism and Black Feminist Thought could live together in culturally responsive harmony and consciousness (Boykin, 1983; Brewer, 2016, 2020; Collins, 1996, 2000; Kotak, 2015; Tally, 1986).

As I share now, these revelations are important as I think about a new generation of African American female scholars in the field of education and the African American learners we serve. African American women are "experts on a Black woman's standpoint" (Collins, 1996, p. 547). I was one of a "large number of African American women who reject the term feminism because of what they perceive as its association with whiteness" (Collins, 1996, p. 19). However, I now better understand the importance of navigating the "need for counter spaces and counternarratives in intersectionality and identity development" (Brewer, 2016; Porter & Byrd, 2021), as it pertains to African American women. We resist domination and "anchor our knowledge claims in and through an Afrocentric feminist epistemology" (Collins, 1996, p. 547). My counternarratives were developed with important African American people along the way. I found mentors who looked like me.

MY MENTORS LOOKED LIKE ME

After I entered my doctoral program, I also faced life as a single mother wanting to pursue the possibility of teaching at the university level. As I pursued my plan of study, I began to join professional organizations and explore where I might teach teachers. I met amazing African American scholars who remain my mentors today. It was amazing to watch scholars talk about the brilliance of African American children.

Dr Scholar

I met a young African American man during my doctoral studies. We were recipients of a fellowship created to prepare more scholars of color for our home state. While we were not at the same university, we saw each other often. I did not know then that Dr Scholar would become the president of a university, however, I did know that he was a "brother" who was committed to African American identity development. He told me to not buy into people referring to me as a "loud and angry" Black woman. He said, "My sistuh, you are powerful." He persisted in telling me to work hard and manifest the greatness inside of me. As an African American man, he was uplifting to every African American woman he met in academia.

Dr Scholar walked and continues to walk to the beat of a spiritual drum that eradicates hopelessness in the African American and general community. He defies gravity as he soars beyond the expectations of most to embody the brilliance and dynamism of African Americans and his campus community. He taught me to say and to manifest, "I do not apologize for loving my people." In concert, he leads a PWI by inviting "all" on his campus to travel with him as they achieve greatness for each of the young people they serve. He inspires and motivates me on a daily basis. All of my "Sistuh" mentors have come to know him over many years.

MY "SISTUH" GIRLS

Dr Peachy

I met Dr Peachy at a special education conference. I developed a reputation with her as the "groupie." I introduced myself while in my doctoral program at a professional conference and said, "I want to get to know you. I want to be your friend." Dr Peachy told me she did not want any more friends and she did not want to get to know me or anyone else. I persisted and as I read her work, I discovered we were both theater majors in college. We both taught children demonstrating behavioral disorders before we joined the academy. Her research incorporated theater rehearsal techniques as a method to improve their decision-making strategies in the area of social skills. I persisted and she finally embraced me. It took almost 2 years to develop a meaningful relationship with Dr Peachy.

She empowered me through her work and her wisdom in the academy. We had intense discussions (she called them arguments) about instructional racism. Because she rejected the status quo, she challenged me regularly and asserted that I was "insane" because the educational world in which we lived was insane. In all her assertions, her genuine and genius nature of love and commitment to African American learners remained rays of sunshine in our work together.

Dr Peachy was often "forced" (by another mentor and me) to share a wonderful story of her meeting The Rev. Dr Martin Luther King Jr at the opening of her brand-new high school in the Midwest. She was a sophomore. The entire student population was excited that he was coming to visit. Dr Peachy had been chosen to sing the national anthem. She could, "sang!" She carefully chose her clothes from a box of hand-me-down clothes given to her family. Her mother instructed her children to choose what they wanted and to throw the other garments away. She chose a blouse, skirt, and pair of socks. She did not realize the blouse was a pajama top. The skirt was too large, so she added a belt. She held her socks in place around her calves with rubber bands. Dr Peachy had "big" legs.

Each time she told this story, she spiced it up with more theatrics. For example, she shared that a popular football player in her high school always warmed her legs on a cold day. After rubbing his large hands together, he massaged her legs. We roared with laughter because she was so tickled at the memory. When it was time for her to sing, one of the football players and Dr King helped lift her to the stage. In the process, the blouse was pulled from inside the skirt's waistband. One of her socks slipped to her ankle. As she sang, Dr King said, "Sing baby." The applause was thunderous.

Her sister ran home crying and told their mother how embarrassed she was because Dr Peachy was wearing a pajama top and it was hanging from her skirt. Her socks were sloppy and she was grinning like she had the best day of her life. Dr Peachy shared that her mother was just proud of her and Dr King could care less about how she looked. She said the top was cute. Every time she told that story, we laughed and cried because she continued to make her point that children should be empowered to be their best and she sang her heart out because the Rev. Dr Martin Luther King Jr visited her school and said he was proud of her predominantly African American student body doing so well in school.

In our frequent conversations, she emphasized that I had to find my own voice, not hers. She supported me while she reminded me, repeatedly, that she did not want to be my friend. We always laughed about that. When she died, she had been my "sistuh gurl," for 22 years.

Dr Dragon Lady

I also met Dr Dragon Lady (a name she called one of her professors) at a special education conference. When we first met, we discussed the virtues of lotion made with Vaseline as a major ingredient. I told her she was a true "sistuh" girl because Vaseline was necessary so one would not be "ashy." We bonded over the fact that one should not look as though they had been "kicking" flour if their ankles were showing. Dr Dragon Lady was also a special education teacher before she earned her doctorate. She became Dr Dragon Lady because she was a stickler as we discussed our writing. Knowing the King's English to prepare manuscripts was important. She was and is a phenomenal writer who will breathe fire into a discussion of a manuscript. She is a stickler for "proper" grammar and "clarity" in one's writing.

It was as if the eight parts of speech were her middle names as we wrote, shared, and critiqued our work. She often gave lectures on writing sanctions. In one lecture on the use of an appositive, she said, "One does not say or write, my sister, she; we already know she is a female." "Can you explain why this sentence is four lines long? How long is the run-on going to run on? How many conjunctions are you going to use? Can we find some periods?" "Are you attempting to make your title a paragraph? That is too many words, Gwennie. Keep it simple." So many of these question-filled conversations were punctuated by Dr Dragon Lady saying, "I'll wait..."

I also followed Dr Dragon Lady's scholarship and attended her sessions on African American men studying to become special education teachers. Her projects transformed her college of education at an urban Research I PWI. She challenged her colleagues to see and value differences, not as deficits, but as differences. I was in awe of the brilliance of the young men with whom she worked, and her ability to showcase and help develop their brilliance as they studied to become educators. She was and is always open and candid about the perceptions of her invisibility in the academy as a loss to those who would dare to attempt to define her in any way. Her vision of her scholarship is deeply steeped in the power of knowing herself and her worth with no apologies on any level. Her mentorship and professional support offer a timeless standard of excellence that is inspirational to African American women.

Dr Peachy and Dr Dragon Lady both served as my mentors and eventually became my dear friends as we shared experiences because we worked at PWIs. Their mentorship was from afar. Colleagues and friends are often baffled by the deep structural importance of our relationships. Dr Peachy has gone on to glory, but Dr Dragon Lady and I continue to talk every day there is a day. Most of our conversations are about our work. While these two women were in different parts of the country, they mentored and supported me unconditionally. I also had two other mentors who taught with me at the same PWI.

Dr First Lady

I first met Dr First Lady when she and her husband, Dr Pastor visited my doctoral program. They were a beautiful couple who were "coordinated," as they presented on multicultural education in the development of preservice teachers. They wore suits the same color, "olive green," and her blouse, his tie, and pocket square were complimented by different shades of green. He was the pastor of a church and she was his first lady. They were both university professors at a Research I PWI. They began as teachers in K-12 settings, earned their doctorates at the same university, and taught at the same university in two different colleges.

They worked together to explore and define the importance of multicultural education in the development of teachers in agriculture and curriculum and instruction. I again was in awe. During their visit, I was one of the doctoral students asked to join them for dinner. Dr First Lady said, "When you finish your program, I want you to come teach with me." She meant what she said. She kept in contact with me and upon completion of my program, I interviewed in her department and was hired.

Dr First Lady has been my ally, advocate, and friend since the beginning of my teaching in higher education. She too gave true meaning to "you my sistuh girl." She was adamant about not wanting to be the only African American tenure track scholar in her department. She invited me to write with her, present with her, and teach some of the same classes. More than 30 years later, I continue to write and present with her. She gave me feedback as she challenged me to do and be my best. "Okay girlie, you can do better." She invited me to her home and her church. When she and Dr Pastor retired, I believe I went into mourning for two years.

To say they are missed is an understatement. Dr First Lady and Dr Pastor taught me the importance of engaging students of color at a PWI. I watched them create a home away from home for many young people. Dr First Lady taught some of her multicultural education classes in her home. She also invited students to their church and for dinner. Students knew they were valued. I watched her challenge students who may have been neglecting their responsibilities. I incorporated her mentoring strategies into my life.

My learning has been a journey of strategic care and protection for the development of myself, my craft, and my destiny. I did not do this alone. As I traveled, culturally responsive mentoring accompanied the shadow following me. My mentors (Bertrand Jones et al., 2020; Davis et al., 2022; Griffin, 2013; Griffin et al., 2020), who looked like me assisted me in finding the research framework most meaningful to me as an African American female scholar. That shadow was joined by some dimensions that further helped to define me.

DISCOVERING THE DIMENSIONS OF AFRICAN AMERICAN CULTURE

As I met my mentors, I still did not understand fully who I was as a racial and cultural being. I often dressed in accents of African fabric. Kente Cloth could have been called a dear friend. I was learning more about African American history and the contributions of African Americans in the United States and the diaspora. However, I had little understanding of what that meant in the context of my own identity development and my desire to effectively and purposefully educate African American learners.

As I pursued my studies, I sought a conceptual framework to guide my new learning for my proposed record of study. I did an ERIC search and discovered A.W. Boykin, a psychologist from Howard University, one of the oldest Historically Black Colleges and Universities in the country. He introduced me to the nine "Dimensions of African American Culture" (DAAC). I was ecstatic.

When I had the opportunity to meet Dr Boykin, he shared with me his reasoning for developing the Dimensions. He said, "Gwen if we study African ethos," we learn that some things just "is." He said there were clear patterns in our culture that one could trace back to Africa. I held on to his assertion of "is" and developed an integrity and strength (IS) ideology to develop strategies to be used in classrooms based on the nine dimensions.

I have used DAAC throughout my career. Most of my research projects addressing the culturally responsive engagement of African American learners have included Boykin's Dimensions. I took Boykin's definitions and expanded them to include a curriculum and instruction context to support principals and teachers in creating classrooms that purposefully transform the engagement of African American learners to IS contexts. Table 1 shares some strategies for embracing the nine dimensions in vibrant classrooms, designed to enhance and strengthen academic development and reduce discipline and suspension consequences among African American learners.

Table 1. Integrity and Strength Models (IS).

Dimension Strategy	Description
Spirituality IS	Organizing instruction with the prospective possibility that more than observable and material aspects of the classroom have value. Encouraging children to act on their curiosity while solving a problem or accepting their convictions is potentially useful in their decision-making processes, even though they may not initially be able to understand or explain the vital force that motivates them. Implementing repeated efforts to acknowledge, accept, and enhance epistemologies (ways of knowing) as an integral part of curriculum planning and implementation.
Harmony IS	Organizing classrooms to highlight the linkage of one to one's surroundings. Initiating activities that are a direct result of previous activities and allowing students to help plan for the acquisition of excellence because he/she is a part of the larger picture. Constructing activities that highlight the versatility of individuals and foster collective harmony within the atmosphere of the classroom, school, community, and home.
Movement IS	Organizing classrooms and instruction to typify the individual and group through movement and music. Designing lessons that flow to a beat of vitality. Students need and want to move from place to place and from concept to concept through ideas, thoughts, reality, and fantasy. Orchestrating movement to allow students to address the possible and the perceived impossible within specific contexts of movement.
Verve IS	Designing instruction that highlights variety in activity levels and variability. Presenting information that addresses the propensity toward energetic, intensive, and lively stimulation and personal actions. Addressing the possibility and reality that students can often attend to more than one concept at a time. Building classroom engagement on the premise of diunital interactions and not merely dichotomous ones. Creating a catalog of choices stressing variability and intense interactions in presentation and participation.
Affect IS	Addressing the importance of "person to person" or "member to member" interactions within the classroom. Facilitating instruction that encourages emotional acknowledgment and commitment from students and creating opportunities to practice skills effectively. Refining the ability to identify, read, be sensitive to, accept, and/or reject the emotional aspects of the classroom interactions to affirm where and how one should reside in their identity development.
Communalism IS	Utilizing the social rather than object orientation of students. Designing programs that take advantage of the use of cooperative group opportunities, creates vehicles for the promotion of sharing, learning, and helping others for its own intrinsic value. Providing practice in determining when it is more appropriate to act for the good of the group and when it is appropriate to make decisions based on individual needs within the context of the classroom.

Table 1. *(Continued)*

Dimension Strategy	Description
Expressive Individualism IS	Stressing the importance of each individual articulating his/her own style. Instructional practice embracing the mixture of many components of an activity to create an individual formula. This strength may be highlighted through a variety of mediums (i.e., speech patterns, interaction styles *(TWA)*, studying techniques, dress, interests, or approaches to a task.)
Oral Tradition IS	Utilizing the historical development of African American language for classroom enrichment. Demonstrating communication and language as a powerful tool through, exaggeration, mimicry, punning, spontaneity, etc. that is integrated into all subject areas to capitalize first on classroom dynamics and secondly to provide a historical perspective on the development of language in America and its impact on the learning environment.
Social Time Perspective IS	Acknowledging that behavior is bound to traditions and customs in a social context. Designing motivational classroom strategies that enhance the use of tradition and immediacy, when appropriate. Providing a dynamic emphasis on the events in which students engage to foster self-definition of learning persistence and needs. Providing more time on an assignment when beneficial, thereby encouraging students to engage in planning and decision-making that supports high expectations and refusal to yield to difficulties that might arise in the pursuit of knowledge.

*Source: *Developed by* Webb based on Boykin's Dimensions of African American Culture (Boykin, 1983).

Note: The above strategies use Boykin's Dimensions of African American culture as a conceptual framework for culturally responsive curriculum and instructional development.
These modes in instructional and curriculum design influence the active participation of African American children in their learning process, highlight the integrity and strength brought to the classroom, and address specific skill challenges through cultural frameworks.

Not Earning Tenure and Promotion Initially and Now Working Toward the "Prize" in Academe

Upon the completion of my doctorate, I began my work in the academy in a curriculum and instruction department dedicated to preparing preservice teachers. I had a secondary position in the Department of Special Education. This was a tenuous marriage because many of my new colleagues knew little about how an Assistant Professor could successfully be a part of these two departments. I was questioned about my research agenda in general and special education. Inclusion was a challenge because each department worked specifically to ensure that programs prepared developing teachers to be successful in all subject areas or the areas of demonstrated disabilities. As I supervised general and special education preservice teachers, they were uncomfortable outside of their "designated" roles. When our program partnered them with one another in the classroom, the developing general education teachers thought their job was to interact only with general education students. Special education teachers thought their job was to interact only with students demonstrating disabilities. Inclusion was stagnant because our departments were not clear on how to "teach" them how to work together. As a result, our students were not clear on how to be culturally responsive partners. The more we discussed these issues, the more confused leadership in both departments was as it relates to me. I was instructed to choose "one home," because it would be difficult to assess the impact of my work collectively.

Leadership in the college and my two departments changed three times in 4 years. Consequently, they did not know how to consistently advise me on how to earn tenure and promotion. Amid this, I was asked to apply to the special education department at another Research I PWI in the state. I applied and was hired. I then spent 6 years (because I had to restart my tenure clock) and focused specifically on special education in an urban setting with concentrated foci on African American cultural contexts in PreK-12 settings. During my fifth year, I was not granted tenure.

One of the most painful incidents I experienced at my second Research I institution was being accused of padding my vita as I sought promotion and tenure. I joined a writing group composed of African American females. I believed we had a good working relationship. We wrote several refereed articles together. We worked together and decided we would equally distribute the percentages of our respective contributions to each article. When my dossier was presented, it was reported to me that the percentages in my vita were different from one of the other authors. I was told to resolve the issue. When I went to that individual, I was told, "Oh, I have already been promoted. I don't think it matters Gwen, just put whatever you want." I was devastated. I wrote in my dossier what we had discussed and adhered to what the group decided. I also received mixed reviews on my teaching. Some students believed I spent too much time using examples about African American learners as I taught about learners who demonstrated emotional disturbances or behavioral disorders. I was given one more year of employment as I sought another position. I spent 6 years at this institution and did not achieve tenure and promotion.

As I began to look for another position, colleagues shared negative opinions about my work, not only in the department, but also at the state level, and throughout the country. I was told that I was not a team player. It was shared that I only wanted to talk and teach about African American issues. I was perceived as the "angry Black woman." Some of this was shared during my interviews at other institutions.

I was then invited to reapply at my first institution. This invitation came from the Acting Provost (a wonderful European American administrator). He spoke with Dr Pastor, and Dr Pastor contacted me. We prepared for my interview. I was rehired and the institution accepted some of my work from the previous 10 years. I earned tenure and promotion 3 years later. I was finally an Associate Professor. I spent 13 years as an Assistant Professor!

I have not yet become a full professor. That is my ultimate goal in academe. Almost 18 years later, I am not a full professor. I have not tried. I have not submitted a dossier. I had a few traumatic incidents in my personal life which impacted my progress. My scholarly production and teaching evaluations are not what they should be. I want developing scholars who are African American women to learn from my experience.

I take full responsibility and ownership for the present state of my academic realities. I am not interested in a "blame" game. I am happy and joyous in my identity and the continuation of my journey. I must actualize my happiness and joy and become a full professor.

ENTERING, SERVING, AND CIRCLING IN THE ACADEMY

My learning has been a journey of strategic care and protection for the development of myself, my craft, and my destiny. What does it mean to be an African American in a race-conscious society? What does it mean to be an African American woman, a womanist, in a race-conscious society? What does it mean to understand how I came to be and how can I use such learning in more strategic and dynamic ways as I conduct research, and teach university classes in the areas of special education, curriculum and instruction, and leadership?

I have served as one who prepared general and special education teachers at two large Southwestern Research I PWIs. Presently, I serve as one who also prepares school principals and superintendents at one of these flagships. In these three positions, I have traveled in circles, seeking to do and be my best as one who "educates" educators.

IN PURSUIT OF MY SANKOFA—LESSONS LEARNED

I am most intrigued by the importance of sociocultural tenets as an important part of how I think and behave as an African American female scholar. As a lifelong educator, I have faced important shortcomings (on my part) that interfered with the effectiveness of my research and teaching. This occurred when I taught in PreK-12 settings, and as I taught in Research I institutions of higher learning. In my former setting, I was impacted by my lack of knowledge and support from those who could have been my professional support. I had no clue about the importance of culturally responsive engagement.

I believe my early teacher preparation program was based on "common" thoughts of teaching and learning. I was prompted to "teach" in particular ways that did not honor the prior knowledge brought to classrooms by diverse learners or myself. Supervisors in my preparation provided me with a "model" of best practices based on research modeled by the dominant population in America's schools. Many of these practices did not work for me as I progressed through elementary, secondary education, and higher education. I was taught to comply. While I remembered that piece of tape covering my mouth on my first day of kindergarten, I was perplexed about how to take that experience and provide something lasting for my students. I knew they had a voice that should be supported, but I did not know the necessary "how," to effectively "teach" and act on their behalf in culturally responsive and sustaining ways (Paris & Alim, 2014).

As I continued to attempt to develop my teaching, I felt I was on the outside, looking in, and I did not want this for my future students. As a result, I launched a journey in pursuit of culturally responsive pedagogy that would honor and make "all" finally mean "all" in American schools. While more challenges were created, I found a pathway to explore what it meant to effectively teach "all" children—the six largest groups of learners in public schools, African American, Asian American, European American, Latinx American, Native/Indigenous American, and Arab American. However, a keen and strategic focus has been and is on African American learners. I will never apologize for loving my people as a member of the African American community.

I have learned that I never want to stop learning. As a lifelong learner, I want to develop a better understanding of how facts and procedures are transmitted to stimulate and facilitate deeper conceptual understandings. I want to better teach the importance of prior knowledge and its connections to authentic reflections which can transform the lives of children and youth as I assist in transforming the lives of the developing scholars I teach. I want a better understanding and action foundation for authentic dynamic processes in learning, socialization, and funds of knowledge in qualitative and quantitative contexts. The icing on my multicultural mosaic is the effective use of a collective "me," who enters to learn, departs to serve, and walks in Sankofa circles to do what I have been gifted to do by a spiritual power for which I also do not apologize. I have learned the power of my faith and know the grace and mercies I am afforded because of my faith (Webb, 2021).

I have learned to take pride in not apologizing for my keen emphasis on African American learners throughout my career, especially in higher education, at a PWI. I realized I needed to expand this pathway into teaching and leadership preparation because concepts of "all" needed pedagogy that would honor the learning processes of many, again with my keen emphasis on African American learners. I do not apologize for loving my people. I do not apologize for loving the promise in "all" people. I have learned to be me, as I have found my muse.

As I continue to mentor new and developing scholars, I want them to know the importance of not procrastinating in the personal and professional search for who they are. I want them to know they will articulate their commitment to scholarship and work in the academy. The eradication of procrastination is an ally that can be accessed by embracing one's identity and the mentors in life who truly "see" and value them. Simply put, find a mentor who looks like you and has similar research interests. Find someone conscious about their racial and socialized identity in the academy. I have not had mentors formally assigned to me during my time in academia. If your institution provides assigned mentors, you must be a part of the process that chooses one from your campus. Reaching out to your professional learning communities can be a great asset in this process. Our world in the academy is a small and powerful one (Griffin, 2019). Leadership and colleagues in leadership positions at both my PWIs talked at me and not to me. Some did try to assist me, but they seldom demonstrated any desire to "know me," from my perspective. Many colleagues meant well, but few discussions deconstructed what it meant to get to know "me" and my commitment to anti-racist leadership (Gunzenhauser et al., 2024).

CONCLUSION

> You have searched me, LORD, and you know me.....
> You discern my going out and my lying down; you are familiar with all my ways....
> I praise you because I am fearfully and wonderfully made;
> your works are wonderful, I know that full well.....
> How precious to me are your thoughts, God! How vast is the sum of them! (Psalms 139: 1-18 NIV)

This scripture now guides what I have learned, how I am serving, and the power of Sankofa, which guides my walking in purposeful circles. Identity is a shadow that has persisted in following me. My identity is my shadow who persisted in following me to be *me* with renewed purpose. My final recommendation to developing African American females in academe, is to find and refine your muse, as you (a) conduct your research, (b) teach developing scholars, and (c) provide service to your array of communities. I close with an example of the axiology of my muse and the collective lessons I have learned as a result.

THE AXIOLOGY OF MY MUSE

There is an African proverb that says it takes an entire village to raise a child. In the school of education at my PWI, we take pride in our efforts to transform lives. I have modified the proverb. "It does indeed take an entire village to *educate* a child, but we must first reconstruct the village because quite frankly, the educational village is messed up." I This is true, especially as it relates to better serving African American learners, especially girls. Indulge my thoughts as I share the present axiology of my muse to eradicate the miseducation of African American learners (Woodson, 1933).

SCENARIO: MY GRANDDAUGHTERS AND ALL MY BABY GIRLS

Imagine you see the pictures of two beautiful African American girls. Those are my grandbabies, Nia and Imani. Are those beautiful faces or what? Thank you for knowing the truth! As you look at their faces, I know you see their physical beauty. But do you see their intellectual beauty? Know that their faces are the faces of thousands of African American girls. As babies, it is often easy for others to see their physical beauty. But do you see that same beauty as it relates to their brilliance and academic potential? By the time they, like many other African American girls, are age four, they are thrust into an educational system that over-disciplines, over-suspends and criminalizes them because of their behavior, their attitude (Webb, 2019), and their choice of dress (Morris, 2016).

Do you realize that their identity is supported by their "attitude?" An African American girl demonstrates verve, one of A. Wade Boykin's (1983) nine dimensions of African American culture. She may rock her neck from side to side, she may put her hands on her imagination (some people call this her hips), she may talk back to an adult, she may "get in your business," and she may give you "side eye." She may tell you exactly what is on her mind with no filter.

Research has focused considerably on African American males because they too embrace challenges because of our systems' lack of respecting who they are. Seven percent of the school-age population comprises African American boys. Eight percent of the school-age population is African American girls. They are 15% of the school-age population in public schools, yet they account for almost 36% of all school suspensions (U.S. Department of Education & Office for Civil Rights, 2023). African American boys are 3 times more likely to be suspended from school when compared to European American males, and an African American girl is 6 times more likely to be suspended when compared to European American female peers (Crenshaw et al., 2015).

In 1905, W.E.B. DuBois, a noted African American scholar wrote:

> Education is the development of power and ideal. We want our children trained as intelligent human beings should be, and we will fight for all time against any proposal to educate black boys and girls simply as servants and underlings, or simply for the use of other people. They have a right to know, to think, to aspire. (p. 2)

It is now 2024, and the mantra remains the same, "We want our children educated! They have the right to know, to think, and to aspire (Du Bois, 1905)."

Some of my current and former doctoral students and I have been working with fifth and sixth-grade African American girls who are experiencing problems in the areas of behavior and the perceptions of their attitude. The research is virtually void in listening to their voices. They deserve to be heard. We meet weekly with these dynamic young women to mentor and empower them to be their academic and behavioral best. They discuss their challenges with teachers and administrators. They are learning about past, present, and local African American Sheroes, so they can see "Talking with Attitude" (TWA) (Koonce, 2012) in positive action. They discuss their future and celebrate who they are as intellectual beings. They will be the narrators, who will transform the negative perceptions of TWA with TWA. We plan to travel with them through their freshman year in college to document the development of their identity as young women of integrity and strength, in a race-conscious society.

Schools are virtually void of systemic and systematic culturally responsive engagement as it relates to African American girls. Adding their voice to the dialog will assist us in meeting them where they are as learners, and taking them where they need to go, as they exercise their right to know, to think, and to aspire (Du Bois, 1905). It does indeed take an entire village to educate an African American girl, and we will reconstruct her educational village. My African American granddaughters and all the African American baby girls across our nation and the diaspora are worthy of culturally responsive academic and pro-social skill engagement. I close with a snapshot of my journey and challenge readers to find their research purpose and serve their communities in culturally responsive and sustaining ways.

MY MUSE OF FIRE IS UBUNTU: MY BLACK LIVES MATTER RE-AWAKENING OF PURPOSE

Strangely, I *knew* Shakespeare before I *knew* me.
My love for *the* theatre, fueled by a Heston
Disguised by a story, poised as the greatest,
And sprinkles of being Mother Earth at age five,
Easter speeches, then high school roles, and college roles
With peripheral visions of being a *star*,
Yet never good enough in the eyes of those who taught me.
My desire for stardom was steeped
In someone else's perceptions of me
and who I *should* or *could* be?

I embraced Shakespeare through Henry the Fifth,
O for a Muse of fire, that would ascend
The brightest heaven of invention.
Fascinated by a professor
Who quoted the chorus and taught of a *Muse*
In deep and dreamy thought
With no *thought* for who I was
And how my stage *should* or *could* be wrought

Galvanized by his passion,
For his Shakespeare and *his h*eaven of invention.
But oh, how excited I was at that muse of a thought.
Yet, led me to genres that did not echo or channel *me*
But on how excited I was, as I was easily bought.

I sought *my stage*, while beaconing Broadway
To welcome *me*
Bought miseducation, as Woodson (1933) did decree
Reality, set for my muse, was not *me*!
Turned to education and found a stage to share,
Then confronted by learners,
Their *Mis-education*
Personified by the fraud in *me*!
With no foundation to teach
What it means to be *me*
What it means to be *them*
In a world where the stage of make-believe
Continued Mis-education of purpose in me!

I needed purpose to see, to live, and to *be*.
My charges, who looked like me,
Had no kingdom for a stage,
A stage of self-identity,

Built on *their* right to *be*
In the context of a world hostile to their beauty and worth
I floundered searching for hope in the thrill
A thrill without foundation of who I was, who they were,
And how I was to reach and teach them to *be*

My world began to change, reflections flooded in …
I taught African American children,
African American learners,

African American young adults.
Became an African American mother
Of an African American girl and an African American boy.
Became an African American grandmother
Of an African American boy and two African American girls.
Fueled by the murder of George Floyd,
Addie Mae, Cynthia,
Carole and Carol Denise,
(three African American girls, bombed to death in 1963),
Trayvon, Tamir, Alhaji,
Michael, George, Daunte,
Ahmaud, and Ryan,
Janisha, Sandra, Breonna,
Atatiana and Ma'Khia

Every day, I saw my life as one without that fire
No flame in my wisdom
No knowledge in my awakening.
Now, I am ***Ubuntu!!*** (Nussbaum, 2003)
I am, because we are,
Because we are, therefore, I am

My re-awakening has been enlightened by the power of "Black Lives Matter!"
Fire is a generator of energy
Fire had been shut up in my bones
The last two years, in a freeze-framed pandemic
Have shown me and taught me
Who I am and who I must be, *...me,*
As a leader, an educator, a researcher, a mother, a grandmother,
Who teaches in and through each *Muse*
I do not and will not apologize for loving my people
For loving our children,
For laboring in my passion better,
For effectively teaching those who lead and *teach* our children
O for a Muse of Black Lives Matter fire, that would ascend
The brightest heaven of invention.
Our children have a right to know, to think, to aspire (TeachingAmericanHistory.org, 2021)...
I have a renewed purpose... to see, to do, to live, to be,
Black Lives Matter and their self-identity development, collectively, must be.... (Webb, 2022)

REFERENCES

Banks, J. A. (1993). Multicultural education: Historical development, dimensions, and practice. *Review of Research in Education*, *19*, 3–49.

Bertrand Jones, T., Ford, J. R., Pierre, D. F., & Davis-Maye, D. (2020). Thriving in the academy: Culturally responsive mentoring for Black women's early career success. In *Strategies for supporting inclusion and diversity in the academy: Higher education, aspiration, and inequality* (pp. 123–140). Palgrave Macmillan.

Bethune, M. M. (1950, January). The Negro in retrospect and prospect. *Journal of Negro History*, *35*(1), 9–19.

Bethune, M. M. (1963, September). My last will and testament. *Ebony*, *18*, 150–156.

Blackwell, B. G. (1979). *The advocacies and ideological commitments of a Black educator: Mary McLeod Bethune 1875–1955*. University of Connecticut.

Boykin, A. W. (1983). The academic performance of Afro-American children. In J. Spence (Ed.), *Achievement and achievement motives* (pp. 323–371). W. H. Freeman and Company.
Brewer, R. M. (2016). Theorizing race, class, and gender: The new scholarship of Black feminist intellectuals and Black women's labor. In *Race, gender and class* (pp. 58–64). Routledge.
Brewer, R. M. (2020). Black feminism and womanism. *Companion to Feminist Studies*, 91–104.
Collins, P. H. (1986). Learning from the outsider within: The sociological significance of Black feminist thought. *Social Problems*, *33*(6), 14–32.
Collins, P. H. (1990). Black feminist thought in the matrix of domination. *Black Feminist Thought: Knowledge, Consciousness, and the Politics of Empowerment*, *138*(1990), 221–238.
Collins, P. H. (1996). What's in a name? Womanism, Black feminism, and beyond. *The Black Scholar*, *26*(1), 9–17.
Collins, P. H. (2000). Coming to voice, coming to power: Black feminist thought as critical social theory. In *Women in higher education: A feminist perspective* (pp. 34–52). Pearson.
Crenshaw, K. W., Ocen, P., & Nanda, J. (2015). *Black girls matter: Pushed out, overpoliced and under protected*. African American Policy Forum.
Davis, T. M., Jones, M. K., Settles, I. H., & Russell, P. G. (2022). Barriers to the successful mentoring of faculty of color. *Journal of Career Development*, *49*(5), 1063–1081.
Du Bois, W. E. B. (1905). *Niagara movement speech*. Teaching American History. https://explorehistory.ou.edu/wp-content/uploads/2020/01/DuBois.Niagara-Address.pdf
Griffin, K. A. (2013). Voices of the "othermothers": Reconsidering Black professors' relationships with Black students as a form of social exchange. *The Journal of Negro Education*, *82*(2), 169–183.
Griffin, K. A. (2019). Institutional barriers, strategies, and benefits to increasing the representation of women and men of color in the professoriate: Looking beyond the pipeline. *Higher Education: Handbook of Theory and Research*, *35*, 1–73.
Griffin, K., Bennett, J., & York, T. (2020). *Leveraging promising practices: Improving the recruitment, hiring, and retention of diverse & inclusive faculty*. https://doi.org/10.31219/osf.io/dq4rw
Gunzenhauser, M. G., Flores, O. J., & Quigley, M. W. (2024). Race-conscious caring for anti-racist leadership: A narrative ethics for cultivating communal responsibility. *Journal of School Leadership*, *34*(1), 3–25.
Jones, L., & Baraka, I. A. (1964). *Dutchman and the slave: Two plays from the African American theatre*. William Morrow and CRDEEP Publications.
Koonce, J. B. (2012). "Oh, those loud Black girls!": A phenomenological study of Black girls talking with an attitude. *The Journal of Language & Literacy Education*, *8*(2), 26–46.
Kotak, N. (2015, October–December). Womanism: Black feminist theory with a difference. *Research Journal of English Language and Literature*, *3*(4).
Leffall, D. C., & Sims, J. L. (1976, Summer). Mary McLeod Bethune – The educator; Also including a selected annotated bibliography. *The Journal of Negro Education*, *45*(3), 342–359. https://doi.org/10.2307/2966912
Livington, R. H., Joseph, S. M., & Schapiro, H. (1970). *The me nobody knows*. [Play].
Morris, M. (2016). *Pushout: The criminalization of Black girls in schools*. New Press.
Nussbaum, M. C. (2003). Capabilities as fundamental entitlements: Sen and social justice. In *Feminist economics* (*vols. 9*(2), p. 1). https://doi.org/10.1080/1354570022000077926
Paris, D., & Alim, H. S. (2014). What are we seeking to sustain through culturally sustaining pedagogy? A loving critique forward. *Harvard Educational Review*, *84*(1), 85–100.
Peare, C. O. (1951). Mary McLeod Bethune. In L. D. Patton, V. Evans-Winters, & C. Jacobs (Eds.), (2023). *Investing in the educational success of Black women and girls*. Taylor & Francis.
Pitts, J. P. (1974). The study of race consciousness: Comments on new directions. *American Journal of Sociology*, *80*(3), 665–687.
Porter, C. J., & Byrd, J. A. (2021). Understanding influences of development on Black women's success in US colleges: A synthesis of literature. *Review of Educational Research*, *91*(6), 803–830.
Sizemore, B. A. (1973). Sexism and the black male. *The Black Scholar*, *4*(6–7), 2–11. https://doi.org/10.1080/00064246.1973.11760853
Sizemore, B. A. (2008). *Walking in circles: The Black struggle for school reform*. Third World Press.
Tally, J. (1986). Why "womanism"? The genesis of a new word and what it means. *Revista de Filologia de la Universidad de La Laguna*, (5), 205–222.

TeachingAmericanHistory.org. (2021, September 10). Niagara movement speech. Teaching American History. https://teachingamericanhistory.org/document/niagara-movementspeech/

U.S. Department of Education & Office for Civil Rights. (2023). *2020-21 Civil Rights Data Collection: Student discipline and school climate in U.S. public schools* [Report]. https://www2.ed.gov/about/offices/list/ocr/docs/crdc-discipline-school-climate-report.pdf

Walker, A. (1988). *Living by the word: Selected writings, 1973-1987*. http://ci.nii.ac.jp/ncid/BA03972319

Webb, G. C. (2019). *Talking with attitude*. Presentation for Voices of Impact, Texas A&M University, College of Education. https://www.youtube.com/watch?v=Yh3Oqt_FP6c

Webb, G. C. (2022). My muse of fire is Ubuntu: My black lives matter re-awakening of purpose. *Journal of Multicultural Affairs*, *7*(2). Article 8.

Webb, G. C. (2021, January). I can't breathe: But, the Holy Spirit can, as I advocate for African American boys and men. Special issue, the tipping point: A faith perspective. *Journal of Faith, Education, and Community*, *5*(1), 1–7.

Woodson, C. G. (1933). *The mis-education of the Negro*. Associated Publishers.

FROM FIRST GENERATION TO HIGHER EDUCATION: I CAN SHOW YOU BETTER THAN I CAN TELL YOU

Clara Y. Young

Tennessee State University (Retired), USA

ABSTRACT

As a person, the author is a sum of her experiences. Whether those experiences are good, bad, or indifferent. The author has learned who she is, how to handle situations and the value of always being honest with others and herself. The sum of these experiences has helped her to be a professional person and to navigate the higher education environment. The author is proud of her contributions to students, as an advocate, to teacher education with the students she encountered, and financially by making contributions to the Foundation. The author truly enjoyed her experiences in higher education and is thankful for the opportunity to pursue a doctorate. As a first-generation college student hailing from a town with a population of 5,900 (1972), the author had monumental experiences. She was able to accomplish her desire to travel, be an author, and work at an HBCU before retiring. It is her hope that what is read from her writing will be enlightening for the life of anyone who reads it.

Keywords: Higher education; student advocacy; mentoring; leadership; professional development

INTRODUCTION

As a young girl from a small town (population – 5,900), I grew up in a family of eight children. There were two sets of children, so I grew up with the second set, which consisted of four girls. Three of the last four were very close in age. Therefore, I was the middle child of the three. I did not experience any middle

Journeys of Black Women in Academe
Diversity in Higher Education, Volume 26, 147–175

Published under exclusive licence by Emerald Publishing Limited
ISSN: 1479-3644/doi:10.1108/S1479-364420240000026008

child syndrome because I always asked for what I wanted. I asked to go to Europe during my senior year in high school, and my parents made that happen financially. We had traditions that I enjoyed and experienced through adulthood. We had Thanksgiving dinner at my elder brother's house, had dinner at home for Christmas, and later in the day, we visited with an older uncle and had dessert; we always had a picnic on July 4, my mother's birthday and everyone received a cake made by my mother on their birthday. Another tradition was attending church, Sunday School, morning worship, B.T.U., and sometimes afternoon services. There was no need to complain because it was not going to change. In church, I learned how to lead; I gave longer and longer speeches for Easter and Christmas programs. Attending church activities helped instill more confidence in me and what I could do. We did activities that caused the family to unite several times throughout the year. I never experienced a time without food, clothes, or shelter. Our parents supported us, and we were secure. I did not know how much money my father made until I went to college. Hindsight, I made more money in 1 month than my father made in 1 year. Life was secure!

I never envisioned having a doctorate. I had yet to learn what a doctorate was or college. I was a good student throughout my formative years of education. From K – second grade, I remember learning the most about the alphabet, words, and how to add, subtract, multiply, and divide. I also remember reading the sight words in the Dick and Jane books. Knowing that information helped me to apply those concepts to learn more details. One monumental experience was in third grade. My teacher asked me if I realized how well I read. I replied to her, "No, I did not know." She informed me that I read well because I read with expression when I saw an exclamation point. I dropped my voice at the period and could pronounce all the words I was reading. That was monumental in my life because, after that comment, I read books that I obtained from the local library. I continued reading information beyond my schoolwork through eighth grade.

Another event that encouraged my learning was my ability to spell. Words and reading were so significant. Reading helped me to experience other places. Homonyms (today, the term is homophones) were exciting. I enjoyed words that sounded the same, had different spellings and meanings, and I could always distinguish the correct spelling by the word's meaning. My teacher, in the fifth grade, because of my love for words, entered me into the spelling bee for the school. I placed second, but it was a great accomplishment for me. I am the only one in my family who participated in the spelling bee.

I primarily made A's and, most often, 1 B. In this small town, each grade level had three classes, and students in each classroom were ranked #1, #2, or #3. The #1 student made all A's, and I strived to make all A's because I believed I was capable. If I received a grade of B in one course, I would work very hard to increase that grade to an A in the next grading period. I accomplished the task; however, I then received a B in another course. This outcome started in fourth grade and continued through eighth grade. I then named myself "Avis" because I always tried harder and still maintained the rank of #2. Trying harder just helped me to continue to establish and accomplish goals. After becoming a teacher, I realized the teacher fixed rankings, and regardless of how hard I tried, I would always have a grade of "B" to maintain me in the #2 position. My best friend (today) was ranked #1. I am not sure psychologically what this did to me; however, I learned that I had to compete with myself to do better and not my best friend.

Math was a subject that I enjoyed, and math in school during my formative years kept me excited. In seventh grade, I asked my math teacher if I could work a chapter ahead. He permitted me to work ahead; however, there was a stipulation. I could only ask questions if the class was on the same chapter. Why he made that decision, I do not know, but I agreed so I could work ahead. I was fortunate because I only had a question from two chapters to clarify how to calculate a problem throughout the academic year. This situation helped me to realize that I was astute enough to learn and learn independently. It would have been good if my teachers had given me more opportunities to learn independently. I enjoyed the challenge of learning and solving problems.

In eighth grade, I had my first opportunity to travel without my parents, even though I traveled with adults from my church. Traveling to another city helped me realize that the world was large, and I wanted to see as much of it as possible. I prayed and asked God to give me a career where I could travel. I had yet to learn at the time that my request would include having a doctorate.

High school progressed well. I knew I wanted to work with my head as a career, so that prompted me to go to college. I applied to college early in my senior year and had an acceptance letter in November. In my graduating class, about 30% of the students attended college. I had a counselor who needed to provide more information about college. I am not sure why, so even though I aspired to attend college, I had to learn about college while in college. As such, I was a first-generation college student. My parents did not have a high school education, but what I appreciated about them was that I was asked in my junior year of high school what I wanted to do, and they supported my choice. That was the protocol in my family. In their junior year of high school, my parents asked their children what they wanted to do after graduation. Their financial support ensured we had what was required to pursue our choices. My brothers also gave my mom money to support me while in college. I learned that later in life, but I hope my brothers realize their money was well-spent.

I had an older brother drafted into the Army and left home and the community first. I was the first girl to leave home to go to college. That was trying for my mother, and I did not realize how she worried about me being away from home even though I was in college. She had not had that experience with my three sisters, who are older than me. They left home by getting married but still lived close enough to visit with my parents daily. As such, my mother called me at least four times a week at 7:00 a.m. I sometimes complained. I did not mind the call; why did she call so early? I do not know the impact of the early calls, but I know today, and for as long as I can remember, I have been an early riser. I have a colleague whom I would call early in the morning with a cheery attitude. She would say, "Why do you call so early with that cheery voice?" That comment reminded me of what I said to my mother, but being awake in the morning with a cheery attitude was a way to thank God for another day.

I also learned that I had to trust people enough to ask questions in college and not feel intimidated. I wanted to be in college and was determined to obtain a degree. Another challenge that helped me to see that I was an independent learner was receiving a B/D on my English 101 paper. I learned that my content was good, but my grammar could have been better. I knew I needed to find a way to improve my grammar, so I asked my mom if I could come home early on a Friday. She agreed, and after arriving home, I went to the middle school I attended and asked for an eighth-grade grammar book. I spent the weekend writing my paper and used the grammar book to verify that I was grammatically correct in my writing. I returned to school and submitted my assignment in class on Monday. My paper was returned to me in class on Friday, and my grade was A/B. My grammar improved tremendously. My professor asked me what I did to improve my grammar. I told her I got an eighth-grade grammar book, began to learn the grammar rules, and checked my writing with the rules. My professor said, fantastic! I was so proud that I found a way to improve my grammar in writing by using my independent learning skills.

Another event in my first year of college helped me realize that I was determined, and that God had a purpose for me. I was diagnosed with Hodgkins, had to be hospitalized at the end of my first year of college, had to have surgery, reacted to the anesthetic, and the doctor was not sure if I would survive the night. I was 19 years old. My hematologist informed me that I had to take Chemotherapy. The plan was to take 6 months of treatment initially. I said to my doctor that I was only going to take 6 months of treatment. That was the Spirit of God guiding my thoughts because I had no idea that I would only take 6 months of treatment. My doctor suggested that I should not return to school until the Spring Semester. In my mind, that was not going to work, so I begged my mother to let me return to college for the Fall semester. I did not want this situation to prevent me from accomplishing my goal of obtaining a college degree. As the saying goes, the rest is history.

After completing my degree in education, I eventually obtained a teaching position in Kansas City, MO. I taught for 4 years, and then I was released from my job due to cutbacks by the district administrators. While in K.C., I pursued my graduate degree. After not being able to secure another position in K.C., I returned home to Illinois. Little did I know this was God's plan. I also realized that God was directing my life; I only needed to follow. I vowed that whatever he led me to do, I would do. One morning, I took my nephew to the community college in the next town that was not there when I was in high school, and I said, "This will be a good place to work." I became employed at the community college a year and a half later.

I became convinced that I should pursue a doctorate in teacher education after serving in a job position as Coordinator of an Early School Leaver Program at the community college. Based on the number of students with whom I interacted and who still needed to complete their high school education, I began to wonder about the preparation of teachers, how teachers contribute to students leaving school, and how I could make a difference. After being in that position for 5 years, I sought to pursue a doctorate. I investigated the criteria for acceptance, took the GRE, and applied for a doctoral program. After receiving a non-acceptance letter, I was surprised because I knew I had met the criteria. I took the liberty of visiting the doctoral coordinator at the institution to assess what standards I still need to meet. I learned that the requirements sent to me regarding admission to the doctoral program had changed. I talked to a professor I knew, and she informed me that I had a legitimate grievance and should appeal the admission. I thought about whether I wanted to file a grievance and decided against it. The score required on the GRE changed. The information I received read a score of 1,000 on the GRE; however, the difference was a score of 1,000 on the verbal and quantitative reasoning. I decided not to grieve the admission and retake the GRE. I wanted my access to the program to be based on meeting the requirements and not on a grievance. I tried to avoid entering the program with faculty, believing I could not be successful. After taking the GRE a second time, I had my scores sent to the university, and I received an acceptance letter for the doctoral program within 2 weeks.

I quit my job, moved out of my apartment, and moved into the graduate dorm to attend my doctoral program in the Spring Semester. I awakened early on Monday morning, dressed, and went to the Department of Curriculum & Instruction to converse with the Doctoral Coordinator. I bring you great joy: the Doctoral Coordinator was a "Brother!" When God opens doors, all we can do is go through it. I had a conversation with the Coordinator. After introducing myself and sharing my reasons for entering the program, he asked me how I would pay for school. It dawned on me then that I had not thought about how I would pay for school. He said me, "You quit your job, left your child with your sister, moved into the Graduate dorm, enrolled in the course, and you do not know how you will pay for college?" I said yes! He said, "Okay, Sister!" You see that short man over there? I said yes! He said, "Go let him know you need an assistantship. The assistantship will pay your tuition for school." Wow! I entered the institution and completed my degree in 3.5 years as a full-time student, only having to pay fees each semester of attendance. "Wow!" While in the doctoral program, I had an opportunity to instruct a course, develop a Retention Program for African American Students in Teacher education, attend conferences, and publish.

As a doctoral student, I had my first introduction to the Academy. As a student and course instructor, I still had much to learn about the Academy. I was fortunate to meet a sister who was also pursuing her doctorate and had entered the fall semester before I joined. Our first conversation, after the meeting, we conversed for about an hour. We were immediately connected and became a robust support system for each other. Another saving grace was our wonderful and supportive Doctoral Coordinator. His guidance was instrumental in the completion of the program. He guided me in obtaining an assistantship, completing the course of study, and submitting a change in the course sequence on the path of study. There were conversations with the Coordinator just about daily. One of the things he often shared was information. The Doctoral Coordinator said, "I will give you some information. You can do what you want with it, but you will have the information when you need it!"

Since I was the only African American doctoral student in the program, the doctoral coordinator's information sharing was very powerful. His support was even more potent after I attended my first class. Students walked into the room and greeted each other. I felt lonely, so the next day, I went to the Doctoral Coordinator and asked, "Why is it the students in class greeted each other and I did not know anyone?" That was not a tricky question; however, it informed the doctoral coordinator that new students in the doctoral program should only come into their first class if they know someone or have met anyone prior when the person is unique to the program. Since I needed an assignment for my assistantship, I was assigned to the Doctoral Coordinator to arrange a meeting for doctoral students entering the program in the Fall Semester. The meeting attendees would be faculty, present postgraduate students, and new doctoral students. Having this assistantship assignment helped me navigate the doctoral program and be successful. One thing is for sure: the faculty knew me by name, and I am sure that was easy since I was the only African American student in the program. However, it allowed me to become acquainted with the professor before I entered the course he or she instructed.

While a full-time doctoral student, I was also a single mother. My child was supportive and helpful at 8 years old. I also had great support from my family. Since I entered the doctoral program in the Spring Semester, my child stayed with my sister so his school and social activities would not be interrupted. In addition to school, my child was on a bowling team, took piano lessons, and participated in a dance club. My sister's children participated in two of the activities, so my child fit in very well with the routine. Before entering the program, I had a conversation with my child. I told him I would attend college to get a degree and needed his help. He was surprised I needed his help, but he kindly asked, "What do you need me to do?"

First, since he would stay with my sister, he had to be obedient, listen to his aunt's instructions, make good grades in school, and be patient until summer when he would come to live with me. After coming to live with me, I asked him to be more helpful with chores in the apartment, laundry, and dishes. He obliged me very well. Even when some of the children in the complex teased him about taking clothes out of the dryer, he continued to complete his chore. He developed an independence that was so helpful to me because he rode his bike to school, made good grades, and played on the Knockers Little League football team. Saturday was his day because I spent every Saturday with him. He bowled in a league, played football, learned to skate, and we shopped for him if needed.

He did very well academically as one of five African American students attending the school. I enjoyed his reading assignments in the third, fourth, and fifth grades. He had to do a book report each month. As such, our venture was that every book read to complete his book report was by an African American author and written about African Americans. He did a book report on the "Black Snowman" in third grade. After the teacher had read his book report and returned the paper to him, she informed him that she had not heard of the book. He told the teacher that he had the book at home. She asked if he would bring it to school. I was not pleased with her request because I asked myself, "Did she believe he made up the story?" His fourth-grade teacher made this same request after he submitted a book report on "The House of Dies Drear" by Virginia

Hamilton. I did not allow him to take the book to school; if the teacher wanted to know if it existed, she could look it up.

I wanted my son to understand that he knew the book was actual and that his teacher should not question him as if he made up information. He enjoyed riding his bike to school, playing football, bowling, and interacting with college students. My son has a degree in electrical engineering but has been on a college campus since age 8. His experiences on a college campus were instrumental in his life and the subliminal message of obtaining a college degree. He attended events with me on campus sponsored by the Black Student Union and the Multicultural Center. He even had the opportunity to talk with Gwendolyn Brooks and have her sign the book he still has today. There were stressful times during my doctoral program, but my son was not a stressor for me.

The assistantship assigned that led to my dissertation was the implementation of a "Retention Program for African American Education majors." The African American female pursuing a doctorate in another field in education, and I organized and implemented the program. Specifically, she devised the activities, and I managed their implementation. We worked well together because I learned using analytical means, and my colleague is a global learner. The program consisted of a monthly meeting, "communal" educational visits (with long-term educators and predominantly African American public-school classrooms), and a three-tier mentoring model. The three-tier mentoring model created consisted of first-year students to faculty. The first and second-year education majors were assigned a mentor who was a third or fourth-year education major; the doctoral students mentored the third and fourth-year education majors, and the Doctoral Coordinator mentored the postgraduate students. What was intriguing about the mentoring model is everyone gained value in the mentoring process. The first- and second-year education majors were receptive to being mentored by the third- and fourth-year education majors who had achieved information about the education program.

As doctoral students, we learned a lot by mentoring the third and fourth year education majors. If a third- and fourth-year education major did not or could not address the needs of the first- and second-year education major, they brought the concern to the doctoral students to resolve the problem. The Education majors in the program had a monthly meeting. In the monthly meeting, we had quest speakers and answered the concerns of the education majors. The coordinators of the Retention Program invited the Dean of the College of Education to a monthly meeting. At the monthly meeting she attended, at least 65 education majors were in the room, and she was surprised to see so many African American students majoring in education. Inviting the Dean to the meeting was a great idea because the Dean supported the program financially to provide opportunities for the education majors to visit classrooms in the inner city. The education majors gained so much insight with the classroom visits.

The communal activity, primarily reserved for education majors taking their methods courses, presented a lesson to their peers to practice teaching. The pre-service teachers had to develop instructional episodes as one of their assignments. The students did exceptionally well with this activity. They planned their lessons, created activities so the students could learn the information, and involved them in the instructional episode. The education majors did not have to sit and take what the pre-service teacher instructed. The education majors interacted with the information.

Another activity in the "communal" was a visit with a retired educator who had worked in education for 44 years, from teacher to principal. We visited her in a fireside chat where she told terrific stories and shared experiences, and the education majors enjoyed hearing them. I still have pictures of that event. She also gave them advice regarding their responsibility to ensure students learned. She believed all students could understand; finding how students learn and teach them that way was essential. In the communal activities, we exposed the education majors to education in unconventional ways. In another "communal" activity, I instructed the education on a study skill concept. The concept was to teach education majors how to make an "A" grade in any course. I required a lot of work, and the method worked if the student was willing to complete the activities.

I completed my program in August of that year and returned to participate in the fall commencement. Students in the program stayed at the university to attend the commencement. A student told me she tried the study method I shared with them and earned a 4.0 GPA. She made the Dean's list that semester. That semester was the only time she had reached an "A" in every subject. She wanted to continue after using the study method for her first exam in each course and earning an "A" grade. Even though it was a lot of work, she enjoyed seeing her grade A on her exams. She also informed me that she would not implement the method in the spring semester but learned how to make an "A" grade and would use it whenever there was a desire to make an "A" grade in any course taken in the future.

Another activity we implemented in the program was to provide the education major with an experience in inner-city schools. The education majors had the opportunity to visit inner-city schools in Milwaukee and Chicago. After the Chicago visit and the students were on the bus, one student said, "That was not a classroom I was in!" He had difficulty believing the behavior of the students he witnessed, the teacher's challenge with instructing the students, and the school's climate. The education major was so surprised by what he saw in the classroom that he questioned whether he should become a teacher. My cohort, who had a lot of experience in inner-city school settings, conversed with the education major while riding the bus back to the university to apprise him of how important it was for them to visit schools in the inner city to be aware of what to expect entering the classroom as a teacher and whether he believed the program he was in would prepare him for the inner-city school environment. Being in the program and completing the activities helped the students realize that being ready for various types of classrooms required more than the education program offered.

I was admitted to the doctoral program based on my GRE scores, my G.P.A. on the last degree received, and a writing sample – however, the writing sample needed to be more scholarly. I needed to learn how to write academically. After I received my grade from my first submitted assignment, which required to be written scholarly, I immediately met with my Doctoral Coordinator to inquire about academic writing. We met for 4 hours, and after that meeting, it was easy to understand scholarly writing. I have used the instructions I received with students to instruct them on academic writing. As such, any doctoral program should implement a course that will teach students on how to write academically. My content writing was good because I enjoyed writing; however, scholarly writing differs from the writing I learned in undergraduate school.

I viewed the doctoral program as a term of "endearment!" I needed something to keep me focused to pursue until the end. I also envisioned the doctoral program as a block of wood. My belief was if I continued to chip away at the wood, something would form. Each course taken was a chip out of the block. Each semester completed was a chip out of the block: each assignment completed, each exam taken and passed, each assistantship, comprehensive exams, proposal hearing, data collection and analysis, review of literature, writing the dissertation, and finally, dissertation hearing the block of wood was now a Doctorate in Education.

EXPERIENCES IN THE ACADEMY

My experiences in the Academy included learning to navigate higher education, challenges with students attaining the standards, having high expectations, student complaints, the administration being candid, obtaining support, not having a mentor, obtaining a mentor, understanding that what a European American faculty could say to a European is not what I could say to the European American student, understanding at the PWI the importance of students liking me, how European American students did not always believe I knew the subject, mistakes I made with students and how students thought it was okay to challenge me when they were the ones learning how to teach. My HBCU experiences included having opportunities to establish myself respectfully on campus, being effective in administrative positions, advocating for students, and following the rules.

Entering higher education, I did not have a mentor. While in my doctoral program, which was a PWI, I helped African American students navigate being an education major and being successful academically. I entered the first PWI and learned that students had the same challenges in education and other majors. I became passionate about assisting students and began interacting with them to help them gain confidence in conversing with their professors and getting what was needed to be successful. I spent too much time assisting students and not spending time conducting research. I attended conferences every academic year but needed to establish how to turn those presentations into publications. Again, a mentor could have been beneficial by providing directions. Presently, even though retired, I am mentoring junior faculty. The conversations were of encouragement, staying focused on tenure and promotion, reading manuscripts for publication, giving advice regarding how to address student and faculty issues, what questions to pose regarding direction in the Department, and developing relationships. Since these young ladies are the only flies in the ointment, it requires a lot of conversations and questions to help them develop those relationships in the Department and trust colleagues. I have also mentored students through the doctoral program, especially helping to create a topic early in the program. I am so committed to mentoring and now know how to mentor based on my mentoring experiences.

I was always held to high standards and graciously met those standards; however, that was different with undergraduate students. So many students came to the institution believing they had skills, so they were not interested in learning any skills. A student was angry at me because I noted grammatical errors on her paper. She said she had always had an "A" grade in English throughout school. The student took the paper to her English teacher at the high school where she graduated. The teacher agreed with the errors identified. She then asked the teacher, "How did I get A's throughout but did so poorly on this paper?" I do not know if the teacher responded; however, the student found a way to improve her grammar.

At my first PWI, the administration was not candid with me. Their experience instructing European American students could have been shared with me by showing me their syllabi and instructional methods or assignments. I was told by my department chairperson that my standards were too high. Another African American junior faculty was encouraged to talk to me about my instruction. Since this was my first position as an Assistant Professor, I would have welcomed the information to improve my situation. There needed to be mentorship as an assistant professor. I did not realize the value of having a mentor, and no one was assigned. There was another African American faculty in the Department who was also a junior faculty, but I believe I was being mentored by someone, not at the university. I did not know to have a mentor and not one outside of the university. I struggled in silence. European Americans did not know how to approach me, and I did not know how to approach them. I could have shared my struggle, but since the complaints had come to the Department Chairperson, then I believed he or she would have shared or made suggestions.

At my second PWI, I was assigned a mentor. I asked that question in my interview because it would be a great help to me. I was assigned a mentor, not of color, but a person who was liberal. I met with my mentor first regarding writing. She was very helpful in getting me to attend a conference and get a manuscript published. I was most appreciative of her assistance; however, I also encountered a person of color at the university who was more than helpful in helping me to get several manuscripts published. He helped me to develop three publications from my dissertation. I was also mentored by another male of color outside of the university who was known for mentoring in his field and encouraged me to conduct research regarding mentoring. I wrote a start-up grant proposal, received funding, and started collecting data. As a result, I obtained a publication and had the opportunity to present at NBSE and AERA.

My mentor at the second PWI listened as I shared the challenges I had with student complaints, especially undergraduates. I was not sure if students believed I should be easy, I did not know the content, or they did not want to do the work.

One student always played devil's advocate regarding any information I shared in class. This behavior was annoying after a while because it disrupted the instruction, and he appeared to want to get some type of acknowledgment from his fellow students. This was also a student who had relegated himself to being an education major after having yet to be successful in another major at a larger campus. The exit activities from the program had changed. Education majors had to demonstrate and explain an educational concept learned in the program. The same student who played the devil's advocate chose the topic I instructed in the course. I was sitting in the classroom, stunned. After students had completed their presentations, the same student came to me and said, "I learned a lot in the course you instructed. Even though I was a nuisance, you instructed the course well. That is why I chose that topic to present." I do not know if that was supposed to mean something to me. Well, it did not.

Another experience was when a student elected to file a grievance on the grade received in student teaching. Even though the grievance was denied at the department head and college level, the student filed the grievance with the Office of the Provost. With the hearing date set, three faculty were selected to attend the grievance meeting and render a decision. The faculty read the documents before the hearing. After explaining why we were at the hearing, the student was asked to speak about why she was grieving the grade. After her explanation, the provost asked why she believed she earned an "A" grade. The rate was based on criteria to accomplish at each level. She responded that she had achieved level 2 before she began student teaching. He asked how she knew she had met the criteria at level 2 before student teaching. She responded that she looked at the requirements and knew she had met the criteria. As a result of the hearing, the committee denied the grade change.

Another experience I encountered was being identified as an "Angry Black Woman." I could have handled a situation with a student better. I agree I was upset but not to be identified as an "Angry Black Woman." As a result, I had to attend an Anger Management Seminar (a one-day seminar) and counseling sessions. I attended three counseling sessions. In the third session, the counselor informed me that I was participating in the sessions because of anger issues. The counselor told me that I was not an angry woman, I did not have anger issues, and I should leave the institution due to having to face a stigma that was not true. That was pivotal advice for me, and it helped me to know it was time to go!

I had the opportunity to serve on the faculty senate as a representative, vice president, and then President. As President of the Faculty Senate, I had a weekly meeting with the Chancellor, which allowed me to become more involved in the campus environment and interact with upper administration. This experience helped me become more acquainted with the responsibilities of upper administration and develop my leadership skills. An event that was the leadership responsibility of the Faculty Senate President and Staff President was to lead the Mardi Gras Activities on campus in February. The community attended the annual event on campus. Before leaving the university, I participated in a Leadership Development Institute that lasted for 8 weeks. I learned a lot about leading, and I was glad I had the opportunity to attend the Institute.

While at the university, it became essential for me to support events related to the Foundation. The College of Education had a Luau for about 5 years to support student scholarships. As a result of support, I had the opportunity to serve on the Foundational Board for the last 2 years and support fundraising.

I asked God to allow me to work at an HBCU before retiring. My desire became a reality after I was selected to be the Department Chairperson for the Department of Teaching & Learning. Learning campus politics was the most challenging. The Department Chairs had developed a Department Chair Counsel support by the provost. During my first month as Department Chairperson, I attended the faculty meeting and was welcomed and supported by other Department Chairpersons. It was a good environment to garner support. I often asked questions in the forum to help me learn a lot about the counsel and made recommendations to improve situations Chairpersons encountered. Attending the Department Chairperson Council meeting and knowing other Department Chairpersons allowed me to gain their assistance in getting students enrolled in courses in their department that were full or students who needed permission to enroll. Likewise, Department Chairpersons could request the same from me, and I obliged.

As the Department Chairperson, I also had the opportunity to continue to advocate for students. My advocacy started as a doctoral student and continued throughout my career. I had an open-door policy, and students visited my office often. Since no one in the Department was designated to advise students, I took the responsibility. Advising students helped me to learn who was in the program, especially since the Department had established students entering the program as a cohort. The advising forms needed to be improved so students could stay on track to gain admission to the education program. Therefore, I reorganized the advising form to make it clear for students. I started establishing folders for students and giving them a copy of the advising form to help them take responsibility for taking courses required to obtain admission to the program and complete the program.

In addition to the student advising form, I also spent time reorganizing the course schedule to reflect current course offerings for each semester. Some courses on the schedule had no enrollment for at least three semesters, so I removed those courses. After completing the task, faculty complimented me on how well I had organized the course schedule for the Fall semester. I also implemented something called the "Wall of Claim," where faculty under their name listed the courses they wanted to instruct. Each faculty came to my office and selected courses. It helped me tremendously to realize what courses would be available each semester.

Education majors were required to take a course, World Geography. Many wanted to avoid taking a particular professor during the advising meeting because they believed they could not pass the course. I convinced several students to enroll in the course he instructed anyway. After a month into the semester, students began to come to me and say they believed they would not pass the course. I talked with the Associate Dean of the College of Liberal Arts and learned that this professor awarded the most failing grades than any professor in the college. That information alarmed me, so I decided to attend his class meeting. After sitting in a 75-minute class meeting, the professor spent 45 minutes of the class meeting time sharing information on a project he required students to attend, even though many did not have transportation. How unfair to students! As the Department Chairperson, I talked with the professor. I shared with him what I witnessed in the class meeting and how so many students majoring in education took this course and believed they would fail. I do not know what he did, but the education majors in the class did not fail, and they encouraged other students to take his course. Our conversation gave him insight to help students be successful and not fail.

I continued giving to the Foundation at the HBCU, a donor at this level the Foundation acknowledged. As such, I had an opportunity to attend events by being a donor. My name was on the donor list, which was a way to become more acquainted with upper administration. In any meeting with upper administration, I shared any facts I had and my opinion professionally if asked. What I shared was taken with great value and recognized by the upper administration as someone who shared facts and always sided with the truth.

Another experience was the opportunity to serve on search committees and to chair two search committees for Research and Sponsored Programs. Serving as the Chairperson of a search committee was another opportunity to use my leadership skills. One thing I disagreed with was giving courtesy interviews. The committee should never get into a situation where a person may become employed in a position and not be qualified. The chairperson asked if a courtesy interview should be allowed on two search committees. My response was always no.

Being asked to serve in an upper administrative position was more than an honor. Hindsight, I do not recall ever being asked to do something I was incapable of doing or had the skills to do, especially in my professional career. When the President called me and asked me to serve as Assistant Vice-President, I was surprised. My immediate response was that I was getting ready to retire. She responded, "Retire to do what?" Then I consulted the Lord, and as I allowed the idea of holding the position to marinate in my spirit, I knew this was for me, and I was very capable of assuming the role. Some of the experiences in the Academy could have deterred me, but as a determined person, I believed my hard work, diligence, preparation, and experiences prepared me for this time, this moment, and this position. After assuming the role, I became acquainted with a team where the Provost assigned responsibilities based on our experience, ability, and background. We accomplished a lot that contributed to the university positively. I appreciated the tasks and responsibilities given to me, and still allowed me to be an advocate for students. While in this position, I had several experiences where faculty did more to prevent students from being successful. Even though I interceded in some of these situations, I included the Dean as the mediator. There was a situation where a student had an excuse for missing a class session when there was an exam. This student also served as the King for that academic year. The professor would not allow the student to take the exam, so I asked him to consider allowing the student to take the missed exam. The student had taken three of the four exams, scoring 96, 80, and 93. The missing exam would lower his grade by one letter. The professor granted the request, and the student scored well on the exam, but the professor then shared that I had forced him to change the grade. The professor filed a grievance with the Dean, Faculty Senate, and the legal office. All interactions between the professor and me had been transmitted via email. None of the messages requested that the professor change the grade. I asked the professor to allow the student to take the exam. I had a conversation with the legal office, and I was requested to keep the conversation private. The person told me he was making a request, but she could not make me not share. My response was that is what I did with the professor. I received no more information regarding the grievance.

In this position, following the rules was so very important to avoid favoritism in forgoing the rules. I had the opportunity to attend meetings with the Deans and contribute to the platform, I worked on the Commencement committee and organized the script, identified the 4.0 students, and created the medallion awarded to the students. I developed the end-of-the-year report submitted by the Deans for the Provost. I also appreciated how the deans respected me in the position and contacted me to address concerns about the assistant vice president's decision. I enjoyed being able to contact personnel to get issues resolved. I learned so much about the operation of the Office of the Provost and its relationship to the university's successes. Since student suspension was one of my responsibilities, I required students seeking readmission to develop a plan regarding what they would do to be better academic students. In this position, I witnessed students who had entered the university from the small hometown where I grew up and graduated with honors. Serving as the Assistant Vice President was the climax of retiring my career in higher education.

WISDOM IN WORDS!

These are comments made by my parents to us as children. The idea was to give us words of wisdom to live by, to be responsible and accountable. Some of these I did not understand until I was an adult. Even though I was a child who asked many questions, I did not ask what the saying meant, even if I wanted to ask. One of my favorite ones from my dad was "That dog won't hunt." What he meant was that what you are saying does not make sense, so you will need to come up with something that does make sense.

"Baby, if the man cannot help you when you need it, then you do not need him." This one did not require a lot of explanation, but it was something I thought about. But my father saw this as a measure of a man.

"It doesn't take all night to do anything." My dad made this comment when we were dating as teenagers. In other words, we could not and had better not stay past curfew. Whatever we were doing on our date, it was not and should not take all night.

"Your name is not blow!" Whenever we were going on a date, the young man had to come and knock on the door. If the young man blew the car horn, we could not go out the door. If the young man did not respect us enough to come to the door, then we could not go. My dad was a quiet man, and teenage males were often uneasy coming inside the house where we lived.

One that my father shared with me based on his experience and what he believed. "You cannot trust white people as far as you can see them." During the time I was growing up, he wanted me to be cautious, especially based on the senseless murders of African Americans in the South. He grew up in the South and did not have cordial experiences with white people.

Whenever, as a child, we were disrespectful or talked back, my dad would often say, "You need to be put a buttonhole lower." In other words, you were out of your place, and a buttonhole lower will put you back in your place as a respectful child.

My son and I lived with my parents for a while. My son was two at the time. One day, I asked my son what he wanted to eat. My dad said, "Who's the Mama?" Baby, feed him. He does not know what he wants to eat. Just feed him. He also used this phrase when we allowed our children to do something disrespectful and we did not correct our child. In other words, as the Mama, you are in charge, not the child.

My mother also shared words of wisdom with us. One is, "You will have to get up early to get one over on me." Whatever was said, she did not believe it, or her facial expression was, do you expect me to believe that? You had to tell the truth because she could sense if you were lying. After all, what was said did not sound true to her.

"I went to school one day in my sister's place." Regardless of how much education she did not have, and we were receiving an education, she also knew things; she had a lot of information that we did not have at a young age, even if she did not get as much education as we did.

"You can do anything temporarily." My mother always wanted us to know that there were things we had to do temporarily to accomplish a larger goal. Even though it seemed we were going to school forever, she informed us we only had to go to school until we graduated. This thought concept helped me to set and accomplish goals. It was good to know that there were things I would not have to do forever. I realized that accomplishing smaller goals will help to achieve larger goals.

"You want too much sugar for a nickel." This idea was quite simple. Her thought was that we wanted more than we deserved, more than the amount of money we had, or what we wanted cost more than the money in hand, or if we did not have the money, then we could not get it. Therefore, we had to work within our financial means. I remember when my sister wanted to borrow $25 from my mother to put a coat in the layaway. My sister told her she could pay her back on Friday after she got paid. My mother suggested that after she got paid on Friday, she should go and see if the coat was there because she did not have the money to pay for the layaway that day. Learning this lesson early, I supported myself financially. I learned if I did not have it, then I could not get it.

"You talk like Ned in the first reader." This saying meant that whatever you were saying was not complete because the first reader was mostly sight words.

I like Proverbs due to the wisdom in it and what can be learned from it. My favorite is Proverb 3:5–6 "Trust in the Lord with all thine heart and lean not unto thy understanding. I all thy ways acknowledge him and He will direct their paths."

"A long life may not be good enough, but a good life is long enough (Benjamin Franklin, 1902. Henry Ketcham, The Autobiography of Benjamin Franklin). It takes less time to do something right than to explain why you did it wrong (Henry Wadsworth Longfellow, 1839)." I have shared this quote with several people after I read it on a wall. The first sentence relates to the fact that most people want to live a long time.

Living a long time does not equate to a good life. We should strive to live a good life because a good life gives us value. The second sentence relates to time and how one values time. We can use our time wisely or waste time. If one has to explain why it was done wrong or must do it over again, the original time spent was wasted.

Another concept I used at the end of presentations I made was called "Food for the Soul."

> Not everybody can be famous, but everybody can be great because service determines greatness. —Martin Luther King (1968)

People strive or want to be famous. It is as if one wants to go where everybody knows their name. No individual can determine if they will be famous. Being famous is determined by people. Dr King encouraged greatness because service brings greatness, and an individual can determine how much service they choose to give.

> My heart is at ease knowing that what is meant for me will never miss me, and that which misses me was never meant for me.—Imam al-Shafi'l, 18th Century Muslim Jurist

Bob Marley also made this one of his quotes. This proverb is so powerful. When I heard this proverb, I began to think about how, as a people, we try to guide our lives. If we live by God's directions, it goes back to the proverb above. Jeremiah 29:11 tells us that God has a plan and purpose for our life. As the Miami Mass Choir recorded: What God has for me it is for me! Adopting this proverb will be good to recall when things do not go as desired, just realize that was not for you and there is a reason it missed you.

> God does not give us what we can handle but helps us to handle what he gives us. (Teaching with T.L.C.)

Proverbs are guiding information that can assist with decision-making, lessen stress in our lives, and assist in gaining wisdom. The above are words we can live by to help maintain a focus on who is guiding our life; we must listen to and for directions and be patient.

POLITICAL CLIMATE

I always believed I was not a politician, but navigating the higher education climate at a PWI required knowing the politics. A mentor could have helped me learn about the political climate. There were situations when I should have said something and I did not, and there were situations where I should not have said anything at that time. I knew my Department Chairperson and Dean; however, I did not navigate upper administration well. I did not realize that even if the person was incorrect, it was not my place to correct them. I would have wanted to be corrected, but that is me and is not the case at a PWI and, more specifically, males. I also believed I was not a politician because I posed too many questions for clarity.

At the PWI, the political climate was if upper administration liked you then you could gain support and be accepted in those venues. I did not achieve that support at the first PWI of employment. I was a larger university, so gaining that support was difficult without a mentor. Not knowing the political climate impacted my personal development. There was a time when I was in a meeting with two females (1 African American and 1 European American), and everyone else around the table was male. I cannot remember why I was in the meeting, but after listening to input from the members, I raised my hand. I do not remember the comment made or question posed, but one gentleman responded to my comment by first acknowledging the name of another African American faculty. My response was, "We all look alike." Politically, that was not the correct response, and I did not respond to the question. Hindsight, maybe he did not know my name and called me by the name of who he knew, maybe it was an innocent mistake, maybe I was too sensitive about the comment, or maybe I could have responded to the question and made him aware of who I am after the meeting. Big political mistake needing to have received tenure. My Department Chairperson said to me, "I cannot believe you responded that way in the meeting." So, politically, it is important to know that the goal should always be to respond to the questions and make corrections later. I do not remember his position; however, he did not like my response. So, it is important to know the political climate and how to navigate within the climate. The political climate at the first PWI was a white boy's network, and you were either in the network or not.

Leaving the first PWI, I entered a second PWI. The political climate was somewhat different, but politics existed. Because it was a smaller university, I had the opportunity to interact with upper administration because those persons mentoring me had upper administration relationships, so my mentor introduced me. Politically, it was still a white boy's network; however, it was not as dogmatic. The upper administration included women who were infiltrating the White Boy's network. Even though the women were European American, it provided room for more sensitivity regarding diversity. I also learned to navigate the political climate by becoming a Senate representative for my college. In those meetings, I knew who was in upper administration and how to interact politically. Later in my tenure, I held an office and eventually served as President of the

Senate. In addition to navigating the political climate, I also gained opportunities to submit a proposal and receive a start-up grant. The research I wanted to conduct related to mentoring African American faculty. I saw the lack of mentorship as a challenge on the campus. The grant funds allowed me to conduct research on mentoring and to have the results published.

The political climate where I was employed was who do you know in what position. I did not experience this aspect of the political environment as an assistant professor, but after being at the university for a time, I witnessed the political climate. As a PWI, I experienced knowing the right people and getting some opportunities; however, in terms of obtaining a position, the odds were against me politically. Regardless of whether I had the extended experience, was very familiar with the operations of the Department and programs, and was ready for leadership, that did not happen. I had to accept that I had not connected with the right people politically. If previous administrations, who had supported me, had been in place, I still would not have attained the position. I witnessed the political climate of who do you know after I became an administrator. It was the same, which may be the political climate on most university campuses.

What I do believe in is policy and rules. At any university I was employed, it was important to know the policies and to follow the rules. The rules and policies were in place long before I arrived. As an administrator, I always referred to the rule when faculty, department chairs, or the Dean wanted to do something for students or other faculty members. My response was this is what it reads in the rules. No policies or rules changed during the time I was an administrator.

EARLY & MID-CAREER FACULTY & ADMINISTRATIVE OPPORTUNITIES

Doctoral students—Pursuing a doctorate is not a walk in the park; it takes time and diligence. Know that you are ready to pursue through completion. Having an A.B.D. (all but dissertation) means nothing. Finding a way to relieve yourself of the stress that comes with the work required in a doctoral program is important. That could be exercising, quiet time for yourself with tea, relaxing with a friend, purchasing something for yourself, or visiting with friends out of town. The stress is going to come.

Remember, you are learning, and learning requires asking questions. Your concern should be to get your questions answered and not concern yourself with what the professor may think. Your confidence in completing the program should increase with every course and writing assignment you complete.

As a doctoral student seeking your first position, consult with a tenured professor regarding questions that should be asked in the interview. The interview committee will ask if you have any questions. Have questions!

You will likely be offered a 9-month tenured track position. Regarding salary, ask for what you want and do not price yourself out of the job, especially if that university is where you want to start your career and that university wants you.

Ask for a salary comparable to the position, but do not cheat yourself. You know your value, and do not undermine your value.

Early Career Faculty—In terms of a person of color, be mindful when you are the only person of color in your Department, whether you are hired because you are a person of color or did you meet the criteria for being hired. It could be both! Nevertheless, do not see this as a bad thing but a way to identify if you will get the support needed to extend your career at that university and decide what contributions you can make to the Department, college, or university. Remember that you are not the spokesperson for all people of color, and sometimes you will be asked advice regarding people of your color.

My advice for early faculty is if you do not want to be tenured and promoted (do not see the university as long-term for you) at the university where you are, then at the end of the third year you should have another position at a university where you want to obtain tenure and promotion. Based on your decision on your potential to advance academically with the institution, not on any service you may be rendering. Even if you do not see the institution as a long-term investment, get tenured and promoted before you leave to take Associate status to your next institution.

Writing is more of a challenge after completing the dissertation than during the dissertation phase. Therefore, just as you planned writing for the dissertation, you must plan to write during the professorship. Get a writing partner to hold you accountable for completing the writing, submitting, and seeking publications.

For any presentation you make at a conference, outline the presentation so you can write a manuscript and submit it for publication. So, develop two or three manuscripts from your dissertation to submit for publication. Take parts of your dissertation and publish. If that is a challenge, a writing partner will be constructive to guide you through the process.

Acclimating to higher education as a new faculty member can be challenging; therefore, during the interview, request assistance in the acclimation process. That person can be your department chairperson or another faculty member who will respond to any questions. This person could or could not be your mentor. But ask for a mentor to assist with professional development. Your mentor should provide adequate assistance to help you obtain a level of comfort. If the mentor does not meet your needs, request another mentor or seek a mentor who can assist you adequately. Your mentor can be a person of color who is a learned professor at another university. This person can suggest who to pose questions to and what questions to pose.

Feel free to pose questions to your department chairperson, a mentor, or others you encounter and feel comfortable with. The objective of asking questions is to get information. After meetings prepared to pose questions. You can always ask if this is the correct venue to pose questions.

If other females of color are on campus, try to connect with them. Ask your department chairperson to assist you in the process. It will give you an idea of how knowledgeable they are in regard to the culture of the campus. It is another way to discern how committed your department chairperson is to your success on campus and in the Department.

Always work toward tenure and promotion. You start this process by knowing the tenure and promotion requirements and developing a timeline to meet the criteria for tenure and promotion. The requirements for tenure and promotion are research, teaching, and service, so you must find a balance to meet the requirements. Be careful to only volunteer for a few service activities. There are a lot of service opportunities, and as a person of color, you may be asked to serve on several committees (representation and new person on the block). You will probably bring new ideas. Just limit how many service activities you need to serve each year. If your service is taking time away from research, then excuse yourself from one or two. Balance, balance, balance! In addition to professional responsibilities, you may have family responsibilities and personal activities to maintain a mental balance.

If you realize that being a professor is not what you want to do after you have entered higher education, get out! My experience has been people who enter and then realize they do not want to maintain in higher education, that person tends not to seek tenure and promotion, primarily because they have not done much to meet the criteria of tenure and promotion. It is senseless to spend time (5 years) not pursuing tenure and promotion and not completing the tenure and promotion requirements. Don't waste time! You can develop yourself in another arena.

MID-CAREER

After tenure and promotion, you should think about your next step. If being a full professor is your desire, then work toward that goal. Also, think of ways you can contribute to the Department or university. Is there a course you can propose or a program you can develop for students in the Department or college? Write a proposal to obtain grant funds related to research or developing students. Develop a research team that includes students.

Become the advisor of an organization. Set up a study abroad program in your field where students can go to enhance their education. I had a faculty to discuss with me her next steps after being tenured and promoted. She had decided on the area she wanted to pursue. Unfortunately, she may not be able to obtain the position at the institution where she is; however, presently, as an interim administrator, she can prepare herself for the goal she desires. Having candid conversations with trusted people can help one put things in perspective.

At this point in your career, it is time to start developing your leadership skills, whether you desire to be in administration or not. Seek faculty awards on campus or within membership organizations. Find a way to become a presenter regarding a specific topic in your academic field. Based on my dissertation, I developed a presentation entitled "Instructing African American Students," which I had the opportunity to share with teachers in public education, parents, students enrolled in courses I instructed, and administrators in the state and other states. I should have developed an assessment to give to participants to continue to obtain qualitative data. If you make presentations in your field, always have an assessment instrument for participants to complete to extend your research and collect additional data.

Be creative with the presentations you develop. I had the opportunity to submit a proposal to the National Title I Conference with a colleague. The title of the presentation was "Advocating for Students: Getting Parents Involved." I devised the idea to give the participants a four-question survey to collect qualitative data. There were at least 150 participants who attended the presentation. The monumental qualitative data collected led to a publication and additional presentations. I also reorganized the presentation to present to parents in the local schools, conferences, and to parents of schools in another state.

Write proposals to obtain grant funds to conduct research, get students involved in research to have an assistantship, earn a stipend, or develop students in your field of study. There are grant opportunities to access Research and Sponsored Programs at the university to identify what proposal opportunities are available, get assistance in writing a grant proposal, and take the opportunity to converse with program officers to gain insight into the types of research the program officer is willing to fund. Write and submit a proposal.

Take this opportunity to serve on university committees and even chair a committee to become acquainted with faculty and administrators on the campus other than those in your department or college. These activities will continue to help you develop and increase your leadership skills. If you desire to be an administrator, you must help other administrators see your leadership skills.

If an administrator is different from your next goal, then decide what you want your next goal to be. Your mentor is an ideal person to have this conversation with. Your mentor can assist in establishing a timeline to accomplish the goal and determine objectives to achieve the next move. Being mentored should not cease, but this is also a good time to become a mentor.

ADMINISTRATION

You must prepare yourself to become an administrator, learn to follow, and understand that someone in administration seeing you as an administrator can determine if you become an administrator. Being an administrator is a challenging position and requires preparation. Preparation can be acquired by volunteering to lead committees, programs within the Department, and university organizations by attending leadership seminars, workshops, or institutes. Being a leader is not automatic; if you have leadership skills, you must learn how to lead.

Learn to follow! Three little words can make a difference in you being an effective leader. If you have issues following a leader, there is a good chance you will not be an effective leader. What motivates you to follow the leader, what is your perception of the leader, and are you progressing under the leadership? Answering these questions will give you an indication of what it requires to be an effective leader. Follow the leader how you would want someone to follow you if you were the leader.

People in academic settings decide they want a leadership position, obtain the credentials to qualify them to lead, and do not get the chance to get a leadership position. I know people who have had this experience because no one in leadership envisioned that person as a leader. The concept seems to be unfair, but leaders know leaders. When a person shows him or herself as a leader, leaders notice.

One scenario was a young man teaching third grade for about 3 years. He asked the principal if he could coach the fourth- and fifth-grade basketball teams. Since the coach was leaving, the principal agreed to allow him to coach. In the first year of coaching, the fourth- and fifth-grade teams went to the state championship and won. The next year, the fifth-grade team went to the state championship and won. The Superintendent of the school district called the principal and asked if the coach had administrative licensure. She told the Superintendent no. His response was to tell the young man he needed to get his administrative license because he saw leadership qualities. The young man pursued his administrative license, obtained a master's degree, and later became an assistant principal in the school district's administrative program. The young man said he had not thought about being a principal, but the Superintendent believed he had the potential due to coaching a winning team for 2 years. Presently, that young man, now older, is a principal and begins his administrative leadership only after 6 years of teaching.

Another scenario is when I met a young lady who had been teaching for about 15 years. She decided that she wanted to be a principal. She pursued her administrative licensure and a master's degree. When I met her, she had her license for 7 years and no opportunity to enter administration. She said she did not know what was causing her not to get the opportunity. I believe the lack of opportunity goes back to the concepts above. She did not show herself as a leader, so no one in the administration envisioned her as a leader, or maybe she had not shown her ability to lead by being a follower of the leader.

In higher education, I believe the concept is the same. Even if the opportunity does not come where you are, it can come at another institution. Regardless, you must show yourself as a leader.

After obtaining a leadership position, take an opportunity to investigate the Department, college, or institution before making any changes. Know what type of leadership style you possess and that the leadership style will fit in the position.

Administration can be lonely, so make alliances with other administrators. The administrators can be within the institution or outside of the institution. The goal is to have someone you can have candid conversations with, keep the conversation confidential, and you can get suggestions to resolve issues or concerns.

Become familiar with the responsibilities of the positions under your leadership. Be aware of whether people are fulfilling their duties in their work. Learn the concept of documenting and having a paper trail of good things, issues or indifferent things. The paper trail requires a lot of work as the position.

After taking a leadership position, make sure personnel are clear about the goals and objectives and put that information in writing. People only sometimes hear what you say, or their interpretation of what you say is different from what you say. There was a department on campus that received many complaints, and I was assigned to meet with the Department. The Department was informed, the meeting was scheduled, and all involved attended. In the first meeting, the personnel made introductions and named their position. I stated the objective was to learn about the department from them because I have limited information about the department. We met weekly for about 4 weeks. During the meeting, I often had personnel who would not respond to questions, were connected to Zoom but were not attending the meeting, and experienced the lead person only responding to questions, even if I asked a particular person. Finally, in the fourth meeting, I asked why it was difficult to get responses, and even when I asked a person specifically, there was no response. Finally, a person shared that the belief was that I was meeting with them to fire them. I restated what I said on the first day, and the response was, "Well, it feels like that is what you were doing"! Their lack of response was due to fear of losing their jobs, so the lead responded to all the questions protecting them. Regardless of what I said I was doing, they did not hear that. What the personnel felt was what they believed, so we could not progress. That is why it is essential to have the objective(s) written and allow the personnel to read it. Then, ask the personnel what they read. Reading it in their voice could make a difference in the interpretation.

For people under your leadership, especially if there are different departments, meet with the leadership of each Department as a group. The goal is to help the Department realize how important it is for the entity to work together to complete tasks. If necessary, meet with each department to assess the organization and how commissions are finished. There may be many meetings, but clarity is vital to accomplishing the goal.

In leadership at the HBCU, personnel want to know who you are to determine how or if they will follow. Determine how much personal information you want to share that will create a connection with the people working under your leadership. Oftentimes, people will ask other people on campus about you. Some are diligent in letting them know they do not know anything, others will gladly tell what little they may know, and some will make it up under the auspices of "I heard." A major question is, "How did he or she get the position?" The candidate applied for the position, interviewed, was the best candidate, and was extended a job offer. If the position is appointed, the same question is asked, "How did he or she get the position?" No one tends to respond; the person is qualified. Someone will ask the question, but all you can do is be as effective as possible in the position, and then your personnel will see that you are qualified.

LESSONS LEARNED

There are so many lessons I learned while in the Academy that helped me during my tenure and through the process. Going into the Academy, this is what I suggest getting through the first process:

Mentor—A new assistant professor requires and should demand to have a mentor. According to my research, a mentor is needed for one of three reasons: professional development, personal development, and personal growth (Young & Wright, 2001). Knowing why the faculty needs a mentor may require one mentor or multiple mentors. A mentor from the same Department is ideal, but the mentor can be from another department or college. The critical fact is that the mentor will give time to the relationship to provide guidance. After meeting the mentor, a conversation should ensue regarding expectations of the relationship, how often you will meet, and the time required to succeed. As a new faculty, you must assess if you are getting what is needed in the mentoring relationship. If a mentor is assigned but is not meeting your needs and giving you time, then seek another mentor. Some professors will accept the mentoring assignment but may not be effective as a mentor. Do not feel bad about seeking someone else because this is your career, and you want to be successful.

Professional development in the Academy assists the new faculty with understanding the professional standard, professional requirements to maintain in the Academy, and what is required to aspire to the next level of promotion or administration. Teaching, Research, and Service are the road to tenure and promotion. The new faculty will need assistance in progressing through the publishing area, instructional prowess, and direction in the extent of service. Mentoring in professional development will also include the mentor making introductions to other professionals, assisting in submitting and developing conference presentations, developing the research agenda, and helping the new faculty increase visibility in the professional arena.

Personal Development in the Academy assists the new faculty in connecting with students, providing advice regarding various academic situations, rehearsing with the new faculty in making presentations, meeting often regarding the academic arena and sharing ideas, and attending conferences with the new faculty. A new faculty may need grooming to navigate the academic arena.

Personal Growth in the Academy is to assist the new faculty in navigating the informal arena of the Academy. Attending academic, social events with the new faculty, impromptu conversations, invitations to lunch, and caring for the new faculty as if that person is his or her son or daughter. The new faculty needs to know how to navigate informal settings in the Academy.

I learned that if one is going through personal challenges, it is a great idea to see a counselor to not allow yourself to be consumed by the situation and let it impact you professionally. One time, I was going through personal challenges in my life. I thought I was separating what I was feeling from my behavior in the classroom. Consequently, I reacted to a student in an unprofessional way. After the incident, I had to attend an anger management seminar and counseling because the Department Chairperson identified me as having anger issues. I needed to handle the personal situation better, and therefore, the situation overwhelmed me. I did not realize I needed to talk to someone professionally. The counselor had received the request from the department chairperson regarding why I was required to attend counseling. I only attended three sessions, and the counselor did not identify me as a person with anger issues. The counselor recommended that I look for another environment to work in because that environment had gotten all I should give.

In terms of the PWI, students have a dire need to see faces that look like them. I know I had the experience, and that experience continues to exist. It is very seldom that an African American faculty in the Academy does not want to help students of color, because these students are looking for someone to trust. However, there must be a balance between advocating for students and meeting the tenure and promotion guidelines. In my first position, I spent a lot of time advocating for students without using that process for research. We cannot turn our back on students, so we must find a way to support and include the advocating in research. It is also a way to help students learn how to conduct research.

In terms of my PWI experience, being liked is a way to gain support. Somewhere in our career, we learned that you do not have to like personnel to work with personnel. That is not true at the PWI. So, how do you get people to like you? It would help if you played the game. Have conversations and limit how much personal information you will share but share personal information. Go to lunches with fellow faculty and administrators if asked. Attend social events organized by the Department, college, and university. Be engaged when you are attending any events. Learn to initiate conversations. Sometimes, you may be the only person of color or one of the few persons of color. In terms of style, as African American females and males, we may often change hairstyle, fingernails, and dress style. Sometimes, comments are made regarding their opinion of these changes. You must respond to the statement, try to give a positive response, and not an answer that informs the person you did not like the comment. That brings me to another lesson learned.

Responding to questions helps clarify your response instead of responding to comments. Develop this habit with students, faculty, and administrators. When a comment is made and you make a comment, what supports your comment? You do not know the essence of the statement, what prompted the statement and therefore, you are responding based on what? Commenting on a statement can cause information to be misconstrued or misunderstood. As such, your response could be, "And the question is?" or "What is it you want to know?" For example, a faculty comments that you change your hairstyle weekly or monthly. After hearing the statement and you know it is true, what comment can you make, or should you make? I would say, "That is true!" or "Thank you for noticing!" You can speculate in terms of why he or she commented, but that would be unfair to you. I shared earlier the value of getting information and then requiring people to get information from you.

I learned that requiring students to reach standards that they do not already have, I had to make a change. It never dawned on me that the standards for them were not the same standards for me. I did not learn about going to a professor and asking for points or extra credit as an undergraduate student. I did not know that I could submit an assignment late with a crazy excuse. After entering the PWI as an assistant professor, I was asked so many times to allow extra credit. Extra credit is more work for me. Developing instructional plans, exams, and grading assignments for at least three courses with at least 25 in each class is a lot of work, in addition to service and research. Asking for extra credit continued at the PWI; however, I did not experience students asking for extra credit at the HBCU. At the HBCU, students did not ask for extra credit, and they just wanted more time to complete the assignments required. My interaction with the students at the HBCU was: what did I do wrong on the assignment, and can I do it over?

Students need to know how to take an exam. When students did not do well on the exam, I suggested the student come to my office to review the exam. The African American students welcomed the invitation, but not the European American students. I only remember one European American student coming to my office to review an exam. She was upset because she did not read the question correctly and believed the point should be received. However, my African American students welcomed the opportunity. I learned that it helped them to realize if they knew the information or addressed any anxiety they had while taking an exam. One thing I shared with students was to ask themselves, what is the question asking me? Several students did not see the value in this exercise because they could repeat the question but could not identify what the question was asking. None of the students completed this task before. Students who used the skill while taking an exam improved their scores. So many African Americans entered college not being able to take exams proficiently and with test anxiety. One student with whom I reviewed an exam learned that she would insert a word if she did not know the meaning of the word in the question. The benefit was asking herself, what is the question asking me? The student learned that inserting or replacing a word she did not know the meaning of did not make sense. Unfortunately, she got the answer incorrect. After practicing what the question asked me a few times on the exam we were reviewing, she used it on each question that she had chosen the incorrect answer and then selected the correct answer. She also realized that she had been making this error on exams in other courses. In another class, she used this method on the final and scored her highest on the exam in the course. The instructor asked her what she did to improve her test taking, and she informed him that another professor helped her see what she was doing wrong while taking an exam. The score on the final assured her of a passing grade in that course. At this PWI, the Department Chairperson told me not to have another student come to my office to review an exam. I don't know why she made this mandate. I know the concept was beneficial for African American students, so I continued as long as an African American student wanted it.

I learned that European American males answer a question, even if it is not the question posed. So, I learned how to rephrase the question to get a response. What I learned to do if I needed clarification on a question was to identify that I needed clarification in terms of what the person was asking or saying to the person. Is this what you are asking?

As an administrator, I learned that you cannot change what you do not know. The first order of business is not to change anything, but to assess what is working, what is not, and when to implement a change if possible. As a new administrator, I entered an environment where I did not know any faculty personally. Even though an administrator gave me information, I believed that if I was going to establish a productive working relationship with the faculty, I had to know them from their perspective. One venture I took was to take each faculty person to lunch. The faculty shared any personal information they wanted with me, and my question was regarding their research agenda. I entered a department of all faculty tenured except two. Therefore, faculty was not conducting research. I only recall getting a little information on previous research. The goal was strictly teaching. The lack of research meant a lack of progress.

As an administrator, I must be fair to all faculty regarding student productivity. At the HBCU, I removed faculty from courses assigned that were not instructing students. I also had to ensure that all students received the same instruction. The change was prompted by a program on and off campus. Only one faculty instructed in both programs. The faculty for the main campus and off-campus program were different personnel. The rule became the same instructor for the course on the main campus and off campus. Faculty had to travel, but it was consistent for students.

I learned at the HBCU that some faculty members do not fulfill their duties, and some faculty members stay too long. When a faculty gets to the point of ineffectiveness or no longer wants to be there, then the person should go home. At this HBCU, there was no means of having those people removed. The biggest challenge was having faculty members who are committed to students' learning. One faculty I inherited was ineffective after I arrived, when I was there, and after I left, but stayed on the payroll until 2023. Another faculty was hired at the age of 70. Why? Age would not have been a factor, but the faculty refused to use technology in the classroom of students who had entered this world via technology. Her response was I wouldn't say I like technology. The underlying message I heard was that she did not want to learn to use technology. That is an indication of age. Some who stay too long believe students need them, or they are committed to helping students outside of the classroom. They continue working until they are requested to leave.

I learned at the HBCU that someone under your leadership will not like you. That person ensures that their dislike for you is known to other faculty and anyone else who will listen. Even if you have done nothing to the person, the dislike is I do not like you. In this situation, the person was antagonistic. Whatever I suggested was not agreed on by this person. While serving as an interim Dean, the person spent time trying to discredit me and gave me the poorest evaluation I had ever received, even though the associate Dean disagreed with the evaluation. Even though the behavior manifested as dislike, the person did not want me in the position. That is okay, but it was not her choice. I have a colleague who is experiencing the same situation at another HBCU. Her situation is that the employee does not want to work for her but wants to work for her previous boss who was promoted to another position. The previous boss could have taken the employee to the next position but did not. So, the employee tried to discredit my friend, spoke to her unkindly, and refused to work in the office due to an excuse of smelling fumes that made her ill. Where did we learn that behavior as people of color? In our community, some of us have difficulty focusing on the true issue. In this situation, the anger was that the previous boss did not promote her to the next level. But her retaliation was with the present boss. The saving grace is "Isaiah 54:17 – No weapon that is formed against thee shall prosper; and every tongue that shall rise against thee in judgment thou shalt condemn."

I learned who to be angry with if you choose to be angry in an academic setting, especially regarding who receives the position. In any academic setting, positions will be available, and candidates can be interviewed and selected within or outside of the university. If the person chosen is not your choice, why is it that anger is exhibited toward the person after the person takes the position? I witnessed this in the PWI and the HBCU. At one institution, two internal candidates were interviewed for the position. Both candidates knew each other and had worked together. The candidate who did not get the position came to work the following week and did not acknowledge the person who was selected for the position. I took the liberty to converse with the candidate who had received the position. I suggested to the candidate who received the position to have a conversation with the candidate. I told her to share with the candidate not selected that she could understand her disappointment in not getting the position, but if she wanted to be angry at someone, then it should be the selection committee and not her. She did not give herself the position. We learned this behavior as early as elementary school. When we vied for something we wanted and did not get it, we were angry at the person who got it. We were immature and learned we could not be angry at the adult in charge. It is amazing how that behavior continued in adulthood. As adults, we should have left that behavior in elementary school. This mindset creates division and interferes with progress. We do not get Everything we want; all we can do is try our best.

Graduate faculty should not assume that a student in a doctoral program knows how to write scholarly. The instructions given to me to learn how to write academically were clear, concise, and doable. Every program should have a course designated for students to learn how to write scholarly and, in that course, an opportunity to develop a dissertation topic. I also learned that if the student has a topic early in the program, then any papers required in courses can relate to their dissertation topic, thereby building the review of literature for the proposal.

CONCLUSION

I am humbled to have had the opportunity to write the book chapter sharing my experiences in higher education from an African American female perspective. Some of the challenges could have deterred me from my purpose. I am so thankful for my experiences from childhood to my professional experiences because I have matured and accomplished my goals to become a Professional.

Just as one goes through experiences, sometimes the idea of getting through is more extended than desired. By being diligent, you can overcome the situation with prayer and supplication. I can do all things through Christ who strengthens me (Philippians 4:13). Everything in my life has not gone as I had planned, but it has progressed as God had planned.

In this writing, I reflected on my life and profession after retirement, which was enlightening. God has been with me as I read about the experiences, triumphs, challenges, and changes. That is how I came through on the other side of the story. Praise God for all the Blessings, challenges, and trials I have experienced to strengthens me, because I can show you better than I can tell you!

REFERENCES

Franklin, B., & Ketcham, H. (1902). *The autobiography of Benjamin Franklin, Poor Richard's almanac and other papers*. The Perkins Book Company.

Iman Al-Shafi'i – 18th Century Muslim Jurist. Islam Practice, 30+ Inspirational quotes by Iman Ash-Shafi'i, https://islampractice.wordpress.com/2017/12/29/30-inspirational-quotes-by-imam-ash-shafii/

King, M. L. (1968, March 3). "The Drum Major Instinct". [sermon]. *Delivered at Ebenezer Baptist Church.*

Longfellow, H. W. (1839). *Voices of the night*. John Owen.

Young, C. Y., & Wright, J. V. (2001). Mentoring: The components for success. *Journal of Instructional Psychology, 28*(3), 202. https://link.gale.com/apps/doc/A79370576/AONE?u=anon~4a4d0904&sid=googleScholar&xid=0c533a2

Printed and bound by CPI Group (UK) Ltd, Croydon, CR0 4YY
14/06/2024
14515251-0001